LYRIC APOCALYPSE
Reconstruction in Ancient and Modern Poetry

John W. Erwin

Scholars Press
Chico, California

LYRIC APOCALYPSE
Reconstruction in Ancient and Modern Poetry

John W. Erwin

© 1984
Scholars Press

Library of Congress Cataloging in Publication Data

Erwin, John W., 1942–
  Lyric apocalypse.

  (Scholars Press studies in the humanities series ; no. 3)
  1. Poetry—History and criticism. 2. Reader-response
criticism. 3. Semiotics and literature. I. Title. II. Series.
III. Title: Reconstruction in ancient and modern poetry.
PN1111.E78 1984   809.1   83-20883
ISBN 0-89130-666-8
ISBN 0-89130-672-2 (pbk.)

Printed in the United States of America

LYRIC APOCALYPSE

Scholars Press
Studies in the Humanities

for
Chandos and Cybèle

CONTENTS

Acknowledgments

Chapter 12 was originally published in a slightly revised version in *Contemporary Literature*, Vol. 21, No. 4 (© 1980 by the Regents of the University of Wisconsin), pp. 588–610.

The illustration on page 223 is from *Les Primitifs flamands*. I: *Corpus de la peinture des anciens Pays-Bas méridionaux au quinzième siècle, 3* (2 vols.; Antwerp, 1953–54). Martin Davies, ed., The National Gallery, London.

INTRODUCTION
The Poetics of Revelation

i

And I saw a new heaven and a new earth; for the first heaven and
the first earth were passed away; and there was no more sea.
And I John saw the holy city, New Jerusalem, coming down from
God out of heaven, prepared as a bride adorned for her husband.
(Revelation 21: 1-2)

As we approach the end of the twentieth century, history seems more
likely to end in nuclear annihilation than in a brilliant cosmic marriage.
But the last book in the New Testament provides a larger view and
reminds us how poetry can challenge all desperate final solutions. For
centuries before and nearly two thousand years after St. John wrote
Revelation, poets have attempted not only to represent the tensions and
ambiguities of historical experience but also to provide models for the
reconciliation of perennial conflicts. Recall how Pindar evoked the wedding of Peleus and Thetis; how the Psalmist compared the Law to a
bridegroom; how Mallarmé and Ashbery played intricate, perverse variations on the descent of the Bride Jerusalem in Revelation.

Yet how can poetry hope to succeed where history so patently fails?
How can such a marginal institution as literature authoritatively propose
radical change? How can even the most polyphonic poetry end the
obsession with univocal definition which has produced the rationale as
well as the hardware for total annihilation?

Indeed the text which most boldly asserts that scripture can renew
culture may even intensify a writer's anxiety about measuring up to the
standards set by his literary authorities. As the Old Testament interprets
the works and words of an invisible Author, it defines authority as transcendent, absolute and unique. But scripture gives back with one hand
what it takes away with the other. The writers of the Law dramatized
the complex dialogues which establish and maintain legitimacy of any
kind. They thereby suggested that a writer can gain the authority which
communities attribute to law if he admits that culture depends upon
continual exchanges of challenge and acknowledgment.

The account of the giving of the Law in Exodus itself anticipates
later writers' attempts to modify the Mosaic deference to transcendent

Authority. If the absolute Lord first writes the Law, Moses rewrites it with his own human hand after he has smashed the first tablets in front of the Golden Calf. The several writers of Exodus probably did not intend this sequence as an allegory of cultural order alternative to the Law. But the Christian writer of Revelation repeatedly elaborated this triadic pattern of writing, challenge, and rewriting. He thus showed later writers how to compensate for vestiges of Old Testament authoritarianism in New Testament prescriptions of fraternal love.

In the book which completes the Christian reinterpretation of the Torah, an angel prevents the writer St. John from deferring to his authority.

> And he saith unto me, Write, Blessed are they which are called unto the marriage supper of the Lamb. And he saith unto me, These are the true sayings of God. And I fell at his feet to worship him. And he said unto me, See thou do it not: I am thy fellowservant, and of thy brethren that have the testimony of Jesus: worship God: for the testimony of Jesus is the spirit of prophecy.
>
> (Revelation 19:9–10)

The angel in effect defines the radiant New Jerusalem as the image of a new kind of historical community: one grounded in understanding that culture is always being made, unmade, and remade in mutual recognition by authorities and interpreters, authors and readers. When the angel refuses to stand as supreme, univocal authority, he defines St. John as his equal in a collaborative reading of Authority. And as I will demonstrate, both ancient and modern literary variants of this dialogue in Revelation strongly imply the paradoxical wisdom that Authority derives from the diverse communal interpretations which it demands.

Of course such concern for reciprocity has seldom survived for very long the institutionalization of religious, political, or economic theories. But Revelation tells us that this is precisely where literature comes in. Far more than other cultural institutions, literature demands that we examine the principles and structures by which we think, feel, and communicate.

A. R. Ammons has quite persuasively defined poems as models for optimum cultural order.

> poems are verbal
> symbols for these organizations: they imprint upon the
>   mind
> examples of integration in which the energy flows
>   with maximum
> effect and economy between the high levels of
>   oneness and the
> numerous subordinations and divisions of diversity . . .
>   the poem
> is the symbolic representation of the ideal
>   organization, whether
> the cell, the body politic, the business, the religious

group, the university, computer, or whatever.

("Essay on Poetics")

I submit, however, that poetry provides *negative* models for the construction and reconstruction of humane communities. Energy flows with maximum effect and economy between the one and the many only if a poem challenges a consistent failure of cultural organizations to work at peak efficiency. Poetry offers an exception to the rule that culture tends to conceal the gaps between many varieties of "oneness" and "diversity": differences between consciousness and the unconscious, tradition and contemporary circumstances, text and interpreters. A poem is a model of ideal organization insofar as it questions the limitations of the cultural codes which it employs or to which it refers. For it thereby makes us acknowledge that we too depend upon similar conventions and prepare to engage in mutual challenge with other self-critical interpreters.

Two twentieth-century Americans, Wallace Stevens and Charles Olson, indicate how for millennia poets have tried to gain the authority to remake the world by directly challenging their readers. In "The Man with the Blue Guitar," Stevens commands:

Throw away the lights, the definitions,
And say of what you see in the dark

That it is this or that it is that,
But do not use the rotted names . . .

nothing must stand

Between you and the shapes you take
When the crust of shape has been destroyed.

You as you are? You are yourself.
The blue guitar surprises you.

In "I, Maximus of Gloucester, To You" Olson is even more imperious:

in! in! the bow-sprit, bird, the beak
in, the bend is, in, goes in, the form
that which you make, what holds, which is
the law of object, strut after strut, what you are,
what you must be, what
the force can throw up, can right now hereinafter erect,
the mast, the mast, the tender
mast!

The nest, I say, to you, I Maximus, say
under this hand, as I see it, over the
waters
from this place where I am, where I hear,
can still hear

from where I carry you a feather
as though, sharp, picked up,

in the afternoon delivered you
a jewel,
                it flashing more than a wing,
than any old romantic thing,
than memory, than place,
than anything other than that which you
                carry
than that which is,
        call it a nest, around the head of, call it
        the next second

        than that which you
        can do!

Both poets define our attentive reading not only of their texts but also of
ourselves as the only ground on which a new Jerusalem can be built.
Although contemporaries could hardly be more dissimilar than Stevens
and Olson, both the Man with the Blue Guitar and Maximus insist that
collaborative self-criticism itself constitutes a new world. Like St. John,
both project a community founded upon mutual acknowledgment that
all communities begin, achieve legitimacy, and develop in continual
tension between prescriptions and the diverse readings which these provoke. For like Revelation, both "The Man with the Blue Guitar" and the
Maximus Poems define ordinary dialogue as a model of order which is
extraordinarily generative because it is on the one hand more open and
on the other more highly structured than any so far established as the
law of a land.

When we take turns as utterer and respondent, we demonstrate that
individual identity is a collaborative creation. Of course there are as
many kinds of dialogue as there are human situations. But even the most
casual speech gives us some degree of the satisfaction which we draw
from the most intense: it confirms that we are members of a community
who are free to enjoy its rights and privileges as well as obliged to follow
its rules. But we alternately suspend our will to self-assertion because we
expect the intersubjective rhythms of dialogue to generate a stronger and
more flexible sense of personal identity than any prescriptive code per-
mits. And when poets in various ways articulate and intensify the
dynamic structure of dialogue, they prove still more clearly that it is
mutual effort and consent which generate strong individual identity. As
both Stevens and Olson show, if a writer is to legitimize his reevaluation
of his authorities, he must not only quite scrupulously interrogate the
basic assumptions of his culture, literary tradition, and personality: he
must also demand such strenuous criticism and self-criticism from his
readers.[1]

---

[1] In *Problèmes de linguistique générale* (Paris, 1966) Emile Benveniste thus describes
the genesis of identity through dialogue:

Anticipating the most rigorous contemporary literary theory, poets since Homer and "Moses" have indicated that writers are at the mercy of cultural, linguistic, and literary codes which began to evolve long before their birth and should continue to develop long after their death. But the best ancient and modern poetry also shows that in the exchange between writers and readers, the questioning of authority and identity can create new, productive definitions. The strongest poets have analyzed the interactions which define both culture and personality as carefully as the most lucid theorists. But by demanding that we help them rebuild extraordinarily vital communities of understanding, they tend to define reading as *reconstruction*.

Semiotics and deconstruction have contributed greatly to our understanding of texts and the reading of texts. Drawing upon projections of a general science of signification by the American philosopher Charles Saunders Peirce as well as the European linguist Ferdinand de Saussure, literary semiotics studies the complex interaction of cultural and linguistic codes in both the genesis and reception of textual utterance.[2] More intensively concerned with the fundamental tension between aspects of the sign discussed by Saussure, deconstruction argues that literary texts call into question the very possibility of stable definition, proving that language itself does no more than play endlessly upon differences among its own elements and can only generate tentative, provisional formulations.[3]

La conscience de soi n'est possible que si elle s'éprouve par contraste. Je n'emploie *je* qu'en m'addressant à quelqu'un, qui sera dans mon allocution un *tu* . . . La polarité des personnes ne signifie pas égalité ni symétrie: "je" a toujours une position de transcendence à l'égard de *tu*; néanmoins, aucun des deux termes ne se conçoit sans l'autre; ils sont complémentaires, mais selon une opposition "intérieur/extérieur," et en même temps ils sont renversibles. Qu'on cherche à cela un parallèle; on n'en trouvera pas. Unique est la condition de l'homme dans le langage. (p. 260)

This account contrasts with the deconstruction of dialogue as compounded narcissism by Jacques Derrida in *De la Grammatologie* (Paris, 1967):

Le colloque est . . . une communication entre deux origines absolues qui, si l'on peut risquer cette formule, s'auto-affectent réciproquement, répétant en écho immédiat l'auto-affection produite par l'autre. L'immédiateté est ici le mythe de la conscience. La voix et la conscience de voix—c'est-à-dire la conscience tout court comme présence à soi—sont le phénomène d'une auto-affection vécue comme suppression de la différance. Ce phénomène, cette suppression présumée de la différance, cette réduction vécue de l'opacité du signifiant sont l'origine de ce qu'on appelle la présence. (p. 236)

2 See Umberto Eco, *A Theory of Semiotics* (Bloomington, 1976); Maria Corti, *Introduction to Literary Semiotics* (Bloomington, 1978); Michael Rifaterre, *Semiotics of Poetry* (Bloomington, 1978); Robert Scholes, *Semiotics and Interpretation* (New Haven, 1982).

3 See Jacques Derrida, Harold Bloom, Geoffrey Hartman, J. Hillis Miller, Paul de Man, eds., *Deconstruction and Criticism* (New York, 1979); Josué Harrari, *Textual Strategies:*

Neither semiotics nor deconstruction, however, is disposed to study a major literary phenomenon. If a writer acknowledges that any text is determined by various cultural codes and sub-codes, he or she can convince readers to analyze their own subjection to diverse systems and thereby project alternative modes of political and social signification. Indeed the post-structuralist definition of the literary text as an opening of infinite play by polysemous signifiers imitates an arbitrary closure that it first opposed: the New Critics too assumed that neither the individual work nor the literary canon primarily refers to non-literary reality. As Gerald Graff notes, "structuralist and post-structuralist critics do not get rid of the concept of autonomy so much as transfer it from the narrow realm of literature to the larger realm of *écriture*."[4]

How then are we to restore to literary study the sense that literature is open to the world and potentially central to the life of our culture? Certainly the totalitarian closure of *écriture* would be broken if linguists were to qualify Saussure's analysis of the linguistic sign as an exclusively differential function in a system, demonstrating that any performance (*parole*) of potential in the linguistic repertory (*langue*) refers to some reality beyond the semiotic system.[5] However, we already possess models for a semiotics of reference: poetry that reflects upon its genesis and performance. Many of the texts which the newer criticism cites in order to question traditional assignments of a mimetic or referential function to literature in fact define it as only relatively autonomous. They thus help achieve for poetry the cultural centrality that theory has recently attempted to achieve for itself.

ii

In response to various degrees and kinds of pressure from both literary tradition and non-literary circumstances, poets have struck many different poses in relation to literary, political, and economic systems. Criticism must therefore weigh the influence of the several historical contexts which compete for any writer's more or less conscious attention. But poetry is also distinctive for its power to criticize established codes and thereby project communities that are more flexible and open than any which have ever existed: communities grounded in mutual self-criticism by authorities and interpreters. As Wolfgang Iser notes,

---

Perspectives in Post-Structuralist Criticism (Ithaca, 1979); Jonathan Culler, *The Pursuit of Signs* (Ithaca, 1981) and *On Deconstruction: Theory and Criticism after Structuralism* (Ithaca, 1982).

[4] *Literature Against Itself* (Chicago, 1979), p. 21.

[5] Jeffrey Barnouw, "Signification and Meaning: A Critique of the Saussurean Conception of the Sign," paper delivered at the American Comparative Literature Association Triennial Conference, Chapel Hill, North Carolina, 1980.

herein lies the unique relationship between the literary text and
"reality," in the form of thought systems or models of reality. The
text does not copy these, and it does not deviate from them either—
though the mirror-reflection theory and the stylistics of deviation
would have us believe otherwise. Instead, it represents a reaction to
the thought systems which it has chosen and incorporated in its own
repertoire. This reaction is triggered by the system's limited ability to
cope with the multifariousness of reality, thus drawing attention to
its deficiencies. The result of this operation is the rearranging and,
indeed, reranking of existing patterns of meaning.[6]

But this rearranging and reranking is necessarily a communal process:
poetic texts at least imply that no single reader can complete their questioning of both tradition and the contemporary world.

As poetry both invites and refuses location in particular cultural circumstances, no one reader can adequately respond to its mutually contradictory attitudes toward response. Works which are commonly called
literary resist a phenomenology of reading which considers only how a
text appropriates a single consciousness. For a literary text does not ask
that we take it entirely on its own terms without referring to other literary and non-literary texts and contexts—as Georges Poulet maintains, in
effect corroborating the New Critics' position.[7]

A text which compels rereading tends to advertise rather than conceal the fact that it derives from the writer's diverse responses to diverse
encodings of experience.[8] It does not so much appropriate the individual
consciousness as invite a mix of openness and resistance similar to its
own. But if a text also prevents one from appropriating *its* multiple
interpretation of past and future readings of reality, it implies that the
only effective counterpart to the responsive, responsible author is a

---

6 *The Act of Reading* (Baltimore, 1978) p. 72.
7 "Phenomenology of Reading," *New Literary History* I (1969), 53–98. Geoffrey Hartman applies Husserlian categories in "The Interpreter: A Self-Analysis," *The Fate of
Reading* (Chicago, 1975), p. 13: "philosophically speaking, the shadow is as much 'before'
as 'after,' a *Vor-Verständniss* which makes both art and its interpretation possible, and
implies thus a virtual community of interpreters." Also, see Stanley Fish, *Is There a Text
in this Class? The Authority of Interpretive Communities* (Cambridge, Mass., 1980),
p. 335:

> The self does not exist apart from the communal or conventional
> categories of thought that enable its operations (of thinking, seeing,
> reading). . . . If the self is conceived of not as an independent entity
> but as a social construct whose operations are delimited by the sys-
> tems of intelligibility that inform it, then the meanings it confers on
> the texts are not its own but have their source in the interpretive
> community (or communities) of which it is a function.

8 My argument will develop the Prague formalists' notion of "foregrounding"; see Paul
Garvin, ed., *A Prague School Reader on Aesthetics, Literary Structure and Style* (Wash-
ington, 1964), pp. vii–viii. See also David Lodge, *The Modes of Modern Writing: Metaphor, Metonymy and the Typology of Modern Literature* (Ithaca, 1977), pp. 2, 8.

gathering of interpreters who are at least somewhat aware that they share the responsibility of interpretation. This community of readers can to some extent be constituted by the various subjective dispositions of an individual reader at various moments in his acquaintance with the text. But the truly compelling text articulates its provocative mix of demand and resistance to others' demands in ways that indicate that its readership must be more diverse than any number of the fairly distinct readers who can be generated by a particular individual.

Even the most private and introspective lyric can only survive its occasion if it speaks to issues or events of more common interest than its author's immediate experience. Indeed a poem can only respond adequately to a personal crisis by locating it in various larger realms of human experience. How then can the reader ignore the fact that his response is being solicited along with that of many other readers? Of course some forms and some periods more emphatically than others define the reader as one among many potential members of an interpretive community. As Milton's "Lycidas" indicates, pastoral elegy written in a period of sectarian conflict tries with remarkable persistance to designate as members of a surviving community both the dead alter ego of the isolated poet and his counterpart, the reader. But all poetry can be distinguished from other kinds of utterance, both public and private, by the degree to which it calls attention to the interpersonal nature of its medium and thus the potential multiplicity of its receivers.

Because poetic texts continually remind us that we are preceded by many other readers and will very likely be followed by still more, they authorize Hans-Georg Gadamer's description of dialogue.

> We say that we "conduct" a conversation, but the more fundamental a conversation is, the less its conduct lies within the will of either partner. Thus a fundamental conversation is never one that we want to conduct. Rather, it is more generally correct to say that we fall into conversation, or even that we become involved in it. The way in which one word follows another, with the conversation taking its own turnings and reaching its own conclusion, may well be conducted in some way, but the people conversing are far less the leaders than the led.[9]

As structural linguistics insists, the repertory of signifying potential in *langue* determines what can be realized in any *parole*. But the immediate context of a *parole* is also some form of dialogue, a relationship which is both particular and interpersonal—and thus seems more binding than one's obligation to the whole linguistic system. Similarly, poets tend to indicate in several ways that they are attempting to open exchange with many interlocutors. Indeed all the deictics which lead

---

[9] *Truth and Method,* trans. and ed. G. Barden and J. Cummings (New York, 1975), p. 345.

Jonathan Culler to define the lyric as a non-dialogic, impersonal object—
its use of first- and second-person pronouns, anaphoric articles and
demonstratives, adverbials of place and time and verb tenses[10]—provoke
readers to break through the text's somtimes flaunted impersonality and
experience the intersubjectivity of language more fully than they do in
non-literary dialogue. For poetry reminds us that when conversation
leads us it allows us to develop a sense of identity which is strong
because it is flexible and open to development.

In an essay entitled "Poetic Listening" (*New Literary History*,
Autumn, 1978) Merle Brown describes the interpersonal nature of reading in a way that nicely complements Culler's emphasis upon impersonal
aspects of the lyric. Whereas for Culler "lyric poetry in general is an
approach to the inscription" (p. 168) and defines itself against other
writing because it is surrounded by "intimidating margins of silence"
(p. 161), for Brown a poem is an extension and intensification of the
"interminable talk or expressiveness . . . that goes on inside most men
most of the time" (p. 124) and does not approach the epitaph but a
"transcendental society of speaking and listening, of expression and criticism, of writing and reading" (p. 126). If for Culler the poem is "an
impersonal object whose 'I' and 'you' are poetic constructs" (p. 162), for
Brown it is itself a complex *subject*: "a transcendental society . . . an act
of rhythmic expression and listening" (p. 133). If Culler studies deter-
minants, seeking to discover in any text "a set of conventions determin-
ing how the sequence is to be read and what kind of interpretation may
be derived from it" (p. 161), Brown considers how the poem projects
greater freedom. If Culler observes that rhetorical figures offer the
reader reassurance, locating him as firmly in a predetermined cultural
system as themselves, Brown interprets them as provocations for self-
conscious response which will generate what we might call a community
of communities—taking a cue from Wallace Stevens, who showed in "An
Ordinary Evening in New Haven" that the poetic text is a "colony of
colonies" (XIX).

> Human community, in any case, is not possible in the fullest sense
> except between two or more persons each of whom is himself a
> human community of doing and thinking, of expressing and criti-
> cizing, of speaking and listening (p. 137).[11]

---

[10] *Structuralist Poetics* (Ithaca, 1975), pp. 164–70.

[11] Although the Prague formalist Jan Mukarovsky classifies the lyric as monologue (*The
Word and Verbal Art*, trans. and ed. John Burbank and Peter Steiner [New Haven, 1977],
p. 56), his description of "dialogues based predominantly on semantic reversals provided
by the interpenetration and alternation of several contextures" can be applied to poetry.

> This . . . dialogue . . . is, relatively speaking, removed to a considera-
> ble degree from a direct dependence on external circumstances, both
> on the interlocutors' emotional and volitional interrelation and on the

But the poetic text is indeed a colony of colonies because poets tend to emphasize the fact that any dialogue alludes to previous and subsequent exchanges.

It is when writers more or less vigorously interrogate earlier literary interrogations of logical, generic, stylistic, rhetorical systems that they attribute more than individual subjectivity to each member of poetic discourse: author, text, and reader. An allusive text indicates that the initiator of poetic discourse is himself multiple in that he writes only after having been a member of many provisional communities of interpretation generated by texts which in turn interpret diverse systems of signification. The reader can thus hardly remain unaware that his own attempt to respond to multiple, often mutually contradictory textual cues is one among many past and future readings.

Post-structuralist criticism is to some extent aware of the intersubjective dynamics of poetic genesis. Maria Corti begins her *Introduction to Literary Semiotics* by alluding to Eliot's argument in "Tradition and the Individual Talent" that if a writer sacrifices his own awareness to "the Mind of Europe" he can achieve a work which will change the whole canon.[12] But Corti is not primarily concerned with the means by which the function (the new work) both derives from and transforms the system (Tradition): the complementary readings that precede and follow writing. A literary text can seem to live long after its emotional, intellectual or cultural occasion because in various ways it demonstrates that it depends upon the expectation of completing response—even that it has been generated from such expectation. An individual talent can change Tradition only if he acknowledges that he has questioned many precursors and also submitted to questioning by them. Correspondingly, he can define his own individuality only by demanding that future readers make equivalent—indeed quasi-sacrificial—efforts to join the community which his interpretations generate.

When poets dramatize the limitations of their readings of common experience they demand from us reciprocal efforts of self-analysis like those demanded by prophecy, as defined by Martin Buber.

> The prophet addresses persons who hear him, who should hear him. He knows himself sent to them in order to place before them the stern alternatives of the hour. Even when he writes his message or has it written, whether it is already spoken or is still to be spoken, it is always intended for particular men, to induce them, as directly as if they were hearers, to recognize their situation's demand for decision and to act accordingly. The apocalyptic writer has no audience turned towards him: he speaks into his notebook. He does not write

---

material situation. . . . Its prerequisite is a concentration of attention on the dialogue itself as a chain of semantic reversals.

[12] Corti, pp. 1–2.

down the speech, he just writes his thoughts—he writes a book.[13]

Precisely when poets acknowledge that they write no more than text-bound apocalypse they challenge us to respond in the manner of the prophet's listeners: as free persons who are critics in the sense that they must respond to a crisis in whatever historical communities claim their allegiance.

But it is the very tenuousness of such allegiances in this century which authorizes literary attempts to transform apocalypse into prophecy. Provocatively self-reflexive modern and contemporary poetry responds to a particular crisis brought on by free-enterprise technology as well as by totalitarian political and economic ideologies: the weakening of demand for responsible critical response in other cultural institutions. Because the poetic text projects a common place for constructive cultural criticism by resisting as well as inviting critical analysis, it can provide the education in sustained commitment and responsible citizenship traditionally expected from church or state.[14]

If no text is any more than a model for the particular complex of interpretations which it projects,[15] the community to be generated by the interaction between text and readers is obviously no more than a model for a possible historical community. However, poetry can prepare us to live more effectively in the world because more than other institutions it respects the potential for interpersonal reciprocity that is

---

[13] "Prophecy, Apocalyptic and the Historical Hour" in *Pointing the Way* (New York, 1957), p. 200.

[14] See Walter J. Ong, *Interfaces of the Word* (Ithaca, 1977), esp. "Transformations of the Word and Alienation" and "The Poem as Closed Field: The Once New Criticism and the Nature of Literature." Though Father Ong is obviously optimistic about the power of the Church, he describes the influence of technology on discourse, in particular a weakening of the agonistic quality of culture.

[15] The classic statement of this view occurs in René Wellek's essay "The Mode of Existence of a Literary Work of Art" included in Wellek and Austin Warren, *Theory of Literature* (London, 1949), p. 152. The context is a discussion of the application of structural linguistics to literature, and Wellek cites Husserl.

> A literary work of art is in exactly the same position as a system of language. We as individuals shall never realize it completely and perfectly. The very same situation is actually exhibited in every single act of cognition. We shall never know an object in all its qualities, but still we can scarcely deny the identity of objects even though we may see them from different perspectives. We always grasp some "structure of determination" in the object which makes the act of cognition not an act of arbitrary invention or subjective distinction but the recognition of some norms imposed on us by reality. Similarly, the structure of a work of art has the character of a "duty which I have to realize." I shall always realize it imperfectly, but in spite of some incompleteness a certain "structure of determination" remains, just as in any other object of knowledge.

grounded in intensive mutual self-criticism.

Of course conscientious reading projects the fusion of horizons which Gadamer prescribes.

> In this the interpreter's own horizon is decisive, yet not as a personal standpoint that one holds on to or enforces, but more as a meaning and a possibility that one brings into play and puts at risk, and that helps one truly to make one's own what is said in the text.[16]

The risk involved in reading poetry, however, can be so high that there is no question of final fusion or accommodation of the alien, mutually resistant languages of poetic text and reader. And just because texts which survive their private or public occasion tend both to intensify and to extend the conflicts inherent in discourse, their readers' inevitable failure to construct an enduring common language projects renewed efforts to achieve that utopia.

As I have noted, Stevens' Man with the Blue Guitar explicitly demands that we reconsider all our definitions of ourselves and the world.

> Throw away the lights, the definitions . . .
> nothing must stand
>
> Between you and the shapes you take
> When the crust of shape has been destroyed.

Yet poets invite us more urgently to help remake the world when they dramatize the interplay among author, text, and reader projected by Stevens' apostrophes: when they provide fictional surrogates not only for themselves but also for their texts and for us, their readers.

In observing that poems represent discourse, Barbara Herrnstein Smith prepares us to interpret poets' representations of *poetic* discourse.

> As a mimetic artform, what a poem distinctively and characteristically represents is not images, ideas, feelings, characters, scenes, or worlds, but discourse. Poetry does, like drama, represent actions and events, but exclusively verbal ones. And as a verbal composition a poem is characteristically taken to be not a natural utterance but the representation of one. A poem represents discourse in the same sense as a play, in its totality, represents human actions and events, or a painting represents visual objects.[17]

This helps us see how poetry can mediate tensions between mimesis and poiesis in which post-structuralist criticism has located the differences between traditional and modern poetics.[18] According to Smith, poiesis *is*

---

[16] *Truth and Method*, p. 350.

[17] *On the Margins of Discourse* (Chicago, 1978), p. 25.

[18] See, for example, Paul de Man, "Lyric and Modernity" in *Blindness and Insight* (New York, 1971).

mimesis. If a poem is a fictive utterance without particular historical context and its characteristic effect is to create (poiesis) its own context—"or more accurately, to invite and enable the reader to create a plausible context for it"[19]—it does so because it represents (mimesis) the operations of language in general. The strongest poetry, however, supports Smith's analysis by representing a particular linguistic operation: the text-mediated exchange between authors and readers. Poetry can read the world authoritatively by providing fictional surrogates not only for authors and texts but also for readers who temporarily abandon the historical world in order to help construct new worlds of words—and thereby prepare to return to ordinary life with renewed determination to question accepted definitions, even to define such questioning as the only valid ground for private or public discourse.[20]

iii

Revelation is one among many provocative dramatizations of literary exchange by which writers from ancient times to the present have acknowledged—and thus tried to transcend—the limits of literature. Destruction is only half the story in this apocalypse. As the annihilation of the old world prepares for the construction of a new City, the context for all the radical discontinuities is sustained interplay among authors and readers whose mutual self-criticism projects an endlessly innovative community.

---

[19] Smith *op. cit.*, p. 33.

[20] In calling attention to the tendency for literature to represent *literary* discourse, I will attempt to extend the masterful analysis of dramatic monologue in *The Poetry of Experience* (London, 1957) by Robert Langbaum—whom Gerald Graff cites as a precursor of the deconstructionists who claim that literary works dramatize the problems of signification ("Deconstruction as Dogma, or Come Back to the Raft Ag'in, Strether Honey!" *Georgia Review*, Summer 1980, 405–21). See Langbaum, p. 191:

> It is the speaker's ultimate purpose that accounts for the curious style of the dramatic monologue. Not only does the speaker direct his address outward as in dialogue but the style of address gives the effect of a closed circuit, with the speaker directing his address outward in order that it may return with a meaning he was not aware of when sending it forth. I say a closed circuit because this utterance seems to be directed only obliquely at the ostensible auditor and seems never to reach its ultimate goal with him. Nor does the essential interchange take place with the auditor; for even where the auditor's remarks are implied, the speaker never learns anything from them and they do not change the meaning of the utterance. If the speaker represents one voice of a dialogue, then his other self is the essential second voice in that it sends back his own voice with a difference.

If we observe how poets have represented the whole complex interchange among themselves, texts, and readers, however, we may find the circuit more often open than closed— and the difference surprisingly large between the voice which the author sends out and the other which is sent back to him.

The text places the writer St. John and his readers across a brilliant "sea of glass" (4:6) from a celebration which praises a Reader as well as an Author, thus generating larger and larger communities of interpreters.

> And I saw in the right hand of him that sat on the throne a book written within and on the backside, sealed with seven seals.
> And I saw a strong angel proclaiming with a loud voice, Who is worthy to open the book, and to loose the seals thereof?
> And no man in heaven nor in earth, neither under the earth, was able to open the book, neither to look thereon.
> And I wept much, because no man was found worthy to open and to read the book, neither to look thereon.
> And one of the elders saith unto me, Weep not; behold the Lion of the tribe of Juda, the Root of David, hath prevailed to open the book, and to loose the seven seals thereof.
> And I beheld, and lo, in the midst of the throne and of the four beasts, and in the midst of the elders stood a Lamb as it had been slain, having seven horns and seven eyes, which are the seven spirits of God sent forth into all the earth.
> And he came and took the book out of the right hand of him that sat upon the throne.
> And when he had taken the book, the four beasts and four and twenty elders fell down before the Lamb, having every one of them harps, and golden vials full of odours, which are the prayers of saints.
> And they sung a new song, saying, Thou art worthy to take the book, and to open the seals thereof; for thou wast slain, and hast redeemed us to God by thy blood out of every kindred, and tongue, and people, and nation. (Revelation 5:1 ff.)[21]

The sea of glass could be seen as an image of the gap between any reader and any text—especially a text that dramatizes reading as Revelation does. And the sacrificed Lion/Lamb who opens a sealed scroll inscribed inside and out ("written within and on the backside") could be read as a surrogate for all interpreters who voluntarily subject themselves to the endless interplay between revelation and secrecy in literature. Indeed in depicting the Lamb "as it had been slain," already sacrificed, St. John defined sacrifice as the condition for successful reading of the Book of Life. And modern European and American poets who can only stand across a sea of glass from St. John's faith in the transcendental Word have offered mirror-reversals of this implied cause-effect sequence. For them, the reading of many books—each smaller than life— generates rigorous criticism of dominant cultural definitions and conventions: a bloodless equivalent of sacrifice which can establish communities even more vital than any maintained by cultic ritual.

But like their ancient predecessors, the strongest modern poets on

---

[21] In view of its stylistic excellence, I will refer to the King James version. But the most thorough and informative analysis of Revelation is to be found in the translation by J. Massynberde Ford in the Anchor Bible series (Garden City, 1975).

both sides of the Atlantic also insist that the radical self-criticism provoked by poetic texts can be fruitful only if it occurs in a community of
interpreters; the opening sequence in Revelation also anticipates this
concern. Once interest is divided between the central throne and the first
Reader of the Law written by the One on the throne ("and he came and
took the book out of the right hand of him that sat upon the throne"),
two groups of secondary interpreters initiate further displacements of
concern from unique center to multiple circumference. They thus begin
to actualize what is potential in correspondent doublings, the writing on
both sides of a scroll and the division of attention between Author and
Reader. If the all-witnessing four beasts ("full of eyes before and behind"
4:6) are personal figures of both the heavens and their earthly witnesses,
the twenty-four elders further signify collaboration by all temporal, historical Creation in the Lamb's reading. On this side of a bright mirror,
the sea of glass, St. John presents himself as a more intensely personal
representative of another company of fellow-witnesses: readers of his
meta-text which reflects many other Scriptural representations of
discourse.[22]

The ritual across the sea of glass explicitly transfers interest from the
unique Author not only to the unique but representative reader but also
to multitudes of other readers. When the beasts and elders turn away
from the throne to respond to the Lamb's reading of the scroll, they
project increasingly large circles of interpreters.

> And I beheld, and I heard the voice of many angels round about the
> throne and the beasts and the elders; and the number of them were
> ten thousand and thousands of thousands; Saying with a loud voice,
> Worthy is the Lamb that was slain to receive power, and riches and
> wisdom, and strength and honour, and glory and blessing. And every
> creature which is in the heaven, and on the earth, and under the
> earth, and such as are in the sea, and all that are in them, heard I
> saying, Blessing and honour and glory and power be unto him that
> sitteth upon the throne, and unto the Lamb for ever and ever.
> (5:11–13)

This first liturgy is completed when the first and second groups of secondary interpreters answer and authorize responses to the Lamb-Reader
as well as to the Author by two matching groups: "and the four beasts
said Amen. And the four and twenty elders fell down and worshipped
him that liveth for ever and ever" (14).

After an angel rises like a sun in the East (7:1–2), many more angels
and a multitude "which no man could number" (7:9) particularizes "all
creatures'" response to the beasts' and elders' praise of both Author and

---

[22] In *Revelation* (Philadelphia, 1979) pp. 124–25, J. P. M. Sweet provides a succinct
description of both the sacrificial force of the Lamb's participation and a good distinction
between different modes of interpretation—notably hearing and seeing—in the text.

Reader. But a brief dialogue between intepreters also corroborates the
initial transference of interest from the Law to the Lamb.

> And one of the elders answered, saying unto me, What are these
> which are arrayed in white robes? And whence came they?
> And I said unto him, Sir, thou knowest, and he said to me, these are
> they which came out of great tribulation, and have washed their
> robes and made them white in the blood of the Lamb. (7.13–14)

When one of the many elders asks the solitary witness across the sea of
glass to identify a second multitude of the Reader's interpreters, John
humbly refuses his invitation. He thus in fact anticipates the elder's
definition of the host as imitators of the self-humbling Lamb. Authority
is to be generated from a consensus among many interpreters, and each
achieves authority only by refusing to perpetuate the authorial tendency
to make exclusive prescriptions.

Another sequence in Revelation still more clearly defines reading as
a sacrificial self-challenge.

> And I saw as it were a sea of glass mingled with fire: and them that
> had gotten the victory over the beast, and over his image, and over
> his mark, and over the number of his name, stand on the sea of glass,
> having the harps of God . . . And after that I looked, and behold, the
> temple of the tabernacle of the testimony in heaven was opened . . .
> And the temple was filled with smoke from the glory of God, and
> from his power; and no man was able to enter into the temple, till
> the seven plagues of the seven angels were fulfilled. (15:2,5,8)

This worship of both the Law and its transference to the self-sacrificed
Reader ("they sang the song of Moses . . . the servant of God and the
song of the Lamb") develops the construction of a distinctively *literary*
temple in chapters 4–5. We are excluded from full participation in this
liturgy, as we are from any text: no man is able to enter into the temple
until the work of destruction is completed.

As poets from Pindar to Ashbery tend to insist, literature implicates
many active witnesses only by making severe restrictions and prohibi-
tions. Yet as the sea of glass is now mingled with the fire of martyrdom,
self-reflexive texts are illuminated if their readers as well as their authors
give themselves up to bearing witness that language is in fact "a book
written within and on the backside" which refuses any absolute differentiation of one from many, of inside from outside.

The angel who announces the marriage of the Lamb and Jerusalem
confirms earlier deconstructions of authority and authorship as opportunities for collaborative interpretation: as we have seen, he refuses to
stand upon ceremony with the human writer.

> And he saith unto me, Write, Blessed are they which are called unto
> the marriage supper of the Lamb. And he saith unto me, These are

the true sayings of God.
And I fell at his feet to worship him. And he said unto me, See thou
do it not: I am thy fellowservant and of thy brethren that have the
testimony of Jesus. (19:9–10)

Yet the angel also thus invites us to interpret the presentation of a violent double of the Lamb as paradigm for the conflict between revelation
and secrecy by which texts provoke our collaboration:

And I saw heaven opened, and behold a white horse and he that sat
upon him was called "Faithful and True," and in righteousness he
doth judge and make war. His eyes were as a flame of fire, and on
his head were many crowns; and he had a name written, that no
man knew, but he himself.
And he was clothed with a vesture dipped in blood: and his name
was called the Word of God.
And out of his mouth goeth a sharp sword, that with it he should
smite the nations: and he shall rule them with a rod of iron: and he
treadeth the winepress of the fierceness and wrath of Almighty God,
And he hath on his vesture and on his thigh a name written KING
OF KINGS AND LORD OF LORDS.
And I saw an angel standing in the sun; and he cried with a loud
voice, saying to all the fowls that fly in the midst of heaven, "Come
and gather yourselves together unto the supper of the great God."
(19:11–17)

The image of the brilliant Word retroactively defines the multi-reflective
"sea of glass" in chapter 4 as an unbridgeable gap between the reader of
the Book and the writer of this book—and, by analogy, between the
latter and *his* readers. Of course the fiery-eyed rider on the white horse
is clearly and unambiguously labelled the Word of God. But he also has
a secret name known only to himself: the Word is secretive as well as
revelatory. Indeed this vision shows how an author can invite us to an
equivalent of a marriage feast only if he continually reminds us that the
written word reveals to the extent that it conceals, provoking us to help
reread literary and cultural tradition by placing obstacles in our way.[23]
     Revelation can also stand as a model for both ancient and modern
poetry because several mockeries of the New Song call attention to the
specifically literary quality of five liturgies on the other side of the sea of
glass. These parodies prepare for a final apotheosis of scriptural self-
reflexivity in this last book of Scripture. In chapter 13 an anti-Lamb has
been worshipped in a demonic mockery of heavenly worship of the
sacrifice which opened the Book of Life.

And I saw one of his heads as it were wounded to death: and his

---

[23] In *The Genesis of Secrecy* (Cambridge, Mass., 1979), Frank Kermode follows the
continental avant-garde in stressing the negative moment of what I will present as a dialectic which is indeed a genesis—but of more than concealment.

> deadly wound was healed: and all the world wondered after the
> beast.
> And they worshipped the dragon which gave power unto the beast:
> and they worshipped the beast. (13:3–4)

This anti-Lamb has been matched by an even more striking parodic
double of the Reader who initiates a still more elaborate deconstruction
of merely deceptive image-making:

> And I beheld another beast coming up out of the earth; and he had
> two horns like a lamb, and he spake as a dragon. And he exerciseth
> all the power of the first beast before him, and causeth the earth and
> them which dwell therein to worship the first beast, whose deadly
> wound was healed. (13:11–12)

These sequences should have reminded us that responsible image-makers
impose many restrictions upon interpreters in order to make them reflect
upon their own eagerness to be deceived—and thus form a community
of iconoclasts as self-critical as the idolatrous are self-indulgent. But the
recreative power of literary negation is still more clearly seen in two
strange reconstructions of the historical Temple of Jerusalem.

The new Jerusalem is to be constructed in challenges between the
Reader and innumerable secondary interpreters.

> And the building of the wall of it was jasper: and the city was pure
> gold, like unto clear glass.
> And the foundations of the wall of the city were garnished with all
> manner of precious stones. The first foundation was jasper; the sec-
> ond sapphire; the third . . . .
> And I saw no temple therein: for the Lord Almighty and the Lamb
> are the temple of it.
> And the city had no need for the sun, neither of the moon, to shine
> in it: for the glory of God did lighten it, and the Lamb is the light
> thereof . . .
> And there shall in no wise enter into it anything that defileth neither
> whatsoever worketh abomination, or maketh a lie; but they which
> are written in the Lamb's book of life. (21:18–19; 22–23; 27)

"Jerusalem" is an apotheosis of the textual utopian common place for
endless reflection upon the lack of genuinely self-critical community in
any historical city. It thus has no need of either the natural sun or an
architectural enclosure like those which cities provide for reflection upon
history. But St. John privileges the member of literary discourse usually
assigned secondary importance: the sun-like light who activates all interchange in the templeless City is the Reader–Lamb.

Indeed St. John closes his book by demonstrating that the actual
reader must initiate revelation. In chapter 11 he has been called across
the sea of glass to measure the temple with a reed like the sword that
emerges from the mouth of the secretive as well as proclamatory Word

(19:15). In chapter 21 he watches the angel measure the City with another substitute for his pen, a golden reed: "and he measured the wall thereof an hundred and forty cubits, according to the measure of a man, that is, of the angel" (17). As St. John measures the City in terms of his counterpart, the angel, the strongest ancient and modern poets invite their counterparts, future readers, to take their own measure and that of the times in which they live. But if the City is exclusive, the communities projected by strong poetry set precise and difficult conditions of entry and exit. Each is made to the measure of a man who knows that he is one among many heralds of an Authority whose power derives from the response of many witnesses.

iv

The prologue and epilogue of Revelation emphasize the fact that writers can only authoritatively project endings to the violent conflicts which move history by insisting that no definitive reconciliation is possible. The beginning and ending of this text which closes Scripture by defining the Lord as Alpha and Omega of universal history (21:6) thus opens *literary* history to constructive rereadings. Together, these passages help us look back to endlessly challenging transformations of conflict into conjugal harmony by Pindar and the Psalmist and forward to modern European and American poets' projections of communities more self-aware than any which history records.

Letters to seven eastern churches from a solitary exile on the island of Patmos prepare us to read the descent of the Bride-City as provocation for perpetual reenactment of matching mutilations: the sacrifice of the Reader and his unsealing of the Book.

> I was in the Spirit on the Lord's day, and heard behind me a great voice, as of a trumpet,
> Saying, I am Alpha and Omega, the first and the last: and What thou seest write in a book, and send it unto the seven churches. . . .
> Unto the angel of the church of Ephesus write: These things saith he that holdeth the seven stars in his right hand. . . .
> And unto the angel of the church in Smyrna write: These things saith the first and the last. . . .
> And to the angel of the church in Pergamos write: These things saith he which hath the sharp sword with two edges. . . . (1:10–11; 2:1,8,12)

The prologue seven times designates the ambiguous words of revelation as the primary subject of a text that describes its own genesis. This makes a supreme virtue of a necessity which Pindar and the Psalmist had already read as a severe challenge to their art, and which modern poets have more explicitly acknowledged as an almost definitive obstacle. Although temporal and spatial distance between writer and reader is the very *raison d'être* of literature, the more widely separated the inter-locutors to be joined by a text the greater the strain placed on this extremely fragile medium of discourse. Yet the dramatization of disso-nance and divorce as well as harmony and marriage in Revelation shows that it is precisely when writers emphasize tensions between themselves and their readers that they project the most radiant images of conjugal reconciliation. Some of the strongest poets before and after St. John—Pindar, the writer of Psalm 19, Hölderlin, Mallarmé, Wallace Stevens—have called attention to the fact that they do not share their readers' time and space; they have thereby demonstrated that in poetry the fail-ure to connect can produce extraordinarily fertile connections. Poets have become more and more alienated from their audiences as the locus of performance has shifted from the ancient temple or dancing-floor at victory-banquets to the printed page in industrialized mass culture—and then again from concentrated Europe to the vast North American conti-nent. But from the time of the Psalmist and Pindar to the present, the writers who have most passionately insisted that their textual interpreta-tions of life do *not* communicate have constructed the most enduring communities of understanding.

The ending of St. John's flagrantly artful rewriting of the natural creation in Genesis also suggests how the marriage projected by the best ancient and modern poetry is animated by mutual challenge between writers and readers.

> And the Spirit and the bride say, Come. And let him that heareth say Come. And let him that is athirst come. And whosoever will, let him take the water of life freely.
> For I testify unto every man that heareth the words of the prophecy of this book, If any man add unto these things, God shall add unto him the plagues that are written in this book:
> And if any man shall take away from the words of the book of this prophecy, God shall take away his part out of the book of life, and out of the holy city, and from the things which are written in this book. (22:17–19)

This final sequence reminds us that the slain Lamb's unsealing of the Book is paradoxically commemorated by the apparition of an absolutely closed, self-reflexive City. Although it invites readers to participate in the wedding feast of the Lamb and the Bride, it also seals the actual book—and the Book which that closes. It prohibits either addition or subtraction as imperiously as the Lord sealed off the Tree of Knowledge from the first human couple in the first book of Scripture. Doubling the dramatic genesis of marriage from violent divorce in the central vision, the mutual contradiction of these two verses helps explain why Revelation has informed so many strong projections of community by modern Euro-pean and American poets.

Poetry can unite us both with geographically distant contemporaries and historically distant predecessors and successors if it prevents us from continuing to accept codes and conventions which keep us apart from people who have lived, are living, or may live in other times and places. In order to bring about this ultimately connective disconnection, poets from Pindar to Ashbery challenge us to turn upon ourselves and our communities the mutually contradictory impulses to add and to subtract, to marry and to divorce, which their texts generate. Denying us the immediate gratification of the quick comeback, the best poetry provokes potentially endless reflection upon the processes of mediation that define us both as individuals and as members of many different communities— including some which history will probably never record.

v

The following experiments in reading will stress a continuity in poetic explorations of discontinuity. Each section will consider works generated by one phase in a progressive widening of the inevitable gap between writer and reader dramatized in Revelation. But I will be arguing that literature is neither the ahistorical "order of words" to which Northrop Frye alludes in his essay on "Lycidas"[24] nor the ineluctably historical heap of ruins which Walter Benjamin evokes in his essays on the German *Trauerspiel*—another seventeenth-century extrapolation from the New Testament apocalypse.[25] Each essay will thus also take a cue from the strange temporality of ordinary dialogue.

Dialogue is anachronic (*ana* = against/*chrónos*). It continually folds time back upon itself by reiterating a rupture: a more or less stressed usurpation of the initiator-role. Time is a primary referent in many dialogues, and many literary variants of speech aim at the total commemoration and resolution of historical conflict which the apocalyptist imagined as a cosmic marriage. But the time of dialogue is always out of joint. It sets alpha against omega, "I" against "you," making them compete for the privilege of directing discourse: of writing as opposed to reading.

My attempts to listen in on dialogues between ancient and modern, European and American reader/writers should therefore be excused what may at first sight seem a taste for anachronism inappropriate in discussions of literary history. Having read first back and then forward from Revelation, I will continue to emphasize a Heraclitean wisdom which T. S. Eliot could have added to his observation in *Four Quartets* that the way up is the way down. For modern poetry the way forward

---

[24] Frye, *Fables of Identity* (New York, 1963) pp. 119–29.
[25] Benjamin, *The Origin of German Tragic Drama*, trans. John Osborne (London, 1977).

has certainly been the way back. But might not the more invigorating reversal of that formula prove equally true?

As scrupulously self-critical as any avant-garde theory, the most compelling modern poetry develops the projections of a City in the final book of Scripture by analyzing the complex dynamics of writing and reading. Having reread projections of community by two other ancient writers besides St. John, Pindar and the Psalmist, we will be able to see how modern European and American poets—Milton, Wordsworth, Höl-derlin, Mallarmé, and Celan on the one hand and Whitman, Stevens, Eliot, Pound, Williams, Ashbery, and Ammons on the other—have built textual New Jerusalems that can withstand the most strenuous decon-struction because they are neither more nor less than prefigurations of continuing self-criticism by readers.[26]

---

[26] Although many of my readings of particular texts and my main argument differ strongly from his, I applaud the effort by W. R. Johnson in *The Idea of Lyric: Lyric Modes in Ancient and Modern Poetry* (Berkeley, 1982) to enlarge the expectations we bring to modern poetry by invoking the rich variety of motives and strategies in the ancient lyric. I will also be arguing that poetry, not only modern but also "post-modern" or contemporary, can meet the objections of two healthily vehement foes of lyric solip-sism, Wendell Berry, "The Specialization of Poetry," *Hudson Review* (1975) and Christo-pher Clausen, "The Decline of Anglo-American Poetry," *Virginia Quarterly Review* LIV (1978), 73–86.

ONE
Other Ancient Models

1

Pindar and the Chorus

i

Kronos castrates his father, Uranus, and throws the bleeding genitals into the sea; from the sea-foam springs Aphrodite, principle of unending fertility. Kronos has children by his sister Rhea but swallows each at birth—except Zeus, whom Rhea saves by substituting a phallic stone for him. Zeus eventually either imprisons or castrates Kronos but also allows him to govern the blessed dead. When Zeus falls in turn, Kronos will return and end all conflict once and for all.

But the Kronos-myth does not respect the stable identity of father or son: it celebrates the process of alternation which transmits life. E. R. Leach finds in the myth a representation of the Greek sense of time (*chrónos*) as a continual reversal, most evident during the sacred time of festival in which roles are continually reversed so that death can be converted into birth.[1] It is therefore not surprising that Pindar built around the story of Kronos one of his most complex and powerful odes, *Pythia* 8.

In his festival-songs Pindar tried to ensure that the identity of men, families, and cities would remain stable by reminding his audience that the course of life is made up of continual conflict between one moment or person and others—like the races at the festival games and the recurrent movement of the chorus in the victory ode through strophe, antistrophe, and epode. He was never concerned with the isolated individual or instant, but with the ways in which persons and times are related by many different kinds of exchange. Dramatizing the alternation of gods and heroes, patron and poet in the active and passive roles of discourse, Pindar established our common subjection to pendulum-swings in moral as well as physical life as an opportunity (*kairós*) to know that end (*télos*) is significantly related to origin (*arché*). Yet his odes show how language can conquer time because he was not only concerned with the dynamics of giving and receiving in general but also repeatedly referred to two particular economies which organize conflict in order to project images of perfection.[2]

---

[1] "Two Essays Concerning the Symbolic Representation of Time" in *Rethinking Anthropology* (London, 1961).

[2] Jacqueline Duchemin, *Pindar: Poète et prophète* (Paris, 1955), p. 317:

In several odes the first of two extraordinary communal assemblies, the athletic games and the victory banquet, serves as model for a gathering of moments in the life of individual and city. *Nemea* 3 presents the athletic contest as the means by which the whole of a person's nature is manifest at once: the three categories in the games correspond to three stages in life.

> The end shines through (*télos diaphaínetai*)
> in the testing of actions where excellence is shown,
> as a boy among boys, a man among men, last
> among the elders, each part that makes
> our mortal life.

The following lines corroborate this metaphoric use of the games, speaking of life as a chariot race: "human destiny (*thánatos aión*) drives four excellences. . . ." *Nemea* 6 defines the race as analogue of the driving of mortal life toward wholeness through oscillation, and also suggests that ends are best related to origins through this particular means: the recurrent gathering of many to witness conflict. (In Lattimore's translation the ambiguity of the English word "race" fortuitously embellishes Pindar's comparison of the passage of time to the running and driving at the games.)

> There is one
> race of men, one race of gods: both have breath
> of life from a single mother. But sundered power
> holds us divided, so that the one is nothing, while
> for the other the brazen sky is established
> their sure citadel forever. Yet we have some likeness in great
> intelligence, or strength, to the immortals,
> though we know not what the day will bring, what course
> after nightfall
> destiny has written that we must run to the end.

> For witness
> even now, behold how his lineage works in Alkimidas.
> It is like cornfields that exchange their estate,
> now in their year to yield life to men from their level spaces
> while again they lie fallow to gather strength. He came
> home from the lively games at Nemea,
> a boy contestant; and steering this destiny from God
> he shows how
> as one not ill-starred in his quest of prizes for wrestling,

le lien étroit entre cette victoire même et le poème qui la chante est attesté sans ambiguité par le role des Charités à la fois dans la proclamation immédiate et dans la célébration ultérieure de cette victoire; il s'agit de deux moments successifs, mais étroitement liées, d'un même acte religieux . . . il [l'hymne] porte le trace de caractères dont les contemporains eux-mêmes avaient pu perdre le souvenir, mais dont les résidus, pour nous très instructif, demeurent visibles.

laying his feet in the steps that are his by blood
of his grandfather, Praxidamas.

As recall of a common maternal origin (*matros amphóteroi*, 1. 2) qualifies the initial distinction between gods and men (*hèn andrón, hèn
theón*), the second opposition between day and night (*ouk eidótes oudè
metà núktas*, 1. 6), is resolved not by reference to a stable point of origin
but to competition on the race course (*dramein potì státhman*, 1. 7).
The image of the competition through which one man emerges as the
symbol of communal vitality and unity authorizes reference to another
pattern for the making of lively unity through alternation: the process of
seasonal change (*ameibómenai*, 1. 9). Nature at one time (*tóka*, 1. 10)
yields fruit and at another (*tóka*, 1. 11) gathers energy by resting. The
reassuring observation that gods and men are not only opposed but also
like each other (*allá ti prosphéromen*, 1. 4) introduces a more striking
likeness: energy passes from potent grandfather to potent grandson
through the fallow father as spring restores the vitality of summer after
winter has passed. Yet this comparison has emerged from a presentation
of the contrast between day and night as a race. Although the sequence
ends with a stress of origin (*patropátoros*) it is an extension of the metaphor of athletic contest which authorizes recall of a patriarch as well as
reference to the seasons. While the boy has been a hunter (*kunagétas*,
1. 15) in the wrestling match, he has pursued (*methépon*, 1. 13) his destiny and stalked his grandfather.[3]

Because Pindar continually stressed the importance of middlemen,
his audiences could recognize a glorious moment in the middle of the
athlete-patron's career as a sign that ends are to be consistent with origins. This is apparent in his presentation of the Hermes myth in
Pythia 2. Hermes goes between the realms of the living and the dead,
his mediatory function represented by phallic stones like the one which
Rhea gave Kronos instead of Zeus—signs of the continual transmission of
life. *Pythia* 2 recalls Hermes the god of athletic contests (*enagónios
Hermas*, 1. 10) and then honors the chariot race of Hieron by evoking
dead Ixion, whose wheeling is a demonic parody of the living hero's
course. Trying to possess divine Hera, Ixion not only subjected himself to
endless nonsignificant repetition but also began the race of centaurs,
grotesque counterparts to *two* figures who stand halfway between
realms—Pindar as well as Hermes. This mockery of both the charioteer's
turning on the race course and the poet's mediation between his patron
and the gods as well as the community is countered by the image of one
who judges properly between alternatives. Rhadamanthys (1. 73) personifies the wisdom which this song can give its listener/readers: personal

---

[3] Charles P. Segal has studied references to seasonal rhythms in *Nemea* 5, "Arrest and
Movement," *Hermes* XXII (1970).

integrity demands continual acknowledgment that convention (*nómos*) and nature (*phýsis*) are not only opposed but also both moved by internal oppositions.

Although Hermes' games often served Pindar as a model of perfection, his proper domain was the victory celebration: the chorus' turning through strophe and antistrophe was his primary metaphor for a progress through alternation which opposes the linear movement of life toward death. The opening of *Pythia* 1 shows how Pindar made the turn and counter-turn of singing dancers represent freedom and wholeness.

> Golden lyre, held of Apollo in common possession
> with the violet-haired Muses: the dance-steps,
>   leaders of festivals, heed you;
> the singers obey your measures
> when, shaken with music, you cast the beat to lead
>   choirs of dancers.
> You have power to quench the speared thunderbolt
> of flowing fire. Zeus' eagle sleeps on his staff,
>   folding his quick wings both ways to quiet,
>
> Violent Ares even, leaving aside the stern pride
> of spears, makes gentle his heart in sleep.
>
> Yet such creatures as Zeus loves not are shaken to hear
> the music of the Pierides, whether on earth or the sea
>   unresting.

Praise for Hieron seems to arise from response to an instrument that only accompanies the words and gestures which are to interrelate the patron's extraordinary moment of success in the special time of the games with the ensuing history of the community and family whom he represents. Usually the Muse-led songs lead the lyre as in *Olympia* 2, "my songs, lords of the lyre (*anaxiphormigges*)." Here the inversion of agency within the limited economy of song supports a more audacious cosmic inversion. This lyre rules the gods as well as the gods' enemies: apostrophe transforms the particular visible instrument into the Pythagoreans' symbol of the universe.[4]

---

[4] R. W. B. Burton, *Pindar's Pythian Odes* (Oxford, 1962), p. 91:

> The impression of unity, clear enough even to us who can only read
> the poem, must have been much more vivid to those who heard it
> performed, because the lyre of the opening verses, the symbol of
> music and of what music stands for in this ode, was visible and aud-
> ible throughout as the unifying instrument.

See also Hermann Fraenkel, *Dichtung und Philosophie des frühen Griechentums* (New York, 1951), p. 625:

> Die Chorlyrik deren Meister er ist, mit ihren Worten und Melodien
> und dem sinnreichen Tanzspiel edler, geschmückter Menschen, ist für
> ihn und seine Kreise selbst schon ein Stück werthafte Wirklichkeit,
> vergleichbar dem stolzen Prunk der Wettspiele. Wie Heraklit in

Like the lyre in *Pythia* 1, all of Pindar's major symbols not only transmit and receive energy to and from other moments in the songs. They also celebrate a self-conscious gathering (*súmbole*) of speakers and listeners in a sacred time-out-of-time to which the poet referred in order to suggest that the whole can always be known through and by the part or member. The context of performance gives symbol (metaphor) the force of synecdoche, a kind of metonymy. The texts of the odes can thus still tease us out of thought into experiencing the present moment of reading as a vital transcendence of linear *chrónos*.

In *Pythia* 3, *Pythia* 8, and *Olympia* 2 Pindar consummately developed his strategy of giving audiences a sense that they were members of a significant whole: of a human time in which ends do not contradict but complement origins. Each in its own manner, these three odes show how the second part of the two-part festival helped Pindar establish a distinctive alternation, dialogue, as the unstable "origin" of a community of times and persons.[5]

ii

Pythia 3 suggests that Pindar could speak with such authority in the first-person singular because his *epinikia* were usually performed by a chorus. This consolation addressed to the ailing Hieron, patron and hero of three other odes, *Olympia* 1, *Pythia* 1, and *Pythia* 2, was apparently not intended for choral performance.[6] However, it is this remarkable poem which perhaps most strongly of all the odes presents the symbolic implications of choral performance. Writing with knowledge that the

---

erweckter Bewusstheit den Sinn der Welt am eigene Dasein erlebt, so lebt sich in Pindars Chorliedern das Gute und Schöne im erleuchteten Bewusstsein und festlichen Darstellen seines eignen Sinnes aus. Verheissung und Erfüllung fallen hier zusammen. Darum darf Pindars Kunst so oft und nachdrucklich von sich selbst reden.

[5] I will attempt to qualify Mary K. Lefkowitz' skillful demonstration of the importance of the single voice in Pindar, "TO KAI EGO: The First Person in Pindar," *Harvard Studies in Classical Philology* LVII (1963), 177–253.

It is difficult to explain why *epinikia* were usually performed by choruses, in spite of their subject matter, and in spite of the fact that the poet speaks in his own person throughout. Perhaps the earlier *epinikia* were purely choral in form, concerned with the celebration and the immediate importance of the victory. But with the growth of humanism in Greece . . . the presence of a professional poet was eventually required at the victory celebration, a poet who would naturally, like his predecessors the epic *aoidai* speak in the first person and concentrate not on local affairs but on the universal significance of the victory. (p. 236)

[6] Ulrich von Wilamowitz-Moellendorff, *Pindaros* (Berlin, 1922), p. 280; Burton, p. 78; Lewis Richard Farnell, *Critical Commentary on the Works of Pindar* (1932; rprt. Amsterdam, 1965), p. 135.

usual conditions of presentation would not prevail, the poet would have been especially alert to the expressiveness inherent in his offering of a self-referential argument to many listeners in several voices. This ode establishes as models for both personal and communal identity the yielding of one voice to many and the recurrent turn and counter-turn of several feet over the same ground.[7]

In *Pythia* 3 Pindar defined his song as a healing drug by contrasting with his own performance several attempts at transcendence by persons who heard or spoke charms: Chiron, Asklepios, Koronis, Peleus, and Kadmos. The argument continually turns on itself and suggests that the individual is himself to the extent that he knows he is a member of a community including the dead, the living, and the unborn: a kind of chorus held together because each member at one moment tries to stop the common return to nonexistence. As the dancers would turn nearly one hundred and eighty degrees in one direction during a strophe and reverse their progress in the antistrophe, thus implying a complete circle, *Pythia* 3 is unified by the recurrence of stories not only about actions that inadvertently turn on themselves but also about self-conscious, self-referential song.

---

[7] In his excellent study of *Pythia* 3 in *Three Odes of Pindar* (Leiden, 1968), David C. Young comments on the climactic evocation of the wedding: "Significantly among these events which rendered Peleus and Cadmus the most blessed of men, Pindar lists as foremost the celebration in song by the chorus of Muses" (p. 53). In a footnote he states: "Pindar's song celebrates Hieron in the same way" (p. 53, n. 4) and notes further, "the lack of marriage-songs performed in Coronis's honor contributed greatly to her misfortune" (p. 54) and "as the suffering men were cured by Asklepios, so the suffering hearts of the two heroes were 'cured' by festivities and songs in their honor" (p. 54). However, Young does not stress the choral nature of the songs mentioned and projected nor the urgency with which the poet presents himself both in the dual role of speaker and listener in choral song, and as an alter ego of the several presenters and audiences of therapeutic song in the past.

As the exception to the rule of choral performance *Pythia* 3 can be read as proof that the mixture of words, music and dance had great expressive value. Fraenkel observed how the texts of the songs allowed the performance to be repeated.

> Die Heimatstadt des Siegers, der nach griechischer Auffassung die Glorie des Erfolgs in vollem Masse zu Gute kam, mochete sich das Gedicht in ihr Archiv legen. Und aus den Handschriften konnten die Gedichte jederzeit wieder zu klingendem Leben erweckt werden. Denn es stand nichts in Wege, dass auch ein einzelner die Lieder sang und sich dazu selbst begleitete. Die Melodien waren ohnehin einstimmig, und alle Mitglieder der guten Gesellschaft waren in der Lyrischen Kunst geschult. (pp. 544–45)

In the Odes the written word is not simply opposed to speech (cf. Plato's *Phaedrus*) but powerful because it recalls and provokes performance. However, if we are to respond strongly to the ancient choral lyrics and modern imitations of them, we must respect the priority which both gave to the spoken word. As the texts of the Odes and Psalms are vital because they are *pre*-texts for performance, modern experiments in restoring the public dimension of song succeed to the extent that they render the multivocal quality of these works.

The bard begins to bring Hieron back to health by wishing for what he knows is impossible: he would bring back from the dead another mediator, the half-man/half-horse Chiron, teacher of yet another go-between, Asklepios.

> I could wish that Chiron, Philyra's son
> (if such a word of prayer from my lips could be published),
> the departed, were living yet . . .
>   as of old when he reared
> the gentle smith (*téktona nodunías*) of pain's ease to heal
>   bodies, Asklepios,
> the hero who warded sickness of every kind.

The poem proves the folly of such a wish to use words to change the course of nature by recalling how both Koronis, mother of Asklepios, and Asklepios himself did violence to song: one ignored its power to affect nature and the other over-asserted it. The bride of Apollo, patron of poetry "could not stay for the coming of the bride-feast,/ not for hymen cry in many voices (*pamphónon*), such things/ as the maiden companions of youth are accustomed to sing/ at nightfall, using the old names of endearment." Carrying Apollo's child, Koronis was in love with what was not there (*ton apeónton*) instead of listening to what *was* there (*epichória*): the choral songs of maidens who are not yet brides but who remember the anticipatory songs of all brides who have come before. The maidens' evening songs (*hesperíais . . . aoidaís*, 1. 19) can legitimize intercourse between an earthly mortal and a heavenly patron of harmony, Apollo: at the moment which is no longer day and not yet night many single voices join and thus enact what they celebrate, an intimate association of one with another and others. (*Choròs*, round-dance, spelled with the small "o," omicron, is not related to *choros*, the space in which a thing is, spelled with the great "o," omega, but in *Pythia* 3 Pindar continually associated here with song and there with a violation of the choral economy.)

When the bride refuses to listen to the hymenal song, the sun-like bridegroom manifests himself as fire that answers her violence to communal tradition.

>   and many a neighbor
> shared, and was smitten together. Fire on a mountain leaping
> from one seed will obliterate a great forest.

Through elaborate indirection, however, the healing god of song restores a community and again marries heaven and earth. Rescuing Koronis' child from the fire, he gives him to the centaur "to be perfected in the healing of sickness that brings pain to men." Asklepios uses words, incantations (*epaoidaís*, 1. 51), as well as drugs. When he is offered another sign of exchange, however, the human mediator exceeds his role: trying

to have what is not here, he brings a man back from the dead. The poet
presents this story as an *exemplum*:

> With our mortal minds we should seek from gods that which
> becomes us,
> knowing the way of the destiny ever at our feet (*tò pàr podós*).
> Dear soul of mine, never urge a life beyond
> mortality, but work the means (*machanán*) at hand to the end.

Pindar thus prepared to make explicit what was implied in the Koronis-
episode—and again suggested that his medium is itself both paradigm
and source of order. What in fact would be here at our feet if the ode
were performed is the turning of the chorus' feet through strophe,
antistrophe, and epode.[8]

The bard then turns to *his* mother, promising to enact the devotion
to what is *pàr podós* and join maidens in their choral dance at a nearby
shrine—at night, as Koronis' song was in the evening. He thereby more
clearly affirms what was rejected by Koronis, mother of the other word-
healer, Asklepios: here and now song can unite here and there, now and
then.

> But I will pray to the Great Mother
> to whom night after night before my doors (*pár emòn próthuron*), a
> stately goddess,
> the maidens dance, and to Pan beside her.

The poet would go to the Mother's shrine not simply because it is nearby
but also because there the dancers enact the gathering of all times and
persons characteristic of *this* song which would be here and now if it
were performed by a chorus. Many dimensions and several particular
actions are related in this promise of worship.

The poet must try to undo the other son's reenactment of a mother's
crime against song which binds all times and places because he himself
has been tempted by the prospect of his patron's money to bring a man
back from the dead. Before promising to take part in another musical
celebration, he has recalled the unspeakable wish which began this song.

> But if only temperate Chiron were living yet in his cave,
> and the charm of these songs I make might have cast some spell
> (*philtron*)

---

[8] Burton, p. 181:
> "That which runs at my feet" is primarily the debt of song due to the
> victor but it includes also . . . the victory itself, whose fame must be
> given wings by the poet's art.

As the first-person singular pronoun in the formula which concludes *Pythia* 3, "I will
work out the divinity that's busy within my mind" (*therapeúon machanán*) can be attributed to both poet and athlete/patron, so here both poet and athlete/patron have skill
(*machana*) in running.

across his heart, I could have persuaded him even now
to give me a healer against the burning sickness of great men.

The hypothetical resuscitation of the dead and the projected prayer to the
ever-living Mother both reflect the conditional quality of a text which was
not to be performed as were the victory odes. Yet just past the midpoint in
the turning of this poem the bard has made a dramatic choice between
models for song. He has rejected Asklepios' solitary, self-serving and thus
self-destroying incantation and promised to attend a reenactment of that
celebration of natural recurrence which Koronis violated. When Pindar
juxtaposed two ways of using language, one which counters the course of
nature and the other which follows it, he defined poetic performance as a
means of affirming not only personal identity but also the interrelatedness
of all times, persons, and places. Of course Pindar's insistent use of choral
song as his standard is all the more striking because this text was itself not to
be performed. But like his many modern emulators who would never hear
any of their texts performed by choruses, Pindar was clearly inspired to
insist upon the chorus' power to maintain community just because he knew
that his poem would only be read in private. As we have seen in Revelation,
which alternately dramatizes writing and choral song, emphasis of the fact
that a text is exclusively literary can generate a very strong appreciation of
choral, communal expression.
    A third evocation of choral song strengthens implications of the
other two.

> When Kadmos married Harmonia, Peleus wed the sea's daughter
>   Thetis.
>   They heard on the mountain
> and at seven-gated Thebes the gold-chapleted Muses singing (*mel-*
>   *pomenan*)
> when one married ox-eyed Harmonia, and the other
> wise Nereus' legendary daughter, Thetis.

But the poet recalls this other musical feast that doubles the one which
would normally be given the hero of the games only after he has
assigned his host the role of interpreting the complex course of life as
well as of this continually self-qualifying song.

> But, Hieron, if you know how to take the straight issue
>   of words (*sunémen koruphán*) you have seen from
>   what came before:
> for every one good thing the immortals bestow on men
> two evils. Men who are as children cannot take this
>   becomingly;
> but good men do, turning the brightness outward.

If the ailing reader acknowledges that contradiction is the rule of existence, *this* perverse song can definitively challenge the human tendency

to define by exclusion. Pindar invited his patron to play Kadmos or
Peleus at a song-banquet—but with the knowledge that the violent con-
sequences of that double celebration, the sufferings of Kadmos' and
Peleus' children, are dissonances which assure the harmony of evening
songs. If the patron–reader has been brought to share the poet's understanding that there-and-then is always opposed to here-and-now (pàr
podós), the hypothetical movement of feet and voices in organized turn
and counter-turn can serve as model for a persistence of the individual
through surrounding and succeeding movements of nature and history.

> Nestor and Sarpedon of Lykia we know,
> men's speech, from the sounding words that smiths (téktones)
> of song in their wisdom
> built to beauty. In the glory of poetry achievement of men
> blossoms long (chronía teléthei).

The poet thus places himself with Hieron as writer/reader in a succession that matches the potentially endless turning of the dancers.

The formula that introduces this final statement interprets contrasts
between the ways in which the poet's several fellow performers and
interpreters have used words. An emphatic repetition of the first-person
singular pronoun finally establishes the analogy between public choral
performances—Koronis' wedding, the dance in the nearby temple,
Harmonia's wedding—and private reading.

> I will be small in small things, great among great.
> I will work out the divinity that is busy within
> my mind
> and tend the means that are mine (therapeúon machanán)

The speaker will concern himself with movements by the divine guard-
ian of his mind (daímon) and not step outside the clearly demarcated
circle of a particular mental economy. But his solitary reflections will
form a microcosm in turn to the dance in praise of the macrocosmic
Mother. And even when Pindar prepared to close by restricting his concern to his own mind, he further intensified the intimacy with another
self-conscious interpreter which he defined as both a model and a source
of regeneration powerful enough to replace public performance. In projecting sustained work within the limits of his own mind he was only
saying what his primary reader should have said if this textual gathering
of allusions to many choral performances had effected the marriage of
true minds which he requested before recalling Harmonia's wedding
feast: "but, Hieron, if you know how to take the straight issue of words,
you have seen from what came before. . . ."

No identity in this weave of analogies is exclusive. Not only are
Chiron, Koronis, Asklepios, Peleus, and Kadmos images of the poet as
teacher, speaker, and listener: they all also reflect the primary reader,

Hieron. The "I" to be produced by the unusually intimate performance is one shared by the two major parties to the exchange which it proposes. When Pindar gave Hieron and himself the roles of Kadmos and Peleus, he clearly suggested that the individual can become immortal by turning through a round of recollective and projective articulations of conflict— honoring a motherly All which dances at our feet at least until the festival song is over.

iii

In *Pythia* 8 Pindar established the language of choral lyric as the medium of strong, free community by calling attention to the dynamics of speech. From the outset the text repeatedly reassigns the roles of speaker and listener, giver and receiver. It begins by addressing communal harmony, Hesychia, as alternative receiver of the homage due the human victor in the games.

> Hesychia, kind goddess of peace, daughter
> of Justice and lady of the greatness of cities:
> you who hold the high keys
> of wars and of councils
> accept for Aristomenes this train of Pythian victory.
> For you understand, in strict measure of season (*kairo*),
> deeds (*érxai*) of gentleness and their experience (*pathein*) likewise.

Pindar gave equal weight to giving and receiving when he presented the athlete's victory as an offering to one who personifies the community's power to receive proof of its collective power to act, honoring her dual powers: active and passive. And if Aristomenes, the victor, first gives honor to a personification of kindness, he next *receives* kindness— not only from the god of poetry and prophecy but also from the poet himself.

> Apollo . . . now in mood of kindness
> has received Xenarkes' son, home from Kirrha and garlanded
> with leaves of Parnassos and with song in the Dorian strain.

As the victor's role is reversible, by singing of his triumph the poet can enter into several different relationships with Apollo, who speaks through the Pythia.

Although Pindar here did not address one of the elements of the actual performance as he did the lyre in *Pythia* 1, this song much more elaborately imitates its principal subject: a community's consistency with itself in giving and receiving.

> This island, that in its city's
> righteousness has touched
> the famed valors of the Aiakidai, has not

> fallen away from the Graces. She keeps
> glory perfect from the beginning (*teléan d'éxei*
>   *do an ap'archas*) and is sung of many (*polloísi* . . . *aeídetai*)
> for her shaping of heroes that surpassed in excellence
> of games, and in the speed of their fighting also.

Halfway through the ode, Delphi, the city of victory, becomes the focus of attention, but the beginning and end of the poem honor Aegina, the victor's place of origin. The cyclical form of this performance is anticipated when the second strophe recalls the first ("Hesychia . . . you understand in strict measure of season . . ."). Each moment in Aegina's history manifests the continuous presence of correspondingly giving and receiving Hesychia. As the female personification honored at the beginning of the second triad is associated with the one addressed at the beginning of the first, and as the end of the poem develops this early praise of Aegina, Pindar's song is to take its place among those which maintain the continual regeneration of the mother-city.

If Aegina is always imitating her origins, this song continually refers to itself. Refusing to imitate the endless extension of Aegina's praise, Pindar in fact still more strongly established the history of universal response to a harmonious city as the pattern for his choral performance.

> In my haste I cannot lay
> leisure of long-drawn speech (*makragorían*)
> on the lyre and the soft singing,
> lest surfeit come to vex.

Addressing to Aristomenes a remark about the race which his own words are to run, the poet confirms his implication that victor, city, and bard similarly triumph over time.

> Let your own need, my child
> and your youngest splendors run the path at my feet
>   (*en posí moi tráchon*)
> made a thing of speed by my fashioning (*machana*)

When Pindar gave himself the role of watching this poem which ran by him as the boy ran on the Pythian fields, he not only continued to affirm that Aegina outruns time itself: he also prepared to focus attention upon her latest glory in a way that showed off his own skill as poet.

Just past the midpoint of this song's course, Pindar recalled how he conversed with a dead prophet while he was journeying to watch the games at Delphi. The spectator-poet first applies to Aristomenes the gnomic phrases that dead Amphiaros spoke of his own son while watching a replay of the expedition which had cost him his life.

> you wear the saying
> Oikles' son spoke darkly once, as he watched
> the young men enduring the spears in the seven gates of Thebes

when the latter-born came again
to Argos, a second journey.
Thus he spoke, in their striving:
"The heritage (*to gennaion*) of valor from their fathers shines
through in the sons' blood. I gaze in wonder and see plain
Alkmaon steering the spangled snake on his bright
shield, foremost in the gates of Kadmos."

As the poet has addressed the boy-hero as his child, he praises him with words spoken by a seer-father. The quotation establishes another, analogous relationship: glory is manifest (*epiprépai* 1. 43) in Amphiaraos' lineage as it is (*emprépei* 1. 28) in the continuing fame of Aegina. Another course holds to its beginning (*teléan . . . ap'archas*). As Aegina is known to be true to herself because her athlete's strong running is sung by many (*polloisi aeidetai*) in choral song, the sons of the first attackers of Thebes are genuine in that they are true to their progenitors.

Yet the implication that two time-transcending circles are congruent only prepares for a more potent association of members and makers of continuity. As the bard has recalled Amphiaraos' words about Alkmaon in order to honor his own "son," his patron Aristomenes, he joins Amphiaraos as praiser of that seer's son.

Thus
the voice of Amphiaraos. And I also take joy
to cast a garland on Alkmaon and drench him in song.

This not only directs the listeners' attention back to the present performance, but also suggests that it is like the riddling oracle.

He is my neighbor and the keeper of my possessions;
he met me in the way as I went to the singing centerstone
of the earth,
and with the sooth that is his by blood made prophecy
(*manteumáton . . . suggonoisi téchnais*).

Explaining his praise of Alkmaon, Pindar invited his audience to identify song and prophecy. As Amphiaraos was allowed to return from the dead to watch his son reenact the battle which sent him under the earth, Pindar—"father" to his boy-patron—has been allowed to meet dead Alkmaon on his way to the prophetic play-place, Delphi. Halfway through his poem the bard tells how in the middle of the journey which he has made to watch the boy from Aegina win at Delphi he has met the original object of the praise which he has given in turn to the boy-athlete. This symmetry complements the matching of references to Aegina as graceful, kind mediatrix and mother of glory at beginning and end of the ode. If the joining of start and finish enacts and guarantees the unity of songs which sustain Aegina's fame, the mimesis of a meeting between the cities in the middle of the ode establishes the poet as a mediator between gods and men who can maintain concord (*hesychía*): as a go-between like the two seers, Amphiaraos and Alkmaon, and even as a double of the Pythia herself.

The first half of the ode having leagued the boy-athlete with the archer-god, the second half associates the poet as well as the boy with Apollo. Why did Pindar recall that he had been privileged to meet one with both the prophetic skill of his kindred (*suggonoisi téchnais*) and the courage which Alkmaon's father observed as genuine because genealogically proven (*gennaion*)? Surely he did so in order to suggest that his own skill (*machana*, 1. 30)—implicitly equated with that of the boy-athlete ("let your youngest splendors run the path at my feet,/ made a thing of speed by my fashioning")—also could join ends and origins as the Graces and Concord linked the moments of Aegina's history. As we have seen, just past the midpoint of his more explicit demonstration of the power in choral song, *Pythia* 3, Pindar told himself to attend to that which is near, at his feet, and soon countered a recurrence of his temptation to break out of the song-cycle as Koronis did by resolving to take part in dances at the neighboring shrine of the Mother. But in *Pythia* 8 the encounter with the extraordinarily gifted prophet is marked as a rediscovery of what is already the poet's *own*. In the middle of the journey to a distant but centering place he is greeted by a remembrance of home that can send his song moving more powerfully along its course. Having told how he met a prophet as a neighbor-double, the bard addresses Apollo as the ultimate giver of his own gift for song:

> But you, archer of the far cast, lord
> of the famed temple, where all gather (*pándokon*)
> in the deep folds of Pytho,
> have granted this boy delight that is highest;
> and before now, a gift to fold in the arms,
> you brought him home in triumph of your own five-contests.

The strange memory of a meeting en route has already represented poetic mediation, which is always in process. But Pindar corroborated this identification of the form and content of his art by placing just beside the all-welcoming Pythian temple set in maternal folds of hills this performance that uses the boy-victor himself as a means of praising the mediatrix-mother Aegina—an image of Hesychia who continually reconciles oppositions by alternating in active and passive roles. The genuine, genealogically appropriate setting of a song to Concord can only be the place of communal gathering which generates it and is regenerated by it.

Yet the single poet's journey to Delphi through memories of other gifted sayings can serve as a model for any joining of ends to origins only if the present performance imitates the turn and counter-turn of dances in the temple ritual. As the poet who has come to watch the games has associated himself with another spectator-seer, Amphiaraos, he must also see his own bright athlete-like progress as it is seen by Apollo, the divine athlete who gives and receives harmony. "My lord, I pray you that of my heart's will/ I look on each thing in my course/ even as you look also." Only when the meeting with a human seer is doubled by conversation between the poet and the god of poetry can it establish the wandering poet as a genuine mediator between times, persons, and dimensions of existence.[9]

It is striking, however, that this invocation of the god does not occur at the beginning but in the middle of the ode. Already many human doubles of the poet and his audience have been associated with each other: Hesychia, Aegina, Amphiaraos, Alkmaon, and, most important, the boy-athlete. The poet refers to the temple and its god only after having approximated the gathering of voices in the liturgy by showing that roles in relationships of generation as well as expression are interchangeable. Even more important, though, his address to Apollo and his claim that Justice is present introduce a series of reminders that Justice is only *briefly* present among men. The poet is a distinctive mediator because he progresses not by simply asserting a harmony but by constantly reminding his hearers of dissonance. Noting that no festival song accompanies his fellows' reunion with their mothers, Pindar warned the victor against assuming that his fame will be as constant as Aegina's. "In brief space mortal/ delight is exalted, and thus again it drops to the ground,/ skaken by a backward doom." Only after emphasizing the prevalence of imperfection could the poet legitimately ask Aegina to lead a choral progress toward freedom that would be true to her glorious origin.

> We are things of a day (*epameroi*). What are we? What are we not?
> The shadow of a dream
> is man, no more. But when the brightness comes, and God gives it,
> there is a shining of light on men, and their life is sweet.
> Aegina, dear mother, bring this city to haven
> in free guise, by Zeus' aid and stong Aiakos,
> Peleus and goodly Telamon aiding, and with Achilles.

When Pindar matched his earlier address to Aegina as receiver of the Graces with another address to her as active giver of grace, we recall the opening apostrophe to Hesychia as both giver and receiver. Circling

---

[9] C. M. Bowra, *Pindar* (Oxford, 1964) p. 8:
Pindar stands to the Muse as the priests at Delphi stand to the Pythia and the god whose voice she is. The god's messages come to him not directly, but through the Muse and he then interprets it and puts it in order.

upon itself through repeated transfers of role, the poem can for a moment create the Concord (Hesychia) which it first addresses. Rather than explicitly referring to analogues of choral performance as he did in *Pythia* 3, here Pindar made his poem itself the primary locus of choral circling. In *Pythia* 8, then, he more clearly anticipated many modern poets' attempts to give their texts the power of public song and challenge any isolation of person or moment.

iv

My songs, lords of the lyre . . .
Anaxiphormigges hymnoi. . . .

When Pindar evoked metempsychosis in *Olympia* 2, he enacted another Pythagorean idea: world-harmony. Again honoring his own self-conscious assumption of the role of mediator, he defined a continuity of times in the midst of incessant discontinuity and dignified the human dilemma of being lost somewhere between origin and end. Stressing means, even implying that a person *is* a medium, the song projects an end commensurate with a potent origin.

Theron is first honored for carrying on the mental labors of fathers who in the time counted out for them (*aiòn d'ephepe mórsimos*) gained a power over Sicily equivalent to that of the solar eye that rules every day: "in strong toil of the spirit/ they were the eye of Sicily (*Sikelías . . . ophthalmós*)." Yet it is not fathers but hymns that rule Pindar's lyre: again the bard offers the articulation of moments in dialogue as model of both private and public governance.

Like *Pythia* 3 and *Pythia* 8, this text defines the distinctive temporalities of speech and song as means of teaching a community how to balance the positive and negative elements in mortal experience. Asking that his songs persuade Zeus, son of Kronos, to guarantee the Acragas' future prosperity, Pindar prepared for the Pythagorean evocation of Kronos' challenge to linear time with which the ode climaxes: "they who endure thrice over/ in the world beyond to keep their souls from all sin/ have gone God's way to the tower of Kronos." Aristotle associates Kronos with Chronos; although Pindar never made the pun, when he played with a larger verbal unit, the triad strophe/antistrophe/epode, he insured that Kronian Zeus answer his prayer, offering a transcendence of time equivalent to that of the three returns to earth by Kronos' pupils in the underworld. Whether or not Pindar shared the Pythagorean belief of Theron for whom he wrote this ode—like *Pythia* 3 not for choral performance[10]—his songs continually suggest that immortality is generated in the interpretation of poetry, either by many singer/dancers or by a solitary reader who

[10] See Fraenkel, p. 609; Duchemin, p. 320ff.; Bowra, p. 121.

can see the larger implications of choral performance.

Olympia 2 gradually subverts its initial definition of identity in terms of paternal origins, substituting for genealogy a stress of linguistic exchange. Just after he has addressed Father Zeus as Kronion, son of the father Kronos, the poet observes that the all-father Chronos himself has no power over ends.

> Of things come to pass
> in justice or unjust, not Time the father
> of all (*Chrónos ho pánton patèr*) can make the end (*télos*)
> unaccomplished.

Although Chronos cannot change what is just or unjust (*en díka te kai parà díkan*), since Pindar's patron is just to guests (*díkaion zénon*, 1. 5) the poet can himself enter into the workings of time and encourage *his* guests to choose between one course and another. He can even lead them to anticipate the moral education which would be effected if Kronos led them three times back through their lives.

Stressing alternations in experience, the ode not only shows that fathers do not inevitably transmit their good fortune: it also begins to establish a neutral model for a distinctively human order of recurrent choice between moral alternatives. Pindar did recall how Kadmos' daughters have been restored from misfortune—which in *Pythia* 3 proved that harmony has to be reconstructed over and over again. And he did report that it is said (*légonti*, 1. 28) that Ino for all time (*amphì chrónon*) has been given endless life (*bíoton áphthiton*). But these passing references to story only serve as foil for the assertion that those who live in the round of sun-fathered days cannot achieve their ends:

> But for mortal man
> no limit in death has been set apart (*kékritai*)
> when we shall bring to an end (*teleutásomen*) in unbroken good
> the sun's child, our day of quiet (*hesúchimon*).

Although the speaker finally presents Oedipus as the grandfather of the successful Thersander, he mentions him first as one who fulfilled (*telessen*) a terrible oracle and thus showed how sons of fortunate fathers (*de Moîr' á te patróion . . . eúphronia*, 1. 35) tend to suffer reverses at another time (*allo chróno*, 1. 37). And Thersander himself is not principally characterized by his lineage but by his association with his offspring Theron, who now receives song which is to soften fathering/fathered Zeus: "stemmed in his stock, it is fit for Ainesidamos' son/ to win songs in his honor and the lyre's sound (*egkomíon te meléon luran te tugchanémen*)."

This song pivots on the second of three encomia: wealth is equivalent to the sun-like fame of the family ("the eye of Sicily") and to the time-transcending movement of souls in and out of Kronos' domain.

> Wealth elaborate with virtue brings opportunity (*kairón*) for various
> deeds; it shoulders the cruel depth of care,
> star-bright, man's truest
> radiance.

As retrospective/prophetic song reorders time and invites its audience to take a greater part in ordering their own time-bound existence, wealth which pays for song is a star that changes the linear succession of days and years into a series of distinctive occasions for choice.

When Pindar evoked teaching that paralleled his own, he most fully established the power of wealth-induced song to generate a perfection which cannot be controlled by Father Time. In a third allusion to a trans-temporal order, the decision of an infernal judge assigns to the good endlessly sunny days and nights: "but with nights equal forever (*aieî*) with sun equal in their days." Rhadamanthys, like the poet and unlike univocal Father-Zeus and Father-Chronos, mediates between alternatives. He sits beside another father, Kronos (*hon patèr . . . páredron*) and oversees a process of learning through reexperience similar to that projected by a poet's reading of lives and commentaries on lives. In *Pythia* 3 and *Pythia* 8 the doctor Asklepios and the seer Alkmaon are doubles of the poet; this Kronian judge in *Olympia* 2 also shadows the poet's power to manipulate time and achieve perfection.

Pindar could not explicitly compare himself with three other mediators if he was to stay within the limits of the means (*machana*) which are here (*pár podòs*)—and thus persuade his readers to accept the gift/message which had usually been carried by choruses. However, two relationships evoked in variations on *Pythia* 8 support the likeness of mortal and demonic arbiters. Rhadamanthys gathers and counts (*alégontai*, 1. 78) a paradisal company which includes Peleus and Achilles—as Pindar did in his final prayer to Aegina in *Pythia* 8. And whereas in *Pythia* 8 Pindar addressed Apollo the lord of the lyre as lord of the similarly shaped bow, in *Olympia* 2 he depicted himself as an archer who depends only on the restricted audience of this intimate performance.

> there are many sharp shafts in the quiver
> under the crook of my arm.
> They speak to the understanding; most men need interpreters.
> The wise man knows many things in his blood; the vulgar
> are taught.

Perhaps Pindar was more assertive than deferential in this song because he wanted to establish his own art as a strong rival to the Pythagorean ritual from which Theron usually derived his sense of moral integrity.

The moralist-bard finally proclaims blessed the Pythagorean whose moral training by Rhadamanthys, Kronos, and Chronos this performance anticipates.

> Toward Akragas
> we will bend the bow and speak
> a word under oath in sincerity of mind (*audásomai enórkian lógon*)

A disclaimer actually confirms the analogy between the poet and the infernal judge: his words also count.

> For sands escape number (*arithmòn*)
> and for all the joy Theron has brought to others
> what man could tell (*phrásai*) the measure?

An undeclared metempsychosis organizes the ode: as Pythagorean doctrine stressed the transference of extraordinary power from one privileged mediator to another,[11] Rhadamanthys' power to tell, number, and establish harmony is passed to the poet. Pindar did not simply depend upon Pythagorean lore but reinterpreted reincarnation on the model of his own profession.

The turn and counter-turn of the argument of *Olympia* 2 as well as *Pythia* 3 and *Pythia* 8 makes a continuity from stress of discontinuity. It invites the reader also not to be simply a member of a world-concert of transferred voices but actively to make a unity from confusion which, like Hamlet's, is always worse confounded. As Pindar generated a kind of immortality for his patron by adapting that principal reader's own arcane philosophy, he invited at least a few other readers also to accept as a ground for human order more vital than patrolinear succession the knowledge that good and bad alternate in any life as speeches alternate in dialogue.

v

Some of the most important modern European and American poets have emulated Pindar. Several have developed the strategies by which he made the lack of choral performance in *Pythia* 3 establish his flagrantly self-contradictory text as a model for self-critical community. For instance, I will examine Wordsworth's and Hölderlin's great Pindarics, the "Ode: Intimations of Immortality" and "Friedensfeier." But Pindar's proofs that violent contradiction is the very ground of generative harmony can also help us read later poetry that refers more directly to another ancient tradition of reflection upon choral performance: the Old Testament Psalms.

---

[11] E. R. Dodds, *The Greeks and the Irrational* (Berkeley, 1951), pp. 143–44.

2

Psalmist without a Temple

i

Most readers have strictly contrasted the Greek and the Hebrew traditions of poetry. Leo Spitzer, for example, followed Ernst Renan, opposing to the Pythagorean idea of music the Hebrew *siah*, "signifiant à la fois méditer, parler bas, parler avec soi-même, s'entretenir avec Dieu, se perdre dans les vagues rêveries de l'infini. . . ."[1] However, to characterize Hebrew song as private meditation is to ignore the public context in which the first Psalms were composed and performed and to which the later Psalms continued to refer.

It is the late Psalm 19 which most strongly suggests the expressive value of choral performance. As Pindar's celebration of choral song in *Pythia* 3 does not seem to have been meant for singing at a banquet, Psalm 19 was probably written after the first Temple of Jerusalem was destroyed: during a time when the written Torah rather than oral praise for the dialogue between Yahweh and Israel was the primary unifying force of the Hebrew community.[2] But the text consummately honors the medium which the poet and his colleagues used in many other performances. And it has served modern European and American poets as a vital model for their efforts to establish order in the midst of continual change.[3]

---

[1] Leo Spitzer, *Classical and Christian Ideas of World Harmony* (Baltimore, 1963), p. 25.

[2] Harvey H. Guthrie, *Israel's Sacred Songs: A Study of Dominant Themes* (New York, 1966), p. 185:

> Psalm 19 is understandable only in terms of the development of wisdom theology . . . the wisdom mythos addressed itself primarily to the individual and to his conduct of his own life. To members of the "we" who lamented the disaster of 587 B.C. it offered no hope of the restoration of the social, communal, historical continuum to which Israel's view of life had previously been attached. It offered a view of life and of the issues involved in life in which attention was focussed on the connection between them and God.

[3] Artur Weiser stresses the public, proclamatory nature and function of Psalm 19, in *The Psalms: A Modern Commmentary* (Philadelphia, 1962), pp. 201–2:

> For the poet the law is the point at which an encounter takes place with the living God who reveals himself in the law, a conception which has its roots already in the pre-Exilic cult of the Covenant. The

Adapting a Canaanite nature-hymn, the poet of Psalm 19 praised a heavenly equivalent of the convocations which generated the Psalter.

> Day unto day uttereth speech, and night unto night
> sheweth knowledge.
> There is no speech nor language
> where their voice is not heard.[4]

Several pairings of phrases evoke a continuous circling of discourse: "heavens declare . . . firmament sheweth," "day uttereth . . . night sheweth," "day unto day . . . night unto night." As speech makes a continuity from repeated reversal—a listener becomes a speaker in turn, then listens again and so on—the sun is a sign of reversible progress which convokes hearer–spectators from one end of the earth to the other.

> In them he hath set a tabernacle for the sun,
> Which is as a bridegroom coming out of his chamber, and
> rejoiceth as a strong man to run a race.
> His going forth is from the end of the heaven and his
> circuit is
> unto the end of it: and there is nothing hid from
> the heat thereof. (4–6)

In Genesis the heavenly bodies are silent means of measurement and definition: "let there be lights in the firmament of heaven to divide the day from the night and let them be for signs and for seasons and for days and for years." When the Psalmist gave them the power of knowing and speaking, he represented the distinctive structure of a community held together by writing which both reported and stimulated self-conscious utterance. In the first part of Psalm 19 the heavenly bodies are speaking signs of a complex One primarily known through His covenant

---

> "law" comprises the testimony which God bears to himself, that is the manifestation of his will in history. . . . But equally it also comprises the attitude which man adopts in response to the revelation of God.

See also C. C. Keat and G. H. Box, *A Liturgical Study of the Psalter* (New York, 1928), pp. 65ff.; Sigmund Mowinckel, *The Psalms in Israel's Worship* trans. D. R. Ap-Thomas, vol. II (New York, 1962), p. 136; Hans Joachim Kraus, *Worship in Israel: A Cultic History of the Old Testament* trans. Geoffrey Buswell (Richmond, VA, 1966), p. 219; A. Arens, "Hat der Psalter seinen 'Sitz im Leben' in der synegogalen Leseordnung des Pentateuch," *Le Psaultier*, ed. Robert de Longhe (Louvain, 1962); Claus Westerman, *The Praise of God in the Psalms* trans. Keith R. Crim (Richmond, VA, 1965), p. 37.

[4] In a more accurate contemporary translation of the Hebrew, Mitchell Dahood, S.J. (*Psalms I, The Anchor Bible* [Garden City, New York, 1966]) renders verse 3 "without speech and without words/ without their voice being heard," thus removing the double negative of the King James "there is no speech nor language where their voice is *not* heard." Whether or not the metaphor of oral communication is marked as a metaphor, however, it continues to inform the primary argument of a text which stresses subjectivity and interpersonal exchange from beginning to end. Indeed the removal of the second negative actually pays further tribute to subjectivity, making the reader privy to the poet's self-conscious adaptation of naive pagan symbolism.

with a people who have often flouted the Law. In the midst of the heavens runs one who impersonates a harmony made of continual contradiction: a wedding authorized by its members' expressed consent and by the hearing of many others ("their line is gone out through all the earth"). The moving point that inscribes a circle among the heavens is an individual who knows himself ("rejoiceth") as a participant in a loving ("bridegroom") rivalry ("to run a race") among several speakers. Rejoicing in his eloquent revolution with the other signs of God's glory, the sun assures the continued self-conscious vitality of a whole made of contrasting member/parts.

Similarly, the depicted reader of the Torah in the second part rejoices in following written signs. He invites *his* readers in turn to take part in a community composed of individuals who know that they too form a corporate medium for endless annunciations that language continually reconstructs a whole by articulating division.

> The law of the Lord is perfect, converting the soul,
> The testimony of the Lord is sure, making wise the simple.
> The statutes of the Lord are right, rejoicing the heart:
> the commandment of the Lord is pure, enlightening the eyes. (7–8)

Although the opening lines which evoke a gathering of heavenly voices recall the Temple liturgy more vividly, the second part commemorates it too, characterizing an individual as a member of an ongoing community rather than as an origin or end unto himself.

The text thus honors corresponding, complementary celebrations of God's glory: oral in the first part, written in the second. Throughout, means rather than origins or ends concern a poet who may once have taken part in the Temple liturgy. This is perhaps most obvious in the first part, in which the bridegroom/athlete–sun is a mediator and transmitter who reflects not only another quasi-animate mediating force, the text of the Law, but also the poet and each of his potentially articulate readers. As in Pindar's odes, juxtaposition of image/echoes of both the members and the medium of choral song evokes continuity that transcends but also thoroughly engages the mortal individual. Both highly self-conscious attempts to regenerate a strong sense of identity from reminders of commonality allude to recurrent articulations of a sacred festival time: the games and victory banquet in one case and the Temple liturgy in the other. Yet Psalm 19 expresses the Temple's challenge to mortality in terms of ordinary language.

Even more clearly than Pindar, the Psalmist presented choral song as an intensification of daily speech which makes a significant whole by repeatedly undermining the identity of each member, giving his role of speaker or listener to another who in turn dispossesses himself. An "I" finally enters, asking the ultimate divine patron for power to speak again like the speaking sun and the Law: "let the words of my mouth, and the meditation of my heart be acceptable in thy sight, O Lord" (14). But this speaker is clearly defined as a medium of response in turn to a universal response to Being. And the specialness of the Interlocutor is less strongly evoked than the reiterative rhythm which this text shares with any other utterance.

Like Pindar, the poet of Psalm 19 celebrated an athletic contest. Yet his hero-athlete has not emerged victorious on a particular extraordinary day: the race in question is not a real event but a metaphor for the ordinary progress of the sun through every day, and that in turn represents the movement of *torah* through many generations. The song does not commemorate an extraordinary action but presents as significant the very principle of ordinariness: ordination day by day, night by night. Whereas Pindar established choral song as his model of order by recalling several stories, there is no story here, only mythopoiea in its simplest form: a demonstration of the tendency for common language to personify natural forces and events. Whereas the Greek poet elaborately evoked distinctive mediators who anticipated the making and remaking of his song in interplay between poet and readers, the Psalmist primarily celebrated his linguistic medium. But these differences are to be expected. If Pindar was summoned to various places to universalize local victories, the Hebrew poet wrote at least in memory of a Temple in which the history of a whole people had been celebrated; he could thus more directly assert the power of language to order time by representing its rhythms.

The distinctive power of Psalm 19 also emerges from comparison of its two parts: contrasting articulations of the perennial conflict between linguistic conventions and nature—*nómos* and *phýsis*—which Yahwist theology emphasized as the ground of its challenge to earlier Canaanite naturalism. If the organizing Canaanite image of the sun is provocative because it is self-contradictory, evoking conjugal union as well as conflict, Psalm 19 itself demands attention because it is composed of contrasting sequences: an adaptation of a public hymn to nature and an individual reader's response to the supernaturalist Law. Indeed by contradicting itself, the text implicitly projects a dynamic reconciliation of these two modes of reading.

The first part reinterprets but does not suppress the concern for multiplicity in the naturalism which the Temple cult challenged. We know the unique glory of God through declarations by the heavens and His handiwork through demonstration by the multiple firmament. Certainly the supernaturalist poet radically revised his naturalist precursors' treatment of the heavens, firmament, days and nights as members of a cosmic body: he redefined them as signifiers of a single disembodied Creator. However, as he chose to praise the One by adapting a hymn to the many, he also consistently stressed the multiplicity of phenomena and measures of time which his theology refused to see as synecdoches of a divine physical whole: "their line . . . their words . . . in them he hath set. . . ." Correspondingly, the Hebrew poet adapted the naturalist preference for synecdochic identification of part and whole by defining a complex, dynamic personification as a self-conscious representative part of the heavens. His explicit attribution of self-awareness to the primary representative member of a community of signifiers implies a potential for reciprocity between self-conscious performer and interpreters—an image of the Hebrew cult of dialogue between One and many.

But the concentration upon individual subjective response in the second part of the Psalm better demonstrates how the substitution of conventionalist scripture for naturalist ritual can encourage mutually enhancing dialogue among interpreters. As the first part assigns some degree of individual subjectivity to one of many natural signifiers, the second implicitly attributes integrative power both to the unique Law and to its individual readers.

> The fear of the Lord is clean, enduring for ever:
> The judgments of the Lord are true and righteous altogether.
> More to be desired are they than gold, yes, than much
> fine gold: sweeter also than honey and the honeycomb.
> Moreover by them is thy servant warned: and in keeping
> of them is great reward.
> Who can understand his errors? cleanse thou me from secret
> faults.
> Keep back thy servant also from presumptuous sins;
> let them not have dominion over me: then
> shall I be upright, and I shall be innocent from the
> great transgression.
> Let the words of my mouth, and the meditations of
> my heart, be acceptable in thy sight, O Lord, my strength
> and my redeemer.

When the Psalmist expanded the parallelism of any Hebrew verse into the structuring principle of a whole text, he implied that the sun who not only couples but also competes represents the exclusively textual, conventional signifiers in Scripture as well as the natural heavens. Like the sun, the Law is a paragon. If the circuit of the sun is unto the ends of heaven and nothing is hid from his heat, the Law of the Lord is perfect and right; the fear of the Lord which the Law generates is clean and eternal; the judgments which it records and prefigures are true and righteous altogether. More strikingly, the second part implies that the Law and its individual reader play *both* roles assigned the sun. The text characterizes as sensuous and desirable the many judgments by which the Lord declares His desire to be united with the congregation that bears witness to His potency: "more to be desired are they than gold, yes, than much fine gold: sweeter also than honey and the honeycomb." But the unique Law makes its readers competitors as well as brides and bridegrooms, requiring that they challenge multiple powers. "Presumptuous sins: let them not have dominion over me."

Of course extraordinary Identity is the primary topic in both parts of the Psalm. But if the first part projects the responsiveness of a destroyed community of witnesses into the heavens, the second glorifies the single Law in terms of responses by many individual readers. The text thus both ratifies and compensates for the challenge of Yahwist monotheism to Canaanite polytheism. Like Revelation, it defines conjugal/competitive interaction among various signifiers and interpreters as an extraordinarily dynamic standard of definition.

ii

The very long Psalm 119 enacts the Hebrew *mythos* of language more directly than Psalm 19. It not only glosses the more complex strategy of the shorter text but also anticipates efforts by modern European and American poets to assign private reading the power to regenerate community.

This long personal response to the book of Law presents language as the means of reconciling antithetical energies: the unstable human reader and the eternal, constant Yahweh. In twenty-two stanzas in which all eight lines begin with the same letter, the speaker alternately asks that the Lord help him understand the written Law and celebrates his achieved understanding. This alternation implies that dialogue has occurred between incommensurate figures, man and God. But the continual nonprogressive reiteration of praise for the covenant also renders the Temple liturgy in more intimate terms. The letter of the Law represents a speaking of Yahweh which is always new if it is retained in human memory and then translated into a coherent course of life.[5]

Whereas Psalm 19 praises the Law under the guise of the circling bridegroom/athlete–sun, in Psalm 119 a human surrogate for the reader articulates a divine movement inscribed in nature as well as in the Text by honoring the career of other mortals who are as exemplary as Pindar's patrons—but anonymous.

> Blessed are the undefiled in the way, who walk in the law of the
> Lord.
> Blessed are they that keep his testimonies, and that seek him with the
> whole heart,
> They also do no inquity: they walk in his ways.

---

[5] See "Absence, Authority and the Text," *Glyph* 3 (1978), pp. 137–47, in which Richard Jacobsen deconstructs the high valuation of writing in Scripture. As my previous remarks should have made clear, however, I am primarily concerned to demonstrate that in poetry, including Scriptural poetry, the deconstructive impulse is only the first moment in a dialectic in which the desire for self-critical reconstruction is ultimately stronger.

However, as Psalm 19 first honors a supposedly oral signifying of glory, this text principally celebrates verbal expressions, the Law and its variants: testimonies, statutes, judgments, words, commandments, precepts.

In Psalm 19 the sun personifies an awareness of wholeness generated in cooperative articulation of unique radiance by many members of a dynamic community. In Psalm 119 those who walk in the way/law of the Lord only lightly anticipate the persons to be formed—*per*formed—when two interpreters, the speaker who reads the Law and the actual reader of his homage to the Law, fully participate in the text's genesis of meaning from recurrence. The much longer poem develops the less mythopoieic second part of Psalm 19. The same thing happens as many times as there are letters in the Hebrew alphabet: twenty-two times two isolated interpreters, poet and reader, are brought into intense relationship with the Text. And twenty-two times their own relationship doubles the dialogue with the One who originally spoke the Text in which this song was to be included. The poem is lively and compelling because when it calls attention to its writtenness it celebrates interpersonal dialogue between creatures and Creator—which so many Psalms praise by more directly evoking the traditional gathering of many voices in communal song.

Although the seemingly endless juxtaposition of writing and speech gives authority and presence to both, one verse makes explicit a principle which is operative throughout: "thy statutes have been my songs in the house of my pilgrimage" (54). The twenty-two stanzas comprise a verbal architecture, a temple to replace the destroyed Temple. The poem is a microcosm which like its stone model imitates nature's lavish display of means that conceal origins and ends. As day speaks unto day, night unto night, each of these little word-rooms communicates with all the others—and thus to the reader—because a similar short song is performed in each. Twenty-two times the speaker prays for understanding, receives it, and asks for it again. In the reading of the Psalm time is effectively transcended as it would have been when the Temple musicians performed hymns which derived much of their power from the fact that they advertised their cultic function.

Associating the generation of children both with the rise and fall of the sun and with praise of the name of God, Psalm 119 interprets solar revolution as an allegory of Israel's history: a continual speaking and hearing of the Law.

> Blessed be the name of the Lord from this time forth and forevermore.
> From the rising of the sun unto the going down of the same
> the Lord's name is to be praised. . . . He maketh the barren
> woman to keep house and to be a joyful mother of children.

Although temple-song is only mentioned once in Psalm 119, the Psalmist was clearly compensating for the loss of a special place for recollection and prophecy when he so relentlessly elaborated his predecessors' paradoxical strategy of praising eternal harmony by stressing temporal conflict. Many variations in order and reference prevent the reiteration from being monotonous. But it is the recurrence itself which primarily carries the positive sense of liveliness sustained by older choral celebrations of the turn and counter-turn of liturgical performance.

When the Psalmist praised the Lord's text in twenty-two written stanzas, he cast himself as the voice of the whole Hebrew alphabet—and thus, by implication, the whole language: all the Israelite community had left as a means of constructing artifices of eternity. Like the poet who adapted the Canaanite hymn to the sun in order to praise the Law, this poet who simply responded to the Law itself achieved a *kairós* by making his readers contemplate their whole history. All the moments of the Law, the history of a spoken but then inscribed covenant, seem present in a written song which continually begins over again and in which each part reflects each other part like the various elements of the cubic Bride–City in Revelation.

Because the ending of Psalm 119 matches its beginning, the reader can accept the circle as a figure of sense rather than nonsense—as he should be able to do after a reading of Psalm 19.

> Let my supplication come before thee; deliver me according to thy
> word.
> My lips shall utter praise, when thou hast taught me thy statutes.
> My tongue shall speak of thy word: for all thy commandments are
> righteousness.

In the partially naturalist mythos of Psalm 19 and in any actual reading of Psalm 119 repetition seems to be generative because in both songs what is repeated is speech, the matrix of variation and development. In Psalm 19 the cycle of the sun adequately represents the Eternity announced by the Law because the poet attributed to the sun a kind of self-knowledge that can be derived from sustained reflection upon any dialogue. Because the dispossessed "I" of Psalm 119 retained the Temple cult's strong sense that dialogue is endlessly creative, he could present himself as a self-conscious synecdoche of a community which is conjugal *because* it is competitive: united by its never-ending tension with an Image of its potential for perfection.

iii

This awareness has been reconstructed by some of the strongest and most influential lyric poets writing during the past two centuries in both Europe and America. The ancient lyre has now been silent for more than two thousand years longer than it had been when the Psalmist adapted an already venerable Canaanite nature-hymn and thereby moderated the intolerance and exclusivity of his monotheism. But in "Lycidas" Milton overcame limitations of seventeenth-century Puritanism by revising several ancient traditions of dialogue–song. And poets are still finding in ancient poetic intensifications of dialogue the means of challenging an exclusive individualism which daily threatens to end history.

TWO

Europe

3
Lycidas and the Sweet Societies

An extraordinarily influential legacy of the Renaissance to modern poetry, "Lycidas" defines its readers as agents of continual renaissance. It thereby overcomes limitations of both its literary kind, monody, and its author's ideology, Puritan individualism.

As we have seen, St. John tried to prevent corruption of the Eastern churches by dramatizing writing and reading as prologues to universal marriage. Milton challenged the accomplished corruption of the English church by proposing the never-to-be-fully-consummated intercourse between writer and reader as a model for community more vital, because more self-critical, than any which had ever existed. In "Lycidas" he gave the Theocritean/Virgilian pastoral elegy the larger resonance and more public responsibility of Pindaric choral writing and the New Testament apocalypse. He thus prophesied how nineteenth- and twentieth-century poets in Europe and America would renew ancient literary strategies and project union by calling attention to a persistent failure to make connections.

Milton's expansion and correction of classical elegy justifies a large ambition of modern European and American poetry, a project which Wallace Stevens would proleptically present as a *fait accompli*: "the poem is the cry of its occasion,/ part of the res itself and not about it" ("An Ordinary Evening in New Haven," section VII). The Argument of "Lycidas" announces that the poem "by occasion foretells the ruin of our corrupted clergy then in their height." In fact the text *became* the cry of its occasion, a synecdochic part of the cultural and political revolution which it foretold. For Milton not only skillfully interwove and reevaluated the competing claims of several ancient traditions, playing exquisite variations upon the solar revolution which they all used to represent the turns and counter-turns of poetic language. He also anticipated many later uses of ancient choral models both to challenge the losses and to celebrate the gains imposed on European and American society by later revolutions. As I will show in the essays which follow, Wordsworth and Hölderlin responded to the potentially generative disintegration of European society in the aftermath of the French Revolution with

magnificent imitations of Pindar.[1] Mallarmé challenged the decadence
of the bourgeois tradition ironically encouraged by that revolution in a
meditation on the irrelevance of ancient choral models which urgently
provokes disagreement. And Paul Celan unforgettably challenged the
Nazi parody of both the revolutionary tradition and one of its Scriptural
models, Revelation, by mocking ancient Hebrew texts as well as Hölderlin's Pindarics. But in Part Three I will also consider how American
poets familiar with Whitman's emulation of "Lycidas," "Out of the Cradle Endlessly Rocking," have questioned individualist declarations of
independence derived from both the Puritan and the American revolutions, further developing ancient and modern European proofs that nuptial song can be vital to the extent that it resists easy assimilation.

From the outset, Milton's poem heralds many later intensifications of
the decentering of paternal authority in Revelation. In order to avenge
the fall of a brother-poet, Milton's rough speaker challenges several
demonic counterparts to the silent Father. Nature has prematurely
silenced Lycidas, the other voice required for pastoral dialogue, and the
anonymous survivor mimes her violence: he snatches laurel, myrtle, and
ivy which might have crowned the dead poet, "with forc'd fingers/
rude/ [I] shatter your leaves before the mellowing year." The abandoned
pastor also recalls how the nymphs were absent when Lycidas drowned
and how the Muse Calliope was absent when her son Orpheus was
murdered by the maenads, "when by the rout that made the hideous
roar,/ His gory visage down the stream was sent . . ." (61).[2]

Yet the speaker has also proposed the course of the sun—the Psalmist's
model for choral community—as a positive model for cultural revolution.

> Together both, ere the high lawns appeared
> Under the opening eye-lids of the morn,
> We drove afield, and both together heard
> What time the grey-fly winds her sultry horn,
> Battening our flocks with the fresh dews of night,
> Oft till the Star that rose, at evening bright
> Toward heaven's descent had sloped his westering wheel.
> Meanwhile the rural ditties were not mute,
> Tempered to the oaten flute,
> Rough satyrs danced, and fauns with cloven heel,
> From the glad sound would not be absent long,
> And Old Damoetas loved to hear our song. (25)

---

[1] See Christoph Prignitz, *Friedrich Hölderlin: die Entwicklung seines politischen
Denkens unter dem Einfluss der Französischen Revolution* (Hamburg, 1976).

[2] In *"Lycidas*: A Poem Finally Anonymous," *Glyph* 8 (1981) 1–18, Stanley E. Fish reads
the poem as a preemption of the individual voice: a dramatization of the defeat of the
anti-communal, individualist spirit in the young Milton. I will argue, however, that from
the beginning the text also prepares for a positive reconciliation of the tensions between
one and many which it portrays.

In several ways this sequence subverts the privileging of action over reaction and original over image in a civilization ruled by the patriarchal concern for identity expressed in Scripture.

1. The singers were first listeners: the speaker and Lycidas "both together heard/ What time the Greyfly winds her sultry horn." They did not follow the Law and assert themselves against nature, but took their cue from the sun's natural revolution.

2. As reaction generated potent verbal action in the past, this commemoration evokes the positive phenomena of sound and presence by negating the negative concepts of silence and absence: a denial of silence recalls sound, "the rural ditties were not mute," and a denial of absence affirms presence: "fauns from the glad sound would not be absent long."

3. The remembered dialogue–song was shaped not by the singers' intentions but by the sonorities of an accompanying instrument: it was "tempered to the oaten flute."

4. Others' response authorized two poets' alternation as auditors of nature, their instrument, and each other: "rough satyrs danced . . . old Damoetas loved to hear. . . ."

This sketch of a non-patriarchal economy invites the actual reader to help recompose the pastoral day-song by taking the part of Damoetas, a venerable figure more receptive than most fathers.[3]

Even the lines which describe the dismemberment of Orpheus suggest that poetry will be revived: in "when by the rout that made the hideous roar,/ His gory visage down the stream was sent,/ Down the swift Hebrus to the Lesbian shore," "roar" echoes in "gory" but yields to "shore," which designates a place where poetry was reborn. The internal rhyme may have reminded Milton's academic audience of two erudite readings of the Orpheus-myth. Not only were Cambridge scholars familiar with interpretations of Orpheus as a pagan type of Christ, resurrected after his fall, but they might also have known George Sandys' allegorization of Ovid:

> *Orpheus* his head and Harp being throwne into Hebrus, are borne away by the murmuring current. So the scattered reliques of learning, expuls'd from one country are transported to another as here unto *Lesbos*: Pittacus, Arion, Sappho and Alcaeus being all of that

---

[3] See John R. Knott, Jr., "The Pastoral Day in *Paradise Lost*," *MLR* XXIX (1968), 168–82. Leslie Brisman, *Milton's Poetry of Choice and its Romantic Heirs* (Ithaca, 1973), p. 79:

> The duration of "Lycidas" is in Bergson's terms a series of states of consciousness and Milton achieves both the sensation of the presentness of each moment and the moving in time of one "still" to the next.

Yet the lines which Brisman glosses, "meanwhile the rural ditties were not mute . . . And old Damoetas loved to hear our song" evoke a time that was and may again be *out* of the mind in a complex of exchanges: between two performers, between each and his instrument, and between them and their listeners.

Island, who succeeded *Orpheus* in the fame of lyrical Poesy.[4]

However, in order to convince his readers that the death of a poet can help reconstruct both literary and cultural dialogue, Milton had to have his speaker challenge and be challenged by several surrogates for the Son who are more controversial than Orpheus.

Vehemently questioning the efficacy of poetry, the speaker calls up the memory of a response which is as authoritative as his protest is authoritarian:

> Alas! What boots it with uncessant care
> To tend the homely slighted shepherd's trade . . .
> Fame is the spur that the clear spirit doth raise . . .
> But the fair guerdon when we hope to find,
> And think to burst out into sudden blaze,
> Comes the blind Fury with th'abhorred shears,
> And slits the thin-spun life. But not the praise,
> Phoebus replied, and touched my trembling ears;
> Fame is no plant that grows on mortal soil,
> Nor in the glistering foil
> Set off to the world, nor in broad rumour lies,
> But lives and spreads aloft by those pure eyes,
> And perfect witness of all judging Jove (64).

The reader might balk at both the intervention of another voice in a monody and the sudden shift of tense, but one discontinuity may justify another—as two negatives make a positive. And we can accept the introduction of a second voice because Phoebus speaks for us: we want to challenge the speaker for ignoring the implications of renaissance in his account of Orpheus' translation to Lesbos ("roar-gory-shore"). Although Renaissance interpretations of Apollo as another pagan "type" of Christ support Phoebus' claim that poetry yields immortality, even Milton's first audience would have accepted the intervention of a second voice mainly because the speaker has demanded response with an urgency inappropriate in lyric monody.[5] But the sudden transformation of soliloquy into

---

[4] *Ovid's Metamorphosis Englished, Mythologized and Represented in Figures by George Sandys*, ed. Karl K. Hulley and Stanley T. Vandersall (Lincoln, NE, 1970). See Caroline W. Mayerson, "The Orpheus Image in *Lycidas*," *PLMA* LXIV (1949), 189–207.

[5] Christopher Grose, *Milton's Epic Process* (New Haven, 1973), p. 108:

> The poem's most immediate context—the bitter reaction of the poet "now"—is framed in a new perspective, one presumably more definitive than the previous words because judging them and—potentially at least—moving beyond them and into an "other" realm altogether. (1. 108)

I am suggesting the contrary: that the shift validates the previous quasi-dramatic engagement of the reader in a collaborative effort of reformation; that the dominant perspective is the interpersonal rather than the impersonal; and that Phoebus is primarily authoritative not because he voices an objective view but because he articulates our own unformulated response to the preceding diatribe.

colloquy is also authorized by the fact that it provokes other representations of dialogue which question more elaborately generic and ideological limits.

After the speaker addresses rivers associated with two literary fathers, Theocritus ("O Fountain Arethuse") and Virgil ("and thou . . . / Smooth-sliding Mincius," [85]), he is forced to challenge the voices of wild ocean—first in a vain search for narrative information, "questioned every gust of rugged wings . . . They knew not of his story," but then in an effective lyric apostrophe to his absent counterpart:

> It was that fatal and perfidious bark
> Built in the eclipse, and rigged with curses dark,
> That sunk so low that sacred head of thine. (100)

If the shift into narration ("Phoebus replied . . .") balanced the equally ungeneric introduction of a second voice and thus distracted our attention from it, here frustration of the narrative impulse prepares us to accept an apostrophe which is generically appropriate but exceeds the limits of pagan pastoral in energy as well as reference. "That sacred head of thine" not only confuses Lycidas with the Logos, a persona of mediation unknown to the pagan speaker, but also implies that address itself can transform and consecrate its object. Like the Orpheus and Phoebus episodes, this sequence uses traditional Christian readings of myth and Scripture to support a demonstration that utterance subverts conventional definitions of relationship between persons and times.

By having his speaker challenge two intruders who indicate dangers in patriarchal, Scriptural conventions, Milton authorizes his use of apostrophe to associate fallen Lycidas with the resurrected/resurrecting Son. Camus and the Pilot are fathers more threateningly associated with texts than the Jove who reads the plant of Fame:

> Next Camus, reverend sire, went footing slow,
> His mantle hairy, and his bonnet sedge,
> Inwrought with figures dim, and on the edge
> Like to that sanguine flower inscribed with woe.
> Ah! who hath reft (quoth he) my dearest pledge?
> Last came, and last did go,
> The pilot of the Galilean lake . . .
> Two massy keys he bore of metals twain . . .
> He shook his mitred locks, and stern bespake,
> How well could I have spared for thee, young swain
> Enow of such as for their bellies sake,
> Creep and intrude, and climb into the fold? . . .
> Blind mouths! . . .
> And when they list, their lean and flashy songs
> Grate on their scrannel pipes of wretched straw,
> The hungry sheep look up, and are not fed,
> But swollen with wind. (123)

Whereas "high-judging Jove" generates life from death by reading leaves on a plant which belongs to others ("Fame . . . spreads aloft by those pure eyes . . . of all judging Jove"), Camus futilely protests an unnatural death by reading flower-like emblems which he wears on his own body.[6] And the Pilot's threat of apocalypse is as fixed and monolithic as any character printed on a page. Although he challenges the travesty of pastoral communication by "blind mouths" who do not listen through oaten flutes but "list"—will—themselves into power, he himself is authoritarian in his demand that his listener accept his willful formulations.[7]

In order to counter the Pilot's willfulness, the speaker elaborates upon the invocation of Greek and Latin pastoral forces ("O fountain Arethuse . . . Smooth-sliding Mincius") with which he answered Phoebus, "return Alpheus, the dread voice is past/ That shrunk thy streams; return Sicilian Muses/ And call the vales . . ." (132). And it seems that the Muse obeys him: "ye valleys low where the mild whispers use . . ." (136). But the verisimilitude of this call by a gentle counter-voice for flowers to decorate Lycidas' grave is greatly heightened when the main speaker interrupts the Muse in turn: "for so to interpose a little ease,/ Let our frail thoughts dally with false surmise." The speaker legitimizes his attempt to conjure a mediatrix by challenging it, reminding himself of what no reader of a funeral elegy can ever forget: that no body is present to be strewn with pastoral texts.

The speaker's self-criticism may also disarm the reader into taking part in an unconventional and provocative exchange which climaxes the poem.

> Ay me! Whilst thee the shores, and sounding seas
> Wash far away, where 'er thy bones are hurled,
> Whether beyond the stormy Hebrides,
> Where thou perhaps under the whelming tide
> Visit'st the bottom of the monstrous world;
> Or whether thou to our moist vows denied,
> Sleep'st by the fable of Bellerus old,
> Where the great vision of the guarded Mount
> Looks toward Namancos and Bayona's hold.
> Look homeward angel now, and melt with ruth (154).

Watery chaos resounds in assonance ("whilst thee the shores, and sounding seas/Wash far away") and in grotesque approximations of rhyme:

---

[6] See Jon S. Lawry, *The Shadow of Heaven* (Ithaca, 1968), p. 100.

[7] Although David S. Berkeley, *Inwrought with Figures Dim* (The Hague, 1974), summons impressive iconographic evidence to identify the Pilot as Christ rather than St. Peter, this reading ignores the poem's emphasis of dialogic reciprocity more than transcendent authority. Mother M. Christopher Pecheux, "The Dread Voice in *Lycidas*," *Milton Studies* IX (1976), 221–41 offers a more suggestive reading of the Pilot as a composite of Moses, Peter, and Christ.

"lies . . . ease . . . surmise . . . seas," "hurled . . . Hebrides . . . tide . . . world . . . denied." Like the weird fade of "roar" through "gory" to "shore," this succession of sounds suggests positive continuity: in "whilst thee the shores and sounding seas/ Wash . . ." we may hear echoes of "Lycidas" as well as of the alien ocean. But we cannot be convinced that Lycidas has been resurrected merely by hearing the melodious singer's name in onomatopoeia for chaos; we require stronger evocation of the missing brother–poet, the second voice needed for pastoral dialogue. Hence the Angel.

But the apostrophe to the Angel is more disconcerting than the questioning of Phoebus.

> Or whether thou to our moist vows denied,
> Sleep'st by the fable of Bellerus old,
> Where the great vision of the guarded mount
> Looks toward Namancos and Bayona's hold;
> Look homeward angel now, and melt with ruth. (159)

How can we accept a demand for comforting response from a vision of the Archangel Michael which Camden's *Britannia* attributed to several monks at St. Michael's Mount,[8] but which could be no more than a legend devised to explain the Cornish place-name? Milton skillfully disarmed this possible objection. The phrase "the fable of Bellerus old" interprets the name "Bellerium" (Land's End) as a commemoration of an actual person, Bellerus, by Roman soldiers who preceded Camden's monks. Displacing the genesis of a person from a name farther back into British history, Milton may have intended to distract us from accusing either Camden or himself of similarly concocting "the great vision of the guarded Mount." Certainly he displaced fabulation forward in time—at least as far as the first readings of his text in Cambridge.

Milton implicated his first audience as co-conspirators in his assignment of very strong interpretive subjectivity to the counterpart of "Bellerus," the Angel. Two subtle allusions to contemporary ideological conflict elaborate a provocative juxtaposition of "vision" and "look" which implies mediation of sectarian dispute.

1. The "great vision" *has* vision. Since it is a vision which "looks toward . . ." the metaphoric animation buried in the phrase commonly used to designate merely spatial relations emerges as its primary content.

2. Because Nemancos and Bayonne were strongholds of Counter-Reformation Catholicism, an English Protestant might have been expected to project upon the Angel his own resistance to contemplating such horrors, and to credit the Angel's turning his gaze so

---

[8] *The Poems of John Milton*, ed. John Carey and Alastair Fowler (London, 1968), p. 252.

passionately away from the continent that it could transport
Lycidas home to England.

3. The synonym for "great vision," "Angel," also activates the poem's
   larger historical context, the longstanding international religious
   controversy. The Angel can look Lycidas homeward because he is
   an Angle, an *English* angel. Like the reader at home, he would be
   more comfortable looking toward England than toward her Catholic enemy. If the Angel is to fulfill future readers' desire to
   restore the second voice to pastoral dialogue, he represents them
   as speakers of the English mother tongue.

Thus, more strongly than either Phoebus or the Pilot, the Angel would
have tempted Milton's first readers to help him reopen cultural and
literary exchanges threatened by the Protestant stress upon individual
intrepretation as well as by the Catholic stress upon external authority.
Playing up to the ideological prejudice which contemporary English
Protestants shared with him as a man, as a poet Milton persuaded them
to activate the non-ideological structure of virtual dialogue between text
and reader which the generic marking "monody" ignores.

Evoking several communities in the final sequence of the poem,
Milton more clearly invited his readers to transcend their religious ideology and help him complicate his literary genre: to take over the role of
mediator from the Angel and define interpretation as a communal
action. If the pagan speaker seems to have assumed the Christian perspective of the Angel, he also addresses a group of present and future
pastores which includes himself as well as his future reader/hearers:
"Weep no more, woeful shepherds, weep no more,/ For Lycidas your
sorrow is not dead" (165). It is by developing this paradoxical location of
singularity on *both* sides of an imaginary dialogue that the speaker projects an articulate pastoral community—religious as well as poetic. He
concentrates several personae of exchange in one complex mediator.

> So sinks the day-star in the ocean bed,
> And yet anon repairs his drooping head,
> And tricks his beams, and with new spangled ore,
> Flames in the forehead of the morning sky:
> So Lycidas sunk low, but mounted high,
> Through the dear might of him that walked the waves. (168)

A repetition of "head," designating the conventional locus of identity,
both echoes the equation of Lycidas with Christ in "that sunk so low that
sacred head of thine" and recalls the translation of Orpheus' head to
Lesbos. Milton also projected a heavenly analogue of the mortal company summoned by his provocative text:

> Other groves, and other streams along,
> With nectar pure his oozy locks he laves,

> And hears the unexpressive nuptial song,
> In the blest Kingdoms of joy and love,
> There entertain him all the saints above,
> In solemn troops, and sweet societies
> That sing, and singing in their glory move,
> And wipe the tears for ever from his eyes. (174)

But as sunny Lycidas is finally a listener, Milton ended by locating the kingdom of heaven on earth: in the intersubjective processes of writing and reading. First he prophesied that Lycidas and the readers will enact the reciprocity which he had projected between Lycidas and the "sweet societies."

> Now Lycidas the shepherds weep no more:
> Henceforth thou art the genius of the shore
> In thy large recompense, and shalt be good
> To all that wander in that perilous flood. (182)

Then, pretending to have been only a listener himself, Milton transferred his responsibilities as author to his many potential interpreters.

> Thus sang the uncouth swain to the oaks and rills,
> While the still morn went out with sandals grey,
> He touched the tender stops of various quills,
> With eager thought warbling his Doric lay:
> And now the sun had stretched out all the hills,
> And now was dropped into the western bay;
> At last he rose, and twitched his mantle blue;
> Tomorrow to fresh woods and pastures new. (186)

Milton's dark, rough speaker has designated smooth, brilliant Lycidas as solar interpreter, but at the end of the poem he himself is in turn seen dressed in a mantle as blue as heaven: a visual prophecy of sunrise shared by poet and reader at sunset ("at last he rose . . .").

Who, then, will go tomorrow to fresh woods and pastures new? Milton evoked a procession of six analogous mediators: Orpheus, Phoebus, Lycidas, Christ, the Angel, and the Swain. But this series awaits completion by a seventh: the reader who can fully appreciate the need for self-critical mediation between past and present, convention and nature, one and many because he or she has *not* been allowed to respond directly to the Swain's various proofs that monody is as impotent as any unvoiced text.

As we will see in the essay which follows, one of Milton's most alert readers, William Wordsworth, passed on his invitation—and challenge— to approximate the unexpressive nuptial song which Lycidas supposedly hears. Yet as I have noted, "Lycidas" also anticipates other European and American poets' efforts to project conjugal community precisely by insisting that the conditions are *not* right for celebrations like those of Pindar and the Psalmist. After following Wordsworth's complex series of variations on the solar imagery and structure of the odes and psalms, I will reread more radically self-critical emulations of both Greek and Hebrew choral song by Hölderlin, Mallarmé, and Celan—and then consider still more problematic efforts by American poets to become the genius of a transatlantic shore.

4
A Wedding or a Festival:
Wordsworth's Intimations Ode

> There was a time when meadow, grove and stream
> The earth and every common sight,
>   To me did seem
>   Apparelled in celestial light,
> The glory and the freshness of a dream.
> It is not now as it hath been of yore;—
>   Turn whereso'er I may,
>   By night or day,
> The things which I have seen I now can see no more.[1]

In these Poems I propose to myself to imitate, and, as far as possible, to adopt the very language of men, and I do not find that . . . personifications make any regular or natural part of that language. . . . Something I must have gained by the practice, as it is friendly to one property of all good poetry, namely good sense; but it necessarily cut me off from a large portion of phrases and figures of speech which from father to son have long been regarded as the common inheritance of poets.[2]

In the "Ode: Intimations of Immortality" Wordsworth overcame a nostalgia for visionary intercourse with nature by contradicting his rejection of literary conventions in the Preface to the 1798 *Lyrical Ballads*. In fact he most authoritatively defined common experience as the matrix of uncommon vision when he drew quite heavily upon the common inheritance of poets. The Intimations Ode develops the structure and imagery of the Psalms as well as Pindar's odes. It thereby reevaluates the devotion to so-called natural truth which underlies both contrasting impulses in Wordsworthian Romanticism: its privileging of extraordinary vision and its mimesis of ordinary language.

Like Milton's lament for the loss of a partner in pastoral song, Wordsworth's lament for a loss of visionary power intensifies the dialectic of nature with convention in Psalm 19 and *Pythia* 3. The Ode reflects

---

[1] *The Poetical Works of William Wordsworth*, vol. IV, ed. E. de Selincourt and Helen Darbishire (Oxford, 1947), p. 279. Dates of composition are discussed on pp. 463–65.

[2] Wordsworth and Coleridge, *Lyrical Ballads 1798*, ed. W. J. B. Owen (Oxford, 1967), pp. 156, 161.

critically upon a naturalism as strong as the devotion to a Mother/Bride
by pre-Scriptural Canaanite and pre-classical Greek poets. It discovers
intimations of immortality in shared analysis of matching tensions:
between nature and convention-determined writing on the one hand,
and between authors and readers on the other. Like "Lycidas," the
Intimations Ode is far more explicit than Psalm 19 and even more explicit than *Pythia* 3 in inviting us to examine the recurrent conflict
between definitions of the individual as unique, original spouse of nature
and as one among many members of a linguistic community.[3]

---

[3] See W. K. Wimsatt, "In Search of Verbal Mimesis" in *Day of the Leopards* (New
Haven, 1976), p. 73:

> In Plato's *Cratylus*, the chief inquiry into mimetic linguistics that
> survives from ancient times, Socrates the fugleman delivers a pro-
> longed etymological discourse in which he attempts, in large part
> playfully, to convince the "conventionalist" Hermogenes that words
> really do embody reasons for meaning what they mean. Then he
> turns to his other friend, the "naturalist" Cratylus, and says in effect:
> "Yes, like paint in pictures, words do bear some kind of resemblance
> to the things they mean. But after all, the resemblance is not per-
> fect. . . ." It is my notion that today we stand at almost the same
> juncture in linguistic–poetic studies—though coming to it from an
> opposite direction. After the sweepingly successful assertion of the
> primacy of convention in language by the father of modern linguis-
> tics, Ferdinand de Saussure, students of the present era, and most
> notably and perhaps initially Roman Jakobson, reach back to the
> earlier insight and authority of C. S. Pierce, to renew and improve an
> awareness of the "natural" powers of language, both imagistic and
> diagrammatic, on a wide front.

I will argue that Wordsworth is one of the primary initiators of the swing of concern
toward linguistic conventionalism which is clearly still dominant, despite efforts by such
critics as Gerard Genette (*Mimologiques* [Paris, 1976]) to restore, with Socratic delicacy,
the interest in naturalism that Romanticism more often explicitly avowed. See also
Derrida, "La Pharmacie de Platon" in *La Dissémination* (Paris, 1972) and de Man,
Allegories of Reading (New Haven, 1979), especially the chapters on Rousseau.

This essay will develop a paradoxical observation about the Intimations Ode by
David Ferry in *The Limits of Mortality* (Middletown, Conn., 1959), p. 47:

> The poem is, in fact, really a lament over the *gain* of poetic power, or
> rather of that sort of imagination, for it is a formal and reluctant
> acceptance of the limiting conditions under which poetry is possible.
> If mortal man can relate himself to the eternal only through the
> mediation of symbols, and mortal nature is the repository of symbols,
> then poetry—vision by means of symbols—is the only imaginative
> means available to him.

M. H. Abrams' *Naturalist Supernaturalism* (New York, 1971) remains the classic study of
Romantic incorporations of Scriptural structures and imagery. See especially Abrams'
stress upon the judiciously conservative impulse in Romanticism:

> The Romantic enterprise was an attempt to sustain the inherited cul-
> tural order against what to many writers seemed the imminence of
> chaos; and the resolve to give up what one was convinced one had to

The manner in which Wordsworth composed the Ode must have encouraged him to define poetry not as an imitation of ordinary speech ("the very language of men") but as a prefiguration of extraordinary intercourse between self-reflexive text and self-critical reader. Although in 1802 Wordsworth set aside the lines that were to become the first four stanzas of the Ode, in 1804 he completed the text by further developing their dramatization of ultimately irreconcilable conflicts. In the 1802 sequence a solitary, self-analytical speaker defines himself against an antiphonal round like the one evoked in a Psalm which adapts a pagan nature-hymn but does not domesticate it for use by the monotheistic anti-naturalist cult as fully as Psalm 19.

---

give up of the dogmatic understructure of Christianity, yet to save what one could save of its experiential relevance and values, may surely be viewed by the disinterested historian as a display of integrity and of courage. (p. 68)

On Wordsworth and Pindar, see John Hollander, "Wordsworth and the Music of Sound," *New Perspectives on Coleridge and Wordsworth* ed. G. H. Hartman (New York, 1972); G. N. Schuster, *The English Ode from Milton to Keats* (Gloucester, Mass., 1964, first publ. 1940) and Carol Maddison, *Apollo and the Nine* (London, 1960). As for the other higher strain in the Ode, see the 1815 Preface to *Lyrical Ballads*:

The grand storehouses of enthusiastic and meditative Imagination, of potential as contradistinguished from human and dramatic Imagination, are the prophetic and lyrical parts of the Holy Scriptures, and the works of Milton.

See also Harold Bloom, *The Visionary Company* (New York, 1963), p. 181; Geoffrey H. Hartman *op. cit.*, p. 274; E. D. Hirsh, Jr., *Wordsworth and Schelling: A Typological Study of Romanticism* (New Haven, 1960), p. 170. In *The Breaking of the Vessels* (Chicago, 1982), p. 14 Harold Bloom notes Wordsworth's debt to Pslam 19 and "Lycidas" for his solar imagery.

See also F. W. Bateson, *Wordsworth: A Re-interpretation* (New York, 1954), pp. 192–93:

Wordsworth always composed orally. Normally he composed aloud. There is some evidence that his voice rose and fell in the process of composition, as though he were reciting the poem before an imaginary audience. Only when the poem had been completed, unless it was an exceptionally long one, was it put into writing. Often it was not Wordsworth himself but his sister who actually wrote down the poem. . . . When he defined the poet as "a man speaking to men" it is possible . . . that he was using the word "speaking" in a literal sense, and that the audience he envisaged when composing was a real audience—composed of auditors. . . . He is the bard, the sacer vates, whose relationship with his little audience is infinitely more intimate and profound than the casual liaison between the modern poet and his readers that is provided by printers, publishers, and booksellers.

But Wordsworth was in fact *not* the bard, the *sacer vates*, only trying to be: his major poetry is indeed animated by the tension between his aspirations and the reality of writing. If both Psalm 19 and *Pythia* 3 live on because the Psalmist and Pindar dramatized the *difference* between texts written for solitary reading and choral performance, so, I will argue, does the Intimations Ode.

> Now while the birds thus sing a joyous song,
>   And while the young lambs bound
>   As to the tabor's sound,
> To me alone there came a thought of grief. (Ode, III)

> The little hills rejoice on every side. The pastures are clothed with flocks; the valleys are also covered over with corn; they shout for joy, they also sing. (Psalm 65)

But many vaguely personified pre-verbal sounds ("the cataracts blow their trumpets from the steep . . . I hear the Echoes through the mountains throng") form a matrix from which the isolated interpreter generates an urgent address to a boy who might help him break out of his solitude: "Thou Child of Joy,/ Shout round me, let me hear thy shouts, thou happy/ Shepherd Boy!" (III). Having called out to one circling voice, the solitary addresses many other members of a communal celebration:

> Ye blessed creatures, I have heard the call
>   Ye to each other make; I see
> The heavens laugh with you in your jubilee;
>   My heart is at your festival. (IV)

The 1802 fragment concludes, however, by opposing one to many. The single nearby Child yields to many distant "Children . . . on every side/ In a thousand valleys far and wide . . . ," while isolated elements of the landscape insist upon their uniqueness.

> —But there's a Tree of many, one,
> A single Field which I have looked upon,
> Both of them speak of something that is gone. (IV)

It is likely that Wordsworth set aside these four stanzas because the personifications of natural energies which he drew from the common inheritance of poets only yielded reiteration of the opening lament: "the things which I have seen I now can see no more." Of course the remaining stanzas never deny this loss. But their more intensive allusion to Scriptural lyrics and their imitation of Pindaric counter-turning expose the initial lament for alienation from nature as proof that the lost vision was itself an alienation from culture. The 1804 additions may even provoke us to observe that the visionary naturalist can be as destructively self-assertive as the bride of Apollo whose annihilation of a community Pindar challenged by praising communal conventions.

Stanza V indicates how the 1804 text rereads the tension between the solitary and various potential communities in the 1802 fragment. The first of the added stanzas develops both the personifications and the allusions to lavish ceremonial display in the earlier text ("every common sight . . ./ Apparelled in a celestial light" [I]; "jubilee," "festival," "coronal," "adorning" [IV]).

> Our birth is but a sleep and a forgetting:
> The Soul that rises with us, our life's Star,
> Hath had elsewhere its setting . . .
> But *trailing clouds of glory* do we come
> From God, who is our home:
> Heaven lies about us in our infancy!
> Shades of the prison-house begin to close
> Upon the growing Boy,
> But He
> Beholds the light, and whence it flows,
> He sees it in his joy;
> The Youth, who daily farther from the east
> Must travel, still is *Nature's Priest*,
> And *by the vision splendid*
> *Is on his way attended*;
> At length the Man perceives it die away,
> And fade into the light of common day.

Wordsworth pictured the Pythagorean procession of the soul from Identity[4] as a liturgical procession of mediators between One and many like those pictured in several Old Testament adaptations of pagan nature-hymns besides Psalm 19. For instance Ecclesiasticus 50 includes the striking image of a Priest as well as major images found in stanza II of Wordsworth's Ode: rainbow, rose, moon, waters, stars and sunshine.

> How was he honored in the midst of the people in his coming out of the sanctuary! He was as the morning star in the midst of a cloud, and as the moon at the full. As the sun shining upon the temple of the Most High, and as the rainbow giving light in bright clouds, and as the flowers of roses in the spring of the year, as lilies by the rivers of waters. (5–7)[5]

And Ecclesiasticus 45 thus describes Aaron, high priest in the microcosmic Temple:

> He beautified him with comely ornaments, and clothed him with pomegranates, and with many golden bells round about, that as he went there might be a sound, and for a noise made that might be heard in the temple, for a memorial to the children of his people.

Because it is obvious that Wordsworth's ornate personification "Nature's

---

[4] *Iamblichus de Mysteriis Aegyptorum, Chaldaeorum, Assyriorum Proclus in Platonicum Alcibiadem de Anima atque Daemone* (Lugduni, 1577), p. 238 (quoted in John D. Rea, "Coleridge's Intimations of Immortality from Proclus," *Modern Philology* XXVI (1928), 201–13, pp. 208.

[5] Frances Ferguson, *Wordsworth: Language as Counter-Spirit* (New Haven, 1977), p. 109:

> It is as though the poet were countering—and banishing—his recollections of the rainbow as God's covenant with man, of the rose as a symbol of the heavenly paradise, of the trackings of the moon in Isaiah and Job.

Priest" derives from the common inheritance of poets which includes Ecclesiasticus, the presentation of the sun-like Youth as an Aaron rather than as a bridegroom/athlete implies a relationship between times and persons even more complex than that projected by Psalm 19.

In this first 1804 stanza, personifications—a common inheritance of poets whose loss Wordsworth regretted in the anti-conventionalist 1798 Preface—implicitly contradict as well as animate his allegory of a loss which is supposedly greater. When Wordsworth followed the Psalmist in describing a solar hero in complementary ways, he in effect deconstructed his overt message of linear decadence. And he invited us to reconstruct in terms of the literary exchange the natural cycle which both Yahwist theology and Romanticism subordinated to a transcendent self.

1. The Youth is alter ego both to the Boy who sees origins ("he beholds the light and whence it flows") and to the Man who sees ends ("at length the Man perceives it die away/ And fade into the light of common day"). For in "by the vision splendid on his way *attended*" the vision itself becomes a secondary personification and thus intensifies the animateness of the Youth–Priest. More important, like the sun in Psalm 19—and the Angel in "Lycidas"—as a Priest, the Youth is the object as well as the subject of vision: one party to an infinitely reversible exchange of the active and passive roles of seer and seen.

2. If as in Psalm 19 many spectators at a public performance in the heavens can see and thus to some extent share the "vision splendid," might these witness/participants not include the Man who sees the uncommon vision fade into common daylight? Certainly *we* see the glory of Nature's Priest more clearly by comparison with the fading of his power. Perhaps, then, we should not deny that potentially reconstructive vision to the Man—whose self-consciousness suggests that he is a double of both poet and reader who have been made extraordinarily self-conscious by the unusual conditions of their text-mediated intercourse.[6]

This provocative implication that the Youth and Man are potentially interchangeable centers of a self-conscious community is supported by two related sequences. Wordsworth wrote one in 1800 as Book I of "The Recluse," subtitled "Home at Grasmere," and the other for *The Prelude*, probably in the fall of 1803: about six months before he seems to have begun the second part of the Ode with this allegory of solar revolution.[7]

---

[6] Wordsworth also noted a stage of development previous to the triadic movement through boyhood, youth, and manhood: "heaven lies about us in our infancy." But he acknowledged the undifferentiated, impersonal, unarticulated nature of the *in-fans* by not personifying infancy as he did the three later phases.

[7] For texts and notes on dating, see *Poetical Works*, ed. E. de Selincourt and H. Darbishire, vol. V (Oxford, 1949) 315 and 475–76; *Wordsworth's Prelude* ed. de Selincourt, second edition, revised by Helen Darbishire (Oxford, 1959), pp. 4, 511.

In the passage in "Home at Grasmere" the poet mocked himself for having waited so long to leave the city.

> And did it cost so much, and did it ask
> Such length of discipline, and could it seem
> An act of courage, and the thing itself
> A conquest? shame that this was ever so,—
> Not to the Boy or Youth, but shame to thee,
> Sage Man, thou Sun in its meridian strength,
> Thou flower in its full blow, thou King and Crown
> Of human nature, shame to thee, sage Man,
> Thy prudence, thy experience, thy desires
> Thy apprehensions—blush thou for them all.

If we recall that the third member of the triad Boy–Youth–Man in the Ode derives from a Man defined as a potent noon who figures ideal virility ("meridian strength . . . full blow . . . King and Crown"), we may be more likely to feel that the visionary/visible Youth who replaces the meridian Man can attract the later, lesser Man's attention away from a failure of vision. For the miniature autobiographical allegory in the Ode records the actual filiation of one figure from another. In the genesis of the 1804 text a Man is father of the Youth in a partial reversal of Wordsworth's deliberately provocative epigraph for the Ode, "the Child is father of the Man."

Yet the Man in the Ode seems to have derived not only from the meridian hero of "Home at Grasmere" but also from a self-contradictory Youth in *The Prelude*: in a properly Pindaric manner the genesis of stanza V also ratifies the epigraph's polemical reversal of natural succession. In the preamble to the text of *The Prelude* as it would appear in 1805 Wordsworth proclaimed his poetic vocation by assigning himself the role of Nature's Priest:

> to the open fields I told
> A prophecy: poetic numbers came
> Spontaneously, and cloth'd in priestly robe
> My spirit, thus singled out, as it might seem,
> For holy services. (11. 59ff.)

He soon qualified that proclamation, however:

> But I have been discouraged: gleams
> Flash from the East, then disappear
> And mock me with a sky that ripens not
> Into a steady morning. (11. 134ff.)

Some months before the Man first gazed at the fading of the "vision splendid," this priestly Youth anticipated his sense of distance from the potent East of dawn. We are thus encouraged to assign the Youth and the Man in the Ode a relationship as reversible as that between the solar

personifications in "Home at Grasmere" and *The Prelude*. But it is
because the Ode puts the burden of proof upon the common reader
rather than any textual authority that it can finally rival Pindar as well
as the Psalmist and "turn the brightness outward," discovering illumination in the dark solitude of exile from Paradise.

In the next stanza Wordsworth honored Pindar's strategy of self-
contradiction by contradicting his ancient authority's subordination of
poetry to nature in *Pythia* 3 ("I will pray to the Great Mother . . ."). Stanza
VI abruptly redirects our attention away from the all-male solar processional of stanza V toward a bride–mother; it thus implicitly restores the
conjugal aspect of the Psalmist's sun which is lacking in stanza V. Yet if
Pindar assured the Mother that he would worship at her shrine, Wordsworth dismissed her.

> Earth fills her lap with pleasures of her own.
> Yearnings she hath in her own natural kind,
> And, even with something of a Mother's mind,
>   And no unworthy aim,
>   The homely Nurse doth all she can
> To make her Foster-child, her Inmate Man,
>   Forget the glories he hath known,
> And that imperial palace whence he came.

Quasi-bridal counterpart to the Boy/Youth/Man-sun ("fills her lap with
pleasures of her own. Yearning . . ."), nature is seen here as no more
than a stepmother. Although Wordsworth acknowledged the propriety
and worth of nature ("her own natural kind . . . no unworthy aim"), he
put her down as a domestic who is unfit for the imperial splendors of
transcendental vision. This helps further establish the implication that
the Man's vision of a failure of vision might turn out to be a success. If
the Mother cannot make Man forget the [sun]rise of his visionary power,
while he watches its sunset he should be able to remember the "vision
splendid" that attends the noonday Priest—and thus perpetuate its
power to focus and organize a community of witnesses even in marking
the difference between noon and sunset.

But this pivotal stanza raises a major question. If Wordsworth first
excluded *eros* from his solar allegory and then explicitly dismissed the
Mother whom his Youth serves as a priest rather than as a bridegroom,
did he not merely imitate the alienation of transcendent Identity from
multiple nature which the Psalmists corrected? Was he not rejecting all
the ancient poets had gained for literary history by adapting nature-
hymns in ways that establish their text-mediated dialogues with many
readers as an alternative matrix of vitality? Indeed when Wordsworth
addressed nature in stanza XI he seems to have acknowledged that halfway through the Ode he had contradicted the Psalmists' reconciliation of
nature and Scriptural convention.

> And O, ye Fountains, Meadows, Hills and Groves,
> Forbode not any severing of our loves!

But between stanzas VI and XI Wordsworth ratified the naturalist image of conjugal union in Psalm 19 by challenging it on several levels. Like the ancient poet who characterized the sun as both bridegroom and challenger, he implicated many readers in his attempt to reconstruct "jubilee" or "festival" by communicating his private reading of youth not only as a receiver but also as a producer of visions.

Mockery of a father as well as of a mother in stanza VII may begin to dispose us to accept the final reassertion of conjugal community with nature. The speaker explicitly demands ("Behold . . . See") that the reader take the Man's role and behold the fading of vision into the light of common day.

> Behold the Child among his new-born blisses,
> A six years' Darling of a pigmy size!
> See, where 'mid work of his own hand he lies,
> Fretted by sallies of his mother's kisses
> With light upon him from his father's eyes!
> See, at his feet, some little plan or chart,
> Some fragment from his dream of human life,
> Shaped by himself with newly-learned art;
>   A wedding or a festival,
>   A mourning or a funeral . . .
>   Then will he fit his tongue
> To dialogues of business, love or strife:
>   But it will not be long
>   Ere this be thrown aside,
>   And with new joy and pride
> The little Actor cons another part:
> Filling from time to time his "humorous stage"
> With all the Persons, down to palsied Age
> That Life brings with her in her equipage;
>   As if his whole vocation
> Were endless imitation.

Contrasting with the procession of Boy, Youth, and Man in stanza V, this even more emphatically allegorical and exclusively linear procession of all the Persons in Life's equipage implies no capacity for reflection and self-awareness like that which Wordsworth implicitly attributed to the spectator–Man by emphasizing the spectacular, publicly visible nature of the "vision splendid." This pigmy-sized Child who performs in a private, intimate setting "fretted by the sallies of his mother's kisses" has not entirely emerged from infantile subjection to unarticulated multiplicity ("among his new-born blisses"). But he is illuminated by his father's eyes and perpetuates the concern for graphic demarcation and imitation associated with patriarchal convention—the concern which the Psalmist modified by evoking many interpreters of divine glory. The tiny poet's use of "some little plan or chart" to shape "a wedding or a festival" mocks the solitary, vaguely paternal speaker/writer's attempt to conjure "jubilee" and "festival" in stanza IV. But the strong implication that the pigmy-sized poet will fail in a non-reversible progress contrasts more provocatively with the hint that the Man can compensate for a loss of visionary power by revealing community as the true context of the supposedly uncommon "vision splendid." Stanza VII thus prepares us to be challenged by further counter-turns in the actual progression of stanzas toward an indirect reaffirmation of the conjugal as well as the competitive aspect of the Psalmist's sun.

Stanza VIII precisely counters the picture of the small author by addressing the Child as a prophetic reader.

> Thou, whose exterior semblance doth belie
>   Thy Soul's immensity.
> Thou best Philosopher, who yet dost keep
> Thy heritage, thou Eye among the blind,
> That, deaf and silent, read'st the eternal deep,
> Haunted for ever by the eternal mind,—
>   Mighty prophet! Seer blest!

This redefinition of the Child–author as a reader encourages us who read the Ode to authorize the suggestion in stanza V that the non-visionary Man can make the absence of unique vision the self-effacing center of a self-conscious community. Certainly the oxymoron-like association of the child "on [his] being's height" with the "eternal deep" helps relate the beginning and the end of the Ode: we should recall that the Man-like speaker of the beginning heard "the cataracts blow their trumpets from the steep" (III) and thereby conjured a "Child of Joy." And in recognizing that Wordsworth has transferred imagery from the Man–speaker in stanza III to the Child–reader in stanza VIII we can reflect upon a potential for a rejuvenating interchange of roles between ourselves and the poet as well as among the contrasting fictional surrogates which we share with him.

The sequence of approximate identifications is as intricate as any in Pindar. To recapitulate:

1. The parodic picture of the Child as author in stanza VII counters the characterization of the Boy, Youth, and Man as interpreters in stanza V.
2. The honorific designation of the Child as reader of nature in stanza VIII ratifies the hint that the Man may regain some of the visible/visionary Youth's potency by contemplating the departure of the "vision splendid" which he embodies.
3. But it does so effectively because it renders the general foregrounding of subjective interpretation in the first processional in terms of

the actual text-mediated exchange between writer and reader. The Child has been subjected to mockery as a would-be unique author and praised as a universal reader. Similarly, the speaker will fail in his effort to reconstruct "a wedding or a festival" if he continues to define himself solely as authority on his alienation as he did in stanzas I–IV, but may triumph if he joins readers in recognizing the continual alternation between heights and depths, between sublime and ridiculous allegory, in his text as a homeopathic means of curing our common subjection to mortal contradictions.

4. Correspondingly, as readers we could fall into sterile self-regard if we were not continually challenged by a master of literary conventions to share the responsibility of advancing an extraordinarily self-critical reading of our shared aspirations to immortality. Certainly the last stanzas of the Ode intimate that the immortality projected by poetry is no more and no less than self-criticism as intense and reciprocal as that which Pindar initiated with his patron.

Transformation of the mocked Child–author into the eulogized Child–reader in turn prepares us to value an explicit shift of concern from active, authorial identity to reactive, interpretive multiplicity. Stanza IX balances the reversal of Pindar's deference to the Great Mother in stanza VI by defining an alternative, non-natural matrix of integration similar to that invoked by the ancient bard.

> The thought of our past years in me doth breed
> Perpetual benediction: not indeed
> For that which is most worthy to be blest—
> Delight and liberty, the simple creed
> Of Childhood, whether busy or at rest,
> With new-fledged hope still fluttering in his breast:—
>   Not for these I raise
>   The song of thanks and praise;
> But for those obstinate questionings
> Of sense and outward things,
> Fallings from us, vanishings;
> Blank misgivings of a Creature
> Moving about in worlds not realized,
> High instincts before which our mortal Nature
> Did tremble like a guilty Thing surprised:
>   But for those first affections,
>   Those shadowy recollections,
>   Which, be they what they may,
> Are yet the fountain light of all our day,
> Are yet a master light of all our seeing.

The climactic ninth stanza of the Ode defines many losses of identity as a master light of vision which can challenge not only the traditional location of identity in the father's eyes but also the enthusiastic subversion of that hierarchy in the paean to the child–prophet "o'er whom

Immortality broods, like a Master o'er a Slave" (VIII). Having mocked
the artist's aspiration to the role of Creator in the picture of the pigmy-
sized artist in stanza IX, Wordsworth still more provocatively testified to
the Judaeo-Christian doctrine of creation *ex nihilo.* He proposed a
poetics that is not only negative (*"not* indeed/ For that which is more
worthy to be blest . . . *Not* for these I raise the song of thanks and
praise") and critical ("not for these . . . but for those obstinate *questionings,*/ Of sense and outward things") but also therefore communal and
conjugal: "fallings from *us,* vanishings . . . those shadowy recollections . . . are yet the fountain light of all *our* day . . . of all *our* seeing/
Uphold us. . . ." We see truths because the poet and his unique, multi-
allusive text remember along with us—"the thought of *our* past years in
me doth breed . . . *I* raise the song . . ."—many indications that the
alienation of an "individual" is a precarious synecdoche for a lack of
stable identity which we can recognize as a common resource only when
our conventional definitions of identity are as consistently challenged as
they are by the Ode.

One entry in this strange list of estrangements explicitly describes a
displacement of creativity from One to many, from Creator to creatures,
author to readers.

> Blank misgivings of a Creature
> Moving about in worlds not realized,
> High instincts before which our mortal Nature
> Did tremble like a guilty thing surprised.

This defines immortality as a much more common—communal as well as
ordinary—project than the Child–prophet's masterful reading. At least
while reading a continually self-qualifying, non-dictatorial text like the
Ode, each of us is this Creature who moves about in many potential worlds
and receives intimations that he can (pro)create many others if he
acknowledges that he is *not* the Creator. In Book I of *The Prelude,* before
Wordsworth anticipated the image of his former self as Nature's Priest in
stanza V of the Ode and "clothed in priestly robe his Spirit," he cast his
single but vaguely guilt-ridden and continually self-contradictory self as
Adam and Eve in *Paradise Lost* XII ("the world was all before them"): "the
earth is all before me" (1. 15). By contrast, here in stanza IX of the Ode he
implied that poetic creation and revelation derive precisely from the questioning of established definitions of identity by two kinds of guilty creature: poets who cast themselves as self-critical readers, and readers who
willingly share the poet's responsibility for self-criticism.[8]

---

[8] In *Wordsworth's Experiments with Tradition: The Lyric Poems of 1802* (Ithaca,
1971) Jared Curtis finds in stanza IX as opposed to stanza VIII
> the syntax of careful exclusion and assertion rather than of accretive
> doubling or of statement and counter-statement. . . . The shift comes

But this climactic sequence also questions the imitation of ancient public song in the solar processional of Boy, Youth, and Man more explicitly than the picture of the pigmy-sized poet.

> Truths that wake
> To perish never;
> Which neither listlessness, nor mad endeavor,
> Nor Man nor Boy,
> Nor all that is at enmity with joy,
> Can utterly abolish or destroy!

In stanza V the Boy had no negative powers and sharply contrasted with the apparently negative Man. Here the speaker dismisses both as falsifiers who are as impotent as the natural Mother whom he dismissed in stanza VI. He thus further establishes losses, vanishings, and blank misgivings as matrix of creative union in self-critical poetry. And by disowning both extremes of his triadic personification of the natural sun, Man and Boy, he again encourages us to expect the Man who sees the sunset of the visionary gleam to counter the turn of vision away from the mediatory Youth.

Correspondingly, once we have followed such a provocative grounding of definition in compounded contradiction we are unlikely to read the plurals which end this stanza as images of either nature or consciousness.

> Hence in a season of calm weather
> Though inland far we be,
> Our Souls have sight of that immortal sea
> Which brought us hither,
> Can in a moment travel thither,
> And see the Children sport upon the shore,
> And hear the mighty waters rolling evermore.

Certainly this is Wordsworth's most audacious application of naturalist imagery to the transcendentalist (Pythagorean) myth of metempsychosis. But the Ode has also defined a fertile matrix alternative to the vague "immortal sea." Wordsworth has both exaggerated the discontinuity of Pindar's challenges to naturalist *epithalamia* and offered many mutually contradictory dramatizations of interplay between authorities and readers. He has thus developed Pindar's definition of intercourse between himself and his readers as a non-mythic source of intimations of immortality. The actual discontinuous progress of the Ode has defined a counterpart to the supposedly continuous "mighty waters rolling evermore": the mutually regenerative fading of distinctions between one poet and

---

about by an act of will, an act signalled by the poet's adopting a different way of shaping his experience linguistically. (p. 133)

If we stress rhetoric rather than syntax—as Wordsworth himself did in the Prefaces—we can describe the ending not as an "act of will" but as a position achieved by various invitations to the reader to help reconcile one and many.

many readers. This implication is emphatically confirmed by the list of
onomatopoeic, sibilant plurals ("those obstinate questionings . . .") which
subvert any exclusive definition of identity or authority.

Indeed stanza X reverses the linear progress of the text itself, providing a crucial counter-turn equivalent to the reversal of linear succession
gently implied in stanza V.

> Then sing, ye Birds, sing, sing a joyous song!
> And let the young Lambs bound
> As to the tabor's sound!
> We in thought will join your throng
> Ye that pipe and ye that play,
> Ye that through your hearts to-day
> Feel the gladness of the May!

Stanza X can open the festival of the 1802 fragment to a much larger
company and in effect realize the pigmy-sized poet's projection of wedding or festival. For the climactic/anticlimactic stanza X ("fallings from
us, vanishings . . ./ Moving in worlds not realized") has countered and
thus confirmed—to follow Pindaric logic—the verbal staging of intersubjectivity between one and many in stanzas I–IV. In stanza IX a catalogue
of present participle–like nouns ("questionings . . . fallings . . . vanishings . . . misgivings") has evoked a positive containment ("our noisy
years seem moments in the being of the eternal Silence") whereas
"adorning . . . morning . . . calling" in stanza IV yielded only the dis-
persing awareness of "a thousand valleys far and wide." As the address to
the Child–reader in stanza VIII ("reading the eternal deep") may have
reminded us of the blowing of trumpets "from the steep" in stanza III,
we should have recognized "and see the Children sport upon the shore/
And hear the mighty waters rolling evermore" as a variant of "the
cataracts blow their trumpets from the steep . . . I hear the Echoes
through the mountains throng" which preceded the verbal genesis of
Child and children in stanzas III and IV. And the final stanza turns our
attention back not only to the orchestration of sunrise at the beginning of
the text but also to the "sunset" of the visionary gleam noted at the end
of stanza V ("at length the Man perceives it die away,/ And fade into
the light of common day").

Stanza XI acknowledges two endings so as to invite us to reflect
further upon earlier implications that such highly conventionalized dis-
turbances of continuity are as recreative as natural marriages are meant
to be.

> And O, ye Fountains, Meadows, Hills, and Groves,
> Forebode not any severing of our loves!
> Yet in my heart of hearts I feel your might
> I only have relinquished one delight
> To live beneath your more habitual sway.

I love the Brooks which down their channels fret,
Even more than when I tripped as lightly as they;
The innocent brightness of a new-born Day
   Is lovely yet;
The Clouds that gather round the setting sun
Do take a sober colouring from an eye
That hath kept watch o'er man's mortality;
Another race hath been, and other palms are won.
Thanks to the human heart by which we live,
Thanks to its tenderness, its joys, and fears,
To me the meanest flower that blows can give
Thoughts that do often lie too deep for tears.

Wordsworth ended his attempt at a Pindaric by describing the traditional emblem of ending, sunset, in a way that recalls previous literary transformations of discontinuity into the very principle of creative continuity. "The Clouds that gather round the setting sun . . . Another race hath been, and other palms are won": this reminds us that Wordsworth's text is a palimpsest, organized by transformations of the double association of the solar cycle with marriage and athletic contest in Pindar and the Psalms. But there is also a debt here to St. Paul: "seeing we are also compassed about with so great a cloud of witnesses, let us lay aside every weight, and run with patience the race that is set before us" (Hebrews 12:1). It is thus a subtle, non-insistent but very strong awareness of literary history that has allowed Wordsworth's elegiac reflections upon personal loss to become an ode: a celebration of our common power to achieve an uncommonly generative identity as members of a literate, self-critical community.

Wordsworth's final acknowledgment that poetic discourse is other than the very language of men (*"another* race hath been and other palms are won") successfully rivals in turn the merely private, priestly challenge to natural sunset in Book II of *The Prelude*.

      an auxiliar light
Came from my mind which on the setting sun
Bestowed new splendor. (1.387)

The visionary gleam of poetic creativity has in fact always come from as many eyes as are able to find "auxiliar light" in countless readers' recognition of personifications, phrases, and figures of speech which from father to son have long been regarded as the common inheritance of poets. The Intimations Ode triumphantly—because soberly—proclaims that in poetry the truths that wake to perish never arise from the obstinate questionings of sense and outward things, fallings, vanishings, blank misgivings of readers who move about in fictional worlds that are unrealized until they take them in hand. Our ordinary awareness may tremble guiltily before potential textual worlds like Psalm 19, *Pythia* 3, and the Ode. But such texts can form the provisional master light of all our seeing because they require that we continually question our desire for conjugal intercourse with either nature or the "very" language of men.

5

Wenn Wir Harmonia Singen: Projections of Community by Hölderlin and Celan

A German contemporary of Wordsworth, Friedrich Hölderlin also reconstructed two ancient forms of choral song, Pindaric and Scriptural. Comparison of Wordsworth's and Hölderlin's complex adaptations of both Greek and Hebrew rhetorical strategies and imagery can prepare us to read later poets who have updated Milton's use of ancient solar imagery to herald a political and cultural revolution. But before approaching self-consciously anachronistic reflections upon choral writing by Mallarmé—perhaps the most challenging precursor of the international modernist movement—it will be helpful to observe how one of Mallarmé's twentieth-century European readers turned to Hölderlin for assistance. Paul Celan used Hölderlin's Pindarics as models for his parodies of the Psalms and other ancient Jewish lyrics. He thereby challenged violence to a community far more radical than the destruction of the Temple in Jerusalem for which Psalm 19 was apparently intended to compensate: the Nazis' systematic attempt to annihilate the Jews of Europe.

i

In "Friedensfeier"—"Celebration of Peace"—Hölderlin proposed the potential exchange between text and readers as a means of reconciling conflicts between maternal nature and patriarchal conventions. The Preface invites us to receive the text for—in place of—the Mother.

> Ich bitte dieses Blatt nur gutmüthig zu lesen. So wird es sicher nicht unfasslich, noch weniger anstössig seyn. Sollten aber dennoch einige eine solche Sprache zu wenig konventionell finden, so muss ich ihnen gestehen: ich kann nicht anders. An einem schönen Tage lässte sich ja fast jede Sangart hören, und die Nature, wovon es her ist, nimmts auch wieder.

> All I ask is that the reader be kindly disposed towards these pages. In that case he will certainly not find them incomprehensible, far less objectionable. But if, nonetheless, some should think such a language too unconventional, I must confess to them: I cannot help it. On a fine day—they should consider—almost every mode of song makes

itself heard: and Nature, whence it originates, also receives it again.[1]

In the ode proper, nature appears as a human festival-space, a "Seeligge-wohnte Saal" which is to be inhabited again only if many readers inter-pret many unconventional inversions.

> um grüne Teppiche duftet
> Die Freudenwolk' und weithinglänzend stehn,
> Gereiftester Früchte voll und goldbekränzter Kelche
> Wohlangeordnet, eine prächtige Reihe,
> Zur Seite da und dort aufsteigen über dem
> Geebneten Boden die Tische.

> upon green carpets wafts
> The fragrant cloud of joy and, casting their brightness far,
> Full of most mellow fruit and chalices wreathed with gold,
> Arranged in seemly order, a splendid row,
> Erected here and there on either side above
> The levelled floor, stand the tables.

The energies which reanimate an old hall are vaguely named ("die Freudenwolk") only after a predicate, "um grüne Teppiche duftet" ech-oes the past participle in the first clause, "gelüftet ist der altgebaute . . . Saal." Another present participle "weithinglänzend" precedes a second main verb, "stehn," and opens it to infinite reference and movement. As several objects are named before the tables on which they stand, each substantive is presented as the product of preceding actions: "gereiftester Früchte," "goldbekränzter Kelcher," "geebneten Boden." By observing these variants of the tendency in the German mother tongue to delay the verb until the end of a sentence, we help reconstruct a banqueting-hall in which a Pindaric ode could be performed.[2]

Two significant mistranslations in Hölderlin's earlier rendering of *Pythia* 3 set the rubric for his attempts to confuse the German here and

---

[1] Friedrich Hölderlin, *Poems and Fragments*, trans. Michael Hamburger (London, 1966). All Hölderlin quotations are drawn from this edition.

[2] See M. R. Benn, *Hölderlin and Pindar* (The Hague, 1962), p. 91:
> An aspect of his thought that is entirely alien to Pindar and to the Greeks in general is his faith in history, his boundless confidence in the possibilities of historical development.

See also "Über Religion" by Hölderlin in the *Sämtliche Werke* IV, 278:
> Jeder hälte demnach seinen eigenen Gott, in so ferne jeder seine eigene Sphäre hat, in der er wirkt und die er erfahrt, und nur in so ferne mehrere Menschen eine *gemeinschaftliche* Sphäre haben . . . nur in so ferne haben sie eine *gemeinschaftliche* Gottheit . . . Hier kann nur noch gesprochen werden über die Vereinigung mehrerer zu einer Religion, wo jeder seinen Gott und alle einen *gemeinschaft-lichen* in dichterischen Vorstellungen ehren, wo jeder sein höheres Leben und alle ein *gemeinschaftliches* höheres Leben, *die Feier des Lebens mythisch feiern.* (my italics)

now (*pár podòs*) with the Greek then and there in several Pindarics, including "Friedensfeier."

> die goldgeschleierten,
> Die singenden auf dem Berge
> Die Musen, als im siebenthorigen
> Athmen, in Thebe, *wenn wir Har-*
> *monia singen* die stieranschauende,
> Wenn des Nereus des wohl-
> Wollenden Thetis das Kind das gehörte.

> Und die Götter waren beieinander zu Gast,
> Und Kronos Söhne die Könige *sah ich*
> Auf goldenen Stuhlen, und Geschenke
> Empfiengen sie. [italics added]

"*Wir* Harmonia singen" renders "*Harmonia gamen* (he, Kadmos, married Harmonia)" and "sah *ich*" translates "*ídon* (*they*, Kadmos and Peleus, saw)."[3] Shifting both singular and plural third-person pronouns into the first person, the poet expressed his eagerness to identify both Germany and himself with Kadmos and Peleus. In "Friedensfeier," however, Hölderlin tried to activate this identification by calling attention to radical *differences* between Pindar's context and his own.

Hölderlin had no athlete–patron to address, and only one name appears in "Friedensfeier"—as a modifier: "unter *syrischer* Palme . . . (stanza 4). The conspicuous absence of names in a simulation of Pindaric intimacy registered Hölderlin's lack of an audience. But it also helped

---

[3] Not noticing the significance of the actual phrasing, Friedrich Beissner (ed. *Friedens-feier* [Stuttgart, 1954]) glosses "wenn wir Har-/ monia sengen": "als er (der einer nämlich Kadmos) die Harmonia heiratete" and "sah ich" "sahen sie," "wieder Peleus und Kadmos." Stanzas 5–6 of "Friedensfeier" suggest that Hölderlin was remembering the other marriage in *Pythia* 3, the ill-fated union of Koronis and Apollo which ended in the burning of Koronis and her neighbors.

> aber Dank,
> Nie folgt der gleich hernach dem gottgegebene Geschenke;
> Tiefprufend ist zu fassen.
> Auch wär uns, spärte der Gebende nicht
> Schon längst vom Seegen des Heerds
> Uns Gipfel und Boden entzündet.
> Des Göttlichen aber empfangen wir
> Doch viel. Es ward die Flamm' uns
> In die Hande gegeben.

> But thankfulness, never at once does this
> follow upon the god-sent gift; deeply probing,
> this must be grasped. For were the giver
> sparing, long ago the blessings upon our hearths
> would have set fire to both roof and floor.
> But of the divine we received much nonetheless.
> The flame was put in our hands.

him protest against the cause of his isolation: a concern for private property and authority more exclusive than any known to Pindar. Exaggerating the anonymity of exchange in any large modern state, Hölderlin simulated the lively mutuality between the ancient writer and his patrons. His speaker is tentative both in assuming the role of bard and in assigning the role of hero-patron. He uses the first-person singular only in the second stanza—and, then only to emphasize the fact that dialogue repeatedly subverts simple definitions of identity.

> Und dämmernden Auges denk' ich schon,
> Vom ernsten Tagwerk lächelnd,
> Ihn selbst zu sehn, den Fürsten des Festes.

> And already with eyes dusk-dim,
> With solemn day-labour smiling,
> I think that I see him in person, the prince of
> the feast-day.

The self is not sure of what it sees ("denk ich") and is subordinated to the process of perception, expressed by an impersonal infinitive, "zu sehn." Two other anomalies define the perceiver as a member of exchange rather than as a power unto himself. The object of his vision is named after a modifier-phrase which could be assigned either to seer or seen, and "dämmernden Auges" associates either "ich" or "ihn" with a third ambiguous quantity: the evening hour in which they are to meet. Another phrase, "vom ernsten Tagwerk lächelnd," separates the subject/agent from the verb for his action; it too might refer to either of two quasi-persons, the self-doubting seer or the unidentified Prince of the Feast.[4]

---

[4] Wolfgang Binder, "Hölderlins 'Friedensfeier'" in *Hölderlin-Aufsätze* (Frankfurt, 1970), pp. 302–20.

> Wenn sich indessen die syntaktischen Bezüge nicht völlig klaren lassen, so kann über die symbolischen kein Zweifel sein. "Dämmern" und "lächeln" deuten also Leitworte und den Sinnbezirk des ewigen Seins; denn Tag und Dämmerung sind oft gebrauchte Bilder für Zeitlichkeit und Ewigkeit und Lächeln ist ein Signum der Götter oder gotterfüllter Menschen in Hölderlins Dichtung.

Yet it is precisely the initial ambiguity which can make a reader in a secular age attribute divine power to the faint apparition, and it is important to see various shadowings of Christ as figures of the word as well as the Word—as in "Lycidas"—totally shaped and energized by the expectation of response from many members of human discourse. In "'The Fürst des Fests' in Hölderlin's 'Friedensfeier,'" *Modern Language Review* LXV (1970), 94–115, P. H. Gaskill summarizes various attempts to identify the Hero/Prince, one of which observes that the poem is primarily concerned with the potential for dialogic communal performance and thus defines its figures as personae of the intercourse between performers and witnesses. Gaskill cites Psalm 19 as a model for this passage, but does not comment on the Psalmist's association of movement in space and speech. Ruth-Eva Schulz, "Der Fürst des Fests: Bemerkungen zu Hölderlins Hymne 'Friedensfeier,'" *Sinn und Form* XIV (1962), 187–213 treats the Prince as "die Sonne in ihrer naturhaften Wirklichkeit."

By addressing the somewhat patriarchal patron-hero, the speaker does more clearly identify both himself and the other.

> Doch wenn du schon dein Ausland verlaugnest,
> Und also vom langen Heldenzuge müd
> Dein Auge senkst, vergessen, leichtbeschattet . . .
>
> But though you like to disavow your foreign land,
> And weary, it seems, with long heroic war,
> Cast down your eyes, oblivious, lightly shaded . . .

"Vom . . . Heldenszuge müd" and "dein Auge senkst . . . leicht-beschattet" lead us to assign to the addressee the earlier epithets, "däm-mernden Auges" and "vom . . . Tagwerk lächelnd." Yet the apostrophe "dein Auge senkst" makes the earlier confusion between speaker and addressee significant—to still further incarnations of ambiguity. If the poet's words are ambiguous, light-shadowed, in becoming readers we have voluntarily blinded ourselves to the light of common day in order to find light in the obscure turns of Pindaric contradiction.

As readers we can be illuminated by obscurity because the text refers to literary and cultural history more explicitly than Wordsworth's Ode. Hölderlin indicated that his text honors two traditions of poetry as well as ordinary dialogue by elaborating his presentation of a Man: the tired Hero/Prince.

> sie hören das Werk,
> Längst vorbereitend, von Morgen nach Abend
>
> only now do they hear
> The work that long has prepared them, from Orient to Occident

"Friedensfeier" retraces the progress of poetry to Germany in the West (*Abendland*) from two Easts (*Morgenlands*): the Psalmist's Israel as well as Pindar's Greece. While the Hero/Prince takes the role of Pindar's patrons, athletic heroes, his counterpart, a Youth (Jüngling) introduced in stanza 4, resembles two figures in Scripture: the Psalmist's bridegroom-sun and the Logos in the Gospel of John.

Before the Youth appears, an interpretation of "leichtbeschattet" helps locate the Pindaric Hero/Prince in the Hebrew-Christian tradition as well as in the Greek.

> Und Freundesgestalt annimst, du Allbekannter, doch
> Beugt fast die Knie das Hohe.
>
> Assuming the shape of a friend, you known to all men, yet
> Almost it bends our knees, such loftiness.

The speaker uses an epithet which explicitly locates authority with the respondent—with many respondents. "Allbekannter" is a striking variant of "Allwissende," the conventional epithet for the patriarchal God in the

Old Testament, and indicates a reversal of the exchange between Creator and creature evoked by St. Paul.

> When I was a child, I spake as a child, I understood as a child; but
> when I became a man, I put away childish things.
> For now we see through a glass, darkly; but then face to face: now I
> know in part; but then I shall know even as also I am known.
> (1 Corinthians 13, 11–12)

Hölderlin's *Allbekannter* knows as he is known by others, disguising himself as one among many because he has been seen face to face by his mirror-image, the speaker. And when Hölderlin presented the counterpart of the light-shadowed Hero/Prince, a "Jüngling" who corresponds to the Youth in the Intimations Ode, he evoked another Pauline text, one which Wordsworth recalled at the end of his Pindaric: "wherefore seeing we are also compassed about with so great a cloud of witnesses . . ." (Hebrews 12, 1). But he did so by recalling John 4.

> Und manchen möcht' ich laden, aber o du,
> Der freundlichernst den Menschen zugethan,
> Dort unter syrischer Palme,
> Wo nahe lag die Stadt, am Brunnen gerne war;
> Das Kornfeld rauschte rings, still atmete die Kühlung
> Vom Schatten des geweiheten Gebirges,
> Und die lieben dich auch, damit der heiligkühne
> Durch Wildnis mild dein Stral zu Menschen kam, o Jüngling!

> And many there are I would invite, but to you,
> O you that benignly, gravely disposed to men
> Down there beneath the Syrian palm-tree, where
> The town lay near, by the well were glad to be;
> Round you the cornfield rustled, quietly coolness breathed
> From shadows of the hallowed mountainsides,
> And your dear friends, the faithful cloud
> Cast shade upon you too, so that the holy, the bold,
> The beam through wilderness gently should fall on men,
>   O Youth.

As in John 4:21 the Logos tells an adulteress that religion will come down from the high places on which the fathers worshipped, in "Friedensfeier" Hölderlin's Youth exchanges light and darkness with many fellow-impersonators of the adulterous linguistic matrix.

Yet like Wordsworth's many light-shadowings of role-exchange between one author and many interpreters, this evocation of discourse primarily asks to be compared with others in Hölderlin's own performance. This Youth is a mirror-image of the paternal Prince of the Feast. As the Hero/Prince is tired after "ernsten Tagwerk" but is "leichtbeschattet" and puts on a "Freundesgestalt," the Youth is "freundlichernst," rests in the shadow of the holy mountains, and is shadowed by friends who allow his light to come to others, thus making him human as well as divine. The congruence of two witnessed meetings of friends alerts the similarly self-contradictory reader to acknowledge what each description implies: a central individual is himself because he is surrounded by many who recognize him.

When the speaker invites us to compare the Hero/Prince and the Youth, he calls together these two figures who reflect each other, himself, and—by implication—all readers of "Friedensfeier."

> denn darum rief ich
> Dich, Unvergesslicher, dich, zum Abend der Zeit,
> O Jüngling, dich zum Fürsten des Festes.

> for that is why
> You to the banquet now prepared I called,
> The unforgettable, you, at the Evening of Time,
> O youth called you to the prince of the feast-day.

Wordsworth and Hölderlin thus articulated solar revolution in complementary ways. While Wordsworth explicitly presented the continuity between Boy and Man mediated by the Youth, he only implied that an exchange between Man and Boy would occur if the reader reconciled several mutually contradictory presentations of youth. Hölderlin did not locate his mature Man-like Hero and Youth on a single solar course, but he vigorously called one to meet the other.

The ending of "Friedensfeier" also contrasts with the ending of the Intimations Ode. Wordsworth closed by turning our attention back to earlier moments in the poem and intensifying their mediation of the severe discontinuities between one and many, then and now which he stressed at the beginning. But Hölderlin concluded by referring for the first time to the two tensions which his performance attempted to mediate: his conflicts with Scripture on the one hand and with nature on the other. Addressing the Father and then the Mother, the speaker commemorates religious history in a way that invites future readers to complete his projection of communal dialogue. First the speaker suggests that a much more fatherly alter ego than the Hero/Prince finish his day-work.

> Schiksaalgesez ist dies, dass Alle sich erfahren,
> Wo aber wirkt der Geist, sind wir auch mit, und streiten,
> Was wohl das Beste sei. So dünkt mir jezt das Beste,
> Wenn nun vollendet sein Bild und fertig ist der Meister,
> Und selbst verklärt davon aus seiner Werkstatt tritt,
> Der stille Gott der Zeit.

> This is a law of fate, that each shall know all others,
> That when the silence returns there shall be a language too
> Yet where the Spirit is active, we too will stir and debate
> What course might be the best. So now it seems best to me
> If now the Master completes his image and, finished,
> Himself transfigured by it, steps out of his workshop,

The quiet God of Time.

The self-effacing manner of this apostrophe itself expresses a resistance to the patriarchal stress upon identity and recalls Kronos/Chronos' castration of the heavenly father, the Titan Uranus. Secondly, the speaker rearticulates the tension between textualist patriarchy and naturalist matriarchy which the writer of Psalm 19 mediated by adapting a hymn to nature.

Wie die Löwin, hast du geklagt,
O Mutter, da du sie,
Nature, die Kinder verloren.
Denn es stahl sie, Allzuliebender, dir
Dein Feind, da du ihn fast
Wie die eigenen Söhne genommen,
Und Satyren die Götter gesellt hast.
So hast du manches gebaut,
Und manches begraben,
Denn es hasst dich, was
Du, vor der Zeit
Allkräftige, zum Licht gezogen.
Nun kennest, nun lässest du dies;
Denn gerne fühllos ruht,
Bis dass es reift, furchtsamgeschäfftiges drunten.

Like the lioness you lamented,
O Mother, when you lost
your children, Nature,
For they were stolen from you, the all too loving, by
Your enemy, when almost
Like your own sons you had nursed them
And with satyrs made gods consort.
So there is much you built
And much you buried,
For you were hated by
That which too soon
All-powerful, you raised to the light.
Now you know the fault, and desist;
For, till grown ripe, unfeeling
What's timidly busy likes to rest down below.

It was Law-giving Yahweh who stole nature's children, demanding that mankind worship Him alone. In several exchanges with women such as the conversation with the Samaritan woman at the well, the Johannine Logos shifted attention from fatherly authorship to brotherly receptiveness and partially restored the suppressed nature-cults' interest in multiplicity. But the modern poet writes a third testament. Hölderlin could justly claim to have reconciled the Great Mother with Father Time in "Friedensfeier" because he elaborated the concern for mediation and reciprocity in pre-Christian choral poetry and explicitly designated his many listener-readers as a spiritual matrix to replace nature.

Ich bitte dieses Blatt nur gutmüthig zu lesen . . . An einem schönen
Tage lässt sich ja fast jede Sangart hören, und die Nature, wovon es
her ist, nimmts auch wieder.

ii

In "Tenebrae" (1959) Celan inverted the relationship between God
and man evoked by the first line of Hölderlin's "Patmos": "nah ist und
schwer zu fassen, der Gott."

Nah sind wir, Herr,
nahe und greifbar.

Gegriffen schon, Herr,
ineinander verkrallt, als wär
der Leib eines jeden von uns
dein Leib, Herr.

Bete, Herr,
bete zu uns,
wir sind nah.

Windschief gingen wir hin,
gingen wir hin, uns zu bücken
nach Mulde und Maar.

Zur Tränke gingen wir, Herr.

Es war Blut, es war,
was du vergossen, Herr.

Es glänzte.

Es ward uns dein Bild in die Augen, Herr.
Augen und Mund stehn so offen und leer, Herr.
Wir haben getrunken, Herr.
Das Blut und das Bild, das im Blut war, Herr.

Bete, herr.
Wir sind nah.

We are nigh, Lord, nigh and graspable.

Already grasped, Lord,
twisted together as though
the body of each of us
were your body, Lord.

Pray, Lord,
pray to us,
we are nigh.

Against the wind we walked,
walked to bend down
to the trough and pond.

We went to be watered, Lord.

It was blood, it was,
which you shed, Lord.

It glistened.

It threw back your image into our eyes, Lord.
Eyes and mouth are so open and empty, Lord.
We have drunk, Lord.
The blood and the image which was in the blood, Lord.

Pray, Lord,
we are nigh.[5]

Mocking the Jewish tradition of song, Celan indicated how parody can help reveal potential in its original. When he provocatively inverted the "I–thou" relationship in the Psalter, he called attention to an ordering force assumed by all the songs performed in the Temple and explicitly acknowledged by many: the co-presence of other articulate members of the congregation.[6]

As we have seen, Psalm 119 has twenty-two stanzas, one for each letter of the Hebrew alphabet; Celan's mock-Psalm has twenty-two lines—and twenty-two apostrophes. The Lord is addressed eleven times: the monotonousness of the call represents his impotence and absence. However, another symmetry suggests that the song does more than mock the ancient economy. If "Herr" occurs eleven times in twenty-two lines, so does the first-person plural pronoun: "wir" seven times and "uns" four. As seven of the eleven first-person pronouns are subjects of sentences, the poem stresses the activeness of descendents of the Temple-congregation. "Tenebrae" is a *reverent* travesty of ancient songs to patriarchal Law; it not only assumes that the Lord has lost his authority but also transfers it to his former suppliants.

In his best known poem, Celan took a larger field for parody and thus still more strongly urged readers to help reconstruct articulate community. "Todesfuge" (1952) opposes Hitler's travesty of Old Testament patriarchal rule by representing the conflict between Nazi master and Jewish people in terms of a tendency in the history of the lyric: the substitution of private, written poetry for public, choral poetry.

Ein Mann wohnt im Haus der spielt mit den Schlangen der schreibt
der schriebt wenn es dunkelt nach Deutschland dein goldenes Haar
        Margarete
er schreibt es und tritt vor das Haus und es blitzen die Sterne er
        pfeift seine Juden herbei
er pfeift seine Juden hervor lässt schaufeln ein Grab in der Erde
er befiehlt uns spielt auf nun zum Tanz

Schwarze Milch der Frühe wir trinken dich nachts
wir trinken dich morgens und mittags wir trinken dich abends
wir trinken und trinken

---

[5] Paul Celan, *Speech-Grille and Selected Poems* (New York, 1971).

[6] Götz Weinold, "Paul Celans Hölderlin-Widerruf," *Poetica* II (1968), pp. 216–28, assumes that Celan's parodies have no restorative effect.

A man lives in the house he plays with his vipers he writes
he writes when it darkens to Germany your golden hair Margarete
he writes it and steps out of doors and the stars are shining he
    whistles his dogs to come up
he whistles his Jews to come out to shovel a grave in the ground
he commands us strike up a tune for the dance

Coal-black milk of morning we drink you at night
we drink you at daybreak and noon and we drink you at evening
we drink and we drink[7]

Celan personified the potential for totalitarianism in scripture as a man
who dwells in a house and plays with snakes. But he had the solitary
writer order the Jews to continue a song whose choral form is traditional:
"er befiehlt uns spielt auf zum Tanz." The demonic substitute for the
Law-giving Lord helps the Jews make day speak unto day, night unto
night: "Schwarze Milch der Frühe wir trinken dich nachts . . . morgens . . . mittags . . . abends. . . ."

In form as well as content, the solitary author's writing mocks an
ancient Hebrew choral poem, the Song of Songs. The chorus of Jews
indicates this when they counter the writer's apostrophe with a self-
conscious topical parody of apostrophes in the ancient text.

    dein goldenes Haar Margarete
    dein aschenes Haar Sulamith

The man writes to a golden-haired Marguerite: this suggests that he is a
descendent of the Romantic hero, Goethe's Faust. But the Jews sing to a
girl with Semitic black hair; they thus commemorate not only the burning of the Jews in the ovens but also an ancient text in which ironic
interplay between single voices and a chorus generates strong personal

---

[7] Karl S. Weimar, "Paul Celan's 'Todesfuge': Translation," *PMLA* LXXXIX (1974),
85–96. Most commentators assume that Celan's negations are final, but some have
acknowledged the provocative force of his obscurity. Wolfgang Menzel, "Celans Gedicht
Todesfuge," *Germanisch-Romanische Monatschrift* XLIX (1968) 422–47; James K. Lyon,
"Paul Celan and Martin Buber: Poetry as Dialogue," *PMLA* LXXXVI (1971), 110–20,
p. 119:

    While the intense, sometimes desperate struggle to enter into a dia-
    logue might fail or at least experience frustration, the basic impulse to
    reach out and establish contact with a higher more meaningful reality
    distinguishes his poems from almost all the poems of the modern
    tradition which trace their origins to Baudelaire and Rimbaud.

Corbet Stewart, "Paul Celan's Modes of Silence," *Modern Language Review* LXVII
(1972), 127–42, p. 130:

    Silence presses heavily upon the poet's consciousness, acting, indeed,
    as a kind of challenge. It seems, in fact, mysteriously to affirm some-
    thing: and hence language, at the very point where its limitations
    become most perceptible, may, precisely in those limitations, be
    expressive of a possible larger affirmation.

identity from violent alienation.

But in "Todesfuge" the interplay between one and many, identity and alienation, is even more complex than in the Song of Songs. The Nazi who writes in the modern private mode is a demonic image of the actual author as well as of the transcendent Author. And Celan attributed to the many Jews the power of self-criticism which he shows in thus exposing the potential for tyranny in authorship. Mocking their own traditional choral song in order to challenge the Aryan private lyric, the chorus represents literary self-consciousness as a potent criticism of political tyranny.

It is in another mockery of Hölderlin more sustained than "Tenebrae," however, that Celan most triumphantly reinterpreted literary history in order to challenge his Nazi writer's obsession with pure, golden identity.

> Zur Blindheit über-
> redete Augen.
> Ihre—"ein
> Rätsel ist Rein-
> entsprungenes"—, ihre
> Erinnerung an
> schwimmende Hölderlintürme, möwen-
> umschwirrt.
>
> Besuche ertrunkener Schreiner bei
> diesen
> tauchenden Worten:
>
> Käme,
> käme ein Mensch,
> käme ein Mensch zur Welt, heute, mit
> dem Lichtbart der
> Patriarchen: er dürfte,
> spräch er von dieser
> Zeit, er
> dürfte
> nur lallen und lallen,
> immer-, immer-,
> zuzu.
>
> ("Pallaksch. Pallaksch.")
>
> Eyes, talked
> into blindness.
> Their ("pure
> origin is an
> enigma"), their
> memory of
> floating Hölderlin Towers, circled
> by whirring gulls.
>
> Visits of drowned carpenters to
> these submerging words:

If there came,
came a man,
came a man to the world, today, with
the bright beard of the
patriarchs: he could,
if he spoke of these
times, he
could
only stutter, stutter,
all, all ways, al-
ways.

("Pallaksch, Pallaksch.")

According to Paul de Man, "Tübingen, Jänner" proves that poets are blind to each other and that literary history and modernity are mutually exclusive. Modern poets write "allegory": they are concerned with "a tension within the language that can no longer be modelled on the subject-object relationship derived from experiences of perception or from theories of the imagination derived from perception." They thus cannot engage in dialogue with their predecessors or successors.

> The worst mystification is to believe that one can move from repre-
> sentation to allegory, or vice-versa, as one moves from history to
> modernity. Allegory can only blindly repeat its earlier model, with-
> out final understanding, the way Celan repeats questions from
> Hölderlin that assert their own incomprehensibility.[8]

I will show, however, that the tension within language which Celan represented is not only the tension between signifiers and signifieds but also the generative conflict between speakers in dialogue; his meta-text thus does considerably more than blindly repeat its models.

"Tübingen, Jänner" demands active, critical response by advertising its derivation from several earlier, provocative variants of dialogue. "Blindheit," "Rätsel," and "Rein-entsprungenes" at the beginning suggest that the Hölderlin who speaks nonsense at the end is the translator and annotator of *Oedipus the King.* Sophocles' hero shows off his self-inflicted blindness to the uncomprehending Theban chorus. He thus provokes the audience to acknowledge that not only their origins but also their means and ends are *im*pure—and to feel regenerated by doing so. Celan evoked this violent mediation of generational conflict which Hölderlin translated into German when he asked his readers both to acknowledge that massive abuses of authority in modern times have reduced everyone to solitary impotence—and to feel provisionally freed from anxiety by this acknowledgment.

But "ein Rätsel ist Rein-/ entsprungenes" comes from "Der Rhein,"[9]

---

8 *Blindness and Insight* (New York, 1971), p. 185.
9 Martin Anderle, "Sprachbildungen Hölderlins in modernen Gedichten (Celan's

one of Hölderlin's projections of fraternity that enacts the dialogic poetics which he drew in part from Sophocles' riddle-like exploration of impure origins. In "Der Rhein" the first of several figures who impersonate both poet's and reader's mediation is the mid-day sun who steps down from mountains that are sacred to ancient patriarchal authorities.

> Im dunklen Efeu sass ich, an der Pforte
> Des Waldes, eben, da der goldene Mittag,
> Den Quell besuchend, herunterkam
> Von Treppen des Alpengebirgs,
> Das mir die göttlichgebaute,
> Die Burg der Himmlischen heisst
> Nach alter Meinung, wo aber
> Geheim noch manches entschieden
> Zu Menschen gelanget; so
> Vernahm ich ohne Vermuten
> Ein Schiksal.

> I sat among dark ivy, at the forest's gate
> Just as the golden noon,
> To visit the source, descended
> From stairs of the alpine heights,
> Which by me are named the divinely built,
> The stronghold of the heavenly,
> Following old opinion, but where
> Determined in secret something
> Still reaches men; and thus
> Without surmise I hear
> A destiny.

When *mid*day visits the point of origins, the speaker places himself at the *source* of the Rhine but in the *midst* of Dionysos' ivy. He thus prepares to demonstrate that identity and authority derive from a multiplication of voices and verse-feet rather than from direct, unmediated reference to pure, univocal origins. One of two mediators who meet at a source, the speaker appropriates the old sacred interpretation of the mountains ("*mir* . . . heisst/ Nach alter Meinung") and anticipates a new mode of interpreting nature in terms of profane, ordinary language. As in the Scriptural scene evoked in "Friedensfeier," the Logos—anti-type of Dionyosos—like a bridegroom-sun visits the well of Father Jacob, now shadowed by the foreign Samaritan adulteress, and predicts that the Father will no longer be worshipped on mountains sacred to the patriarchs (John 4:20–24).

As Sophocles/Hölderlin's Oedipus shows that the acknowledgment of ignorance and impotence generates strong selfhood when he publicizes

---

'Tübingen, Jänner' and Brobowski's 'Hölderlin in Tübingen')," *Seminar* VIII (1972), 100–116 discusses different relationships between "Der Rhein" and "Tübingen, Jänner." See also Bernhard Boschenstein, "Hölderlin in der deutschen und französischen Dichtung des 20. Jahrhunderts" in *Hölderlin Jahrbuch* XVI (1969–70), pp. 60–75.

his self-blinding, the god-like Rhine is potent *because* he is blind and does not know where to go.

> Die Blindesten aber
> Sind Göttersöhne. Denn es kennet der Mensch
> Sein Haus und dem Tier ward, wo
> Es bauen solle, doch jenen ist
> Der Fehl, dass sie nicht wissen wohin,
> In die unerfahrne Seele gegeben.

> Sons of gods, however,
> Are the blindest of all. For man knows
> His house and the animal where he
> It must build, but to the inexperienced
> Souls of these the fault
> That they know not whither is given.

Many doubled negations, echoes of the negative/intensive prefix "ver-" and references to the destruction of all images are provocative; they represent the remembrance of origins by the (*rein*) Rhein, the poet's primary alter ego, as an annihilation of the historical sense which animates most of his poetry, including "Friedensfeier."

> Doch *nimmer, nimmer vergisst* ers.
> Denn eher muss die Wohnung *vergehn*
> Und die Satzung, und zum Unbild werden
> Der Tag der Menschen, ehe *vergessen*
> Ein solcher dürfte den Ursprung
> Und die reine Stimme der Jugend.

> But he never, never, forgets it.
> For sooner the house must perish,
> And the statutes, and the day of men
> Become an insult, before such a one
> Could forget his origin
> And the pure voice of youth. [italics added]

Intensifying existential riddles, the poet attempted to purify and illuminate ordinary experience and expression; since he defined "Ursprung" by playing like a virtuoso on his riddling, impure medium, it is the latter which emerges as the true origin of sense and value. Hölderlin thus anticipated Celan's use of his punning phrase "ein Rätsel ist Reinentsprungenes" to imply that riddling generates integrity rather than that integrity is an enigma.

But negation can be creative only if it provokes corrective negations by other speakers—as Oedipus shows when he uses his self-mutilation to provoke debate with his community. As the speaker has first enunciated the principle of purity by addressing the river ("Denn/wie du anfängst, wirst du bleiben"), he addresses Rousseau as one who speaks "die Sprache der Reinesten." But he also acknowledges the paradoxicality of defining purity in language, his impure medium. With a formula that verges on oxymoron, "törig göttlich," Hölderlin identified Rousseau with perverse Dionysos ("wie der Weingott") rather than with straight Apollo. He thus exploited the tendency of apostrophe—a theatrical, Dionysiac device—to disturb chronological succession and to subvert pure, Apollonian distinctions.[10]

Likewise, in the last stanza Hölderlin authorized his initial presentation of "Der Rhein" to a friend of his youth ("an Isaak von Sinclair") by completing a gradual shift of concern from paternal/maternal origins to the light-shadowing of the linguistic medium.

> Dir mag auf heissem Pfade unter Tannen oder
> Im Dunkel des Eichwalds gehüllt
> In Stahl, mein Sinklair! Gott erscheinen oder
> In Wolken, du kennst ihn, da du kennest, jugendlich,
> Des Guten Kraft, und nimmer ist dir
> Verborgen das Lächeln des Herrschers
> Bei Tage, wenn
> Es fieberhaft und angekettet das
> Lebendige scheinet oder auch
> Bei Nacht, wenn alles gemischt
> Ist ordnungslos und wiederkehrt
> Uralte Verwirrung.

> To you on the hot path under fir-trees or
> In the oak-forest's darkness, wrapped
> In steel, dear Sinklair, God may appear
> Or in clouds, you know Him, since youthfully you know,
> The Good One's power and never do you
> In day-time, when
> It seems fettered and febrile,
> The living, or also
> By night, when all is mixed
> In disorder and ancient
> Confusion returns.

Acknowledging that another interpreter may meet Authority either under dark fir trees or amid clouds, Hölderlin suggested that he himself can provoke future interpreters to challenge conventional privilegings of

---

[10] Kurt Wais in "Rousseau et Hölderlin," *Annales de la Societé Jean-Jacques Rousseau* XXXV (1962), 287–315, observes that it is not the Rousseau of the *Confessions* who figures in Hölderlin's poetry:

> Son Rousseau est bein plutôt un de ces héros et demidieux que les divinités nous envoient à titre de consolation, en attendant le moment ou les hommes auront trouvé le chemin de la communauté. (pp. 298–99)

Paul de Man, "L'image de Rousseau dans la poésie de Hölderlin," *Deutsche Beitrage zur Geistigen Überlieferung* V (1965), 157–83, p. 174:

> Rousseau . . . apparaît avant tout comme l'homme du language: . . . il écoute (vers 143), il parle (vers 144), il offre le langage (vers 146) et le chant (vers 160).

unclouded solar Authority.

He also shifted attention away from either of the classic polarities, light-dark and father-mother, by honoring the mediator who contemplates both the source and the course of the time-like river along with several doubles: the sun, the Rhine itself, Rousseau, Socrates, Sinclair— and any reader. Although Hölderlin was ostensibly praising purity, consistency with one's beginnings, his Pindaric primarily celebrates the interdependence of human middlemen as a doubling in turn of the reciprocity between men and gods.

> Die Seligsten nichts fühlen von selbst,
> Muss wohl, wenn solches zu sagen
> Erlaubt ist, in der Götter Namen
> Teilnehmend fühlen ein Andrer,
> Den brauchen sie.

> The most blessed feel nothing themselves,
> Another, if to say such a thing
> Is permitted, must, I suppose,
> In the gods' name, sympathetically feel,
> They need him.

The complex, self-contradictory progress of "Der Rhein"—like that of "Freidensfeier"—makes pure nomination ("Namen") depend upon many interpreters' participation ("Teilnehmend") in reevaluating the concepts of purity and origination.

Thus, although in "Tübingen, Jänner" Celan mocked "Der Rhein" and the name of its author, he thereby invited his readers to elaborate the earlier poet's ironic and self-critical projection of articulate community.

> Zur Blindheit über-
> redete Augen.
> Ihre—"ein
> Rätsel ist Rein-
> entsprungenes"—, ihre
> Erinnerung an
> schwimmende Hölderlintürme, möwen-
> umschwirrt.

> Besuche ertrunkener Schreiner bei
> diesen
> tauchenden Worten:

> Käme,
> käme ein Mensch,
> käme ein Mensch zur Welt, heute, mit
> dem Lichtbart der
> Patriarchen er dürfte,
> spräch er von dieser
> Zeit, er
> dürfte
> nur lallen und lallen,

immer-, immer-
zuzu
("Pallaksch, Pallaksch.")

The reader comes to "Augen" through a participial phrase that denies
the power to which it refers, "zur Blindheit über-/ redete"; he must ask,
"whose eyes?" The second non-sentence does not explain the first but
only elaborates its denial of sense: once again there is no primary verb.
No one remembers and there is no one to have a memory. But if the
reader resists giving up his habitual association of speech, vision, and
memory with persons, he to some extent reenacts the major violation of
the *Muttersprache* which Celan challenges: the tendency of any authority to reduce language to no more than a means of defining and retaining personal name and property.

Completing the second non-sentence which he has interrupted by
quoting "Der Rhein," Celan developed his Hölderlinian critique of identity and authority. "Erinnerung an/ schwimmende Hölderlintürme,
möwen-/ umschwirrt." "Hölderlin" loses its status as a proper name in
two ways: it both serves as modifier in a constructed substantive and
describes an arbitrary pluralization of the single patriarchal tower in
which the poet lived out his madness. The memory like the eyes is
unowned; it is not even a memory of the arbitrarily pluralized unique
tower, but of the flow of water: a natural, prelinguistic process which
generates many images of the tower. The water's motion in turn is
imitated by circling gulls: in "möwen-/ umschwirrt," another word-
break like that in "Rein-/ entsprungenes" stresses motion and further
weakens the visual points of reference which the flagrantly constructed,
emphatically textual word circumscribes. The umlaut-weakened first elements of the two constructions ("Hölderlin," "möwen") are dominated by
the indefinite, nearly assonant second elements ("türme," "umschwirrt");
their consonance extends an already long motion begun by the present
participle "schwimmende" which alliterates with "umschwirrt."

But another pluralization which is more disconcerting than "Hölderlintürme" invites us to read the loss of identity as a means of achieving
articulate community. "Besuche ertrunkener Schreiner bei/ diesen/
tauchenden Worte." A single carpenter, a man by the name of Zimmer,
often visited the mad Hölderlin in his tower[11]—yet Celan gives his
many potential readers the role of "carpenter"-visitor to the mad words
of this text. As he pluralized the tower and evoked the river's proliferation of tower-images, he cast readers who have vicariously experienced
this drowning ("ertrunkener") of identity as replacements for Zimmer.
Correspondingly, the more elaborate de-articulations in the second half

[11] Bernhard Boschenstein, "Tübingen, Jänner" in *Über Paul Celan*, ed. Dietland
Meinecke (Frankfurt, 1970), p. 104.

of this text ("dieser tauchenden Worte") can serve as replacements for the unique historical Hölderlin.

Replacing a person—albeit an inarticulate person—with a text, Celan emphatically denied that communication is possible. But his exaggeration of textual self-referentiality is provocative. Urgently demanding critical response, it invites us to stand in for the discredited prophet Hölderlin as well as for the carpenter Zimmer.

The second half of the poem projects an apparition which is absurd enough to have caused the various displacements and confusions of priority recorded in the first half—but which can also provoke us to rectify these discontinuities.

> käme
> käme ein Mensch
> käme ein Mensch zur Welt, heute, mit
> dem Lichtbart der
> Patriarchen: er dürfte
> spräch er von dieser
> Zeit, er dürfte
> nur lallen und lallen,
> immer-, immer-,
> zuzu.

A second group of eleven lines precisely contradicts the first eight-plus-three. As Celan mocked the Psalms in "Tenebrae," in breaking up several compound words in the second half of "Tübingen, Jänner" he adapted the technique of Psalm 119: the celebration of patriarchal Law in which twenty-two stanzas correspond to the letters of the Hebrew alphabet. When Celan parodied this ancient play upon textuality, however, he demanded that we respond to the madness of "dieser Zeit" with a critical intelligence and vocal potency not required by exclusively textual apocalypse. For as if he were enacting the literal sense of the first verb in his text, "über-redete," he exceeded the twenty-two line schema of the Psalm. An extra line, "('Pallaksch, Pallaksch')," requires us to reread political and religious history in terms of the virtual dialogue between authorities and interpreters which animates literary history.

When Celan over-spoke the Psalmist by one line—a parenthetical recollection of a nonsense word which was apparently spoken by the mad Hölderlin—he presented the dead father-poet's historical utterance as more provocatively text-bound than the Psalmist's response to the Law. "Pallaksch" stands in mutually contradictory relations to the page on which it is printed. On the one hand, the parentheses bury this quotation farther *inside* the text than the enigmatic but sane line quoted from "Der Rhein," "ein Rätsel ist Reinentsprungenes." On the other hand, the quotation marks identify what they contain as a transposition of actual speech, which is always *outside* the time/space of a text—after as well as before it: to be present again when the reader reads the text aloud, discusses its enigmas, or talks about anything else while influenced by its exclusion of speech. The diacritical marks' slight mutual contradiction helps us read the doubled non-word as a double negative which implies a positive statement.

To begin with, "Pallaksch" itself has positive as well as negative resonance. Not only does it recall two earlier pluralizations of the tower and of Zimmer; it is also an onomatopoiea which tempts us to reverse our negative reading of both "Hölderlintürme" and "Schreiner." "Pallaksch, Pallaksch" sounds like the lapping and splashing of the river against its banks. It reads Hölderlin's madness as an identification with recurrent, ever-young nature. And it may remind us that the singer of "Der Rhein" can communicate his vatic power to many future readers because he identifies himself with the river.

Yet in "Tübingen, Jänner" as in "Der Rhein"—and "Lycidas"—the disconcerting merge of human articulation and natural flow sounds positive primarily because it matches another tense association of counterparts. As we have seen, in "Der Rhein" Hölderlin addressed two other doubles, the non-patriarchal Rousseau and Sinclair. In "Tübingen, Jänner" Celan assigned no proper name to the alter ego who will authorize his critique of authorship. All the signs in the text—diacritical marks as well as words—imply that it is the anonymous reader who has been blinded to the conventional priorities of "dieser Zeit" by "*diesen* tauchenden Worte." Casting his readers as Zimmers who visit his text as the carpenter visited Hölderlin's tower, Celan played upon the fact that members of dialogue continually subvert previous definitions of priority and role and generate a vital sense of identity by repeatedly abdicating the role of active authority. Halfway through the poem Celan presented the potential exchange between text and reader as an impure and highly unconventional origin of the first Hölderlin-quotation, "ein Rätsel. . . ." He thus invited us to observe that language is a matrix of identity which *un*like nature generates positive order by continually negating or reversing previous formulations. For in recognizing "('Pallaksch, Pallaksch')" as a mimesis of the river that has multiplied images of Hölderlin's tower, we may be persuaded ("über-redete") to challenge the text's increasingly provocative denials that communication is possible. Indicating that the second half of the poem has generated the first, Celan suggests that we too can turn literary history back upon itself. If we react against his hyperbolic and mutually reflecting negations, we project a reopening of dialogue between modern apocalyptist and Romantic prophet and counter the alienation of a survivor of the Holocaust from both communities honored by Wordsworth: "the common inheritance of poets" and "the very language of men."

But in denying Hölderlin authority over "dieser Zeit," Celan also honored his literary authority as much as he did his future interpreters. For as we have seen, Hölderlin too tried to recreate himself in the image of readers who might stand in for nature and acknowledge his many proofs that dialogue continually subverts conventional priorities: "ich bitte dieses Blatt nur gutmüthig zu lesen . . . und die Nature . . . nimmts auch wieder." When Celan treated Hölderlin not as a father but as a medium for transmitting the message that transmission itself is the definitive human action, he elaborated the subversive—indeed revolutionary—economy of "Der Rhein." If Hölderlin came back as an author, he would speak nonsense not only because men of this time cannot understand him: he would also betray his own work, in which acknowledgments of ambiguity rather than transcendental unity and authority project lively convocations. However, if the dead poet came back as a persona of his self-mimicking yet also self-contradictory medium, he would be the other fraternal voice required for pastoral song—which can never end because it only begins again "yet once more and once more," as Milton said in his inversion-filled heralding of revolution.

6

Mallarmé and the Bride

Displacing attention from the unique author to many interpreters more emphatically than St. John, Mallarmé also represented violent and erotic aspects of literary exchange more vividly than Milton, Wordsworth, Hölderlin—or even Celan, his own reader. Although his poetry is generally read as the ultimate in hermetic self-reflexivity, some of his most compelling texts develop ancient choral poets' strategy of dramatizing the complex dynamics of poetic genesis and performance in order to project a community animated by continual exchanges of self-criticism.[1]

Solar imagery in the elegy in prose for Victor Hugo, "Crise de Vers" (1886–1892–1896), prepares us to read "Hérodiade," a poem on which Mallarmé worked for at least thirty years and in which he consummately developed the association of the Psalmist's annunciatory bridegroom-sun with cruel violence in Revelation 19. "Crise de Vers" responds both to the setting of a giant patriarchal sun, Hugo, and to the rise of many poets who write in free verse *against* the mother tongue, "par abus de la cadence nationale."

> le cycle présent, ou quart dernier de siècle subit quelque éclair absolu—dont l'echévèlement d'ondée à mes carreaux essuie le trouble ruisselant, jusqu'à illuminer ceci—que, plus ou moins, tous les livres contiennent la fusion de quelques redites comptées: même il n'en serait qu'un—au monde, sa loi—bible comme la simulent des nations. La différance d'un ouvrage à l'autre, offrant autant de leçons proposées dans un immense concours pour le texte véridique, entre les âges dites civilisés où—lettrés.

The present cycle, or last quarter of a century, is undergoing an

---

[1] In *The Aesthetics of Stephane Mallarmé in Relation to his Public* (Rutherford, New Jersey, 1975), Paula Gilbert Lewis counters Hugo Friedrich's claim that Mallarmé's poetry "refuses to interfere with the present . . . rebuffs the reader and imposes inhumanity upon itself" (*Structure of the Modern Lyric*, trans. J. Neugroschel [Evanston, Illinois, 1974], p. 106). See also her "Stephane Mallarmé: Literature as Social Action," *Romance Notes* XVII, 13–20. In *La Révolution du langage poétique* (Paris, 1974), Julia Kristeva places Mallarmé's self-referentiality in the context of tensions in the bourgeois, patriarchal culture of his time, but does not consider the dynamics of reciprocity between text and readers for which Mallarmé provides; she thus characterizes literary "revolution" as an activity which is as solipsistic as the nihilism described by Friedrich.

absolute illumination—from which the downpour's streaming on my
windowpanes wipes the flowing trouble to the point of making this
clear: that, more or less, all the books contain the fusion of some
calculated pronouncement. There will even be only one bible simulated by the nations, the world's law, the difference from one work to
another offering as many proposed lessons in an immense competition for the true text among the so-called civilized or literate ages.[2]

The poet sits in his library on one of many ordinary rainy afternoons ("une
après l'autre après-midi") and sees lightning-flashes reflected in the glass of
bookshelves opposite his window. But he proclaims a new common place
for poetry: competitive dialogue between parts of a Book that is to rival
Scripture, "une disposition fragmentaire avec alternance et vis-à-vis, concourant au rhythme total." The unity of the new Bible will be generated
from a contest involving several mother tongues: the new gentile scripture
is to be composed of member-parts that gather in a concert which defies
Father Time. If we have been disconcerted by the death of a giant paternal
chef d'orchestre ("ses habitudes interrompues à la mort de Victor Hugo ne
peut que se déconcerter"), we must resist the anarchic individualism of
free verse, the inevitable counterpart to Hugo's authoritarian stress upon
authorship: "pour la première fois, au cours de l'histoire littéraire d'aucun
peuple, concurrément aux grandes orgues générales et seculaires . . . quiconque avec son jeu ou son ouie individuels se peut composer un instrument"; "For the first time in the course of the literary history of any people,
along with the great general and secular organs, anyone can compose himself as an instrument with his individual play or ear."

The poetics implied in "Crise de Vers" is dramatized in the three
fragments that compose "Hérodiade." In the "Ouverture de l'ancienne
Hérodiade," the Nurse sings an incantation which evokes the miniature
drama's setting and heroine: a virgin abandoned to solitary reveries by a
warrior-father. In the "Scène" Salomé/Hérodiade (Herod's stepdaughter)
gazes into a mirror and tells the Nurse how she glories in her absolute
sterility and isolation, but also acknowledges that she fears and desires an
unknown event that will destroy both. Finally, the "Cantique de
St. Jean" reinterprets the decapitation of St. John the Baptist as an
intensely erotic, quasi-mystical union between the virgin and the dead
precursor of Christ the Word. Both individually and together, the three
parts provide an analysis of poetic signification and interpretation which
is among the most concentrated and powerful ever written. And it is
more urgently aware of the dynamics of literary history than any poetry
written until Mallarmé's American readers constructed even more
intensely provocative self-critical songs.

In the "Ouverture" the Nurse helps establish ancient choral song as

---

2 *Oeuvres complètes*, ed. Henri Mondor and G. Jean-Aubry (Paris, 1945), p. 367.

primary model for a modern poetic apocalypse by denying that modern poetry can emulate ancient epithalamia.

Une voix, du passé longue évocation,
Est-ce la mienne prête à l'incantation?
Encore dans *les plis jaunes de la pensée*
Traînant, antique, ainsi qu'une étoile encensée
Sur un confus amas d'ostensoirs refroidis
Par les trous ancients et par *les plis roidis*
Percés selon le rhythme et les dentelles pures
Du suaire laissant par ses belles guipures
Désespéré monter *le vieil éclat voilé*
S'élève: (ô quel lointain en ces appels celé!)
Le vieil éclat voilé du vermeil insolite
De la voix languissant, nulle, *sans acolyte*
Jetera-t-il son or par dernières splendeurs,
Elle, encore, l'antienne aux versets demandeurs . . .
Elle a chanté, parfois incohérente

Que des rèves *par plis* n'a plus *le cher grimoire* . . .
Depuis longtemps la gorge ancienne est tarie. (42) [italics added]

A voice, long-drawn, evocative of the past,
(Is it mine ready for the incantation?)
Languishing among the yellowed folds
of thought, and aged as a cloth perfumed
with incense over a pile of cold church vessels,
arises through the ancient holes and through
the stiffened folds matching the rhythm and pure
lacework of the shroud that lets the desperate
old veiled brilliance mount through its meshes;
(Oh, what distance hidden in these calls!)
the old veiled brilliance of a strange vermilion
of the languishing voice, toneless, without acolyte
will it cast its gold among the final splendors,
still the antiphony of petitioning verses,
she has sung, sometimes incoherently

No more the dear gramarye of dreams
from wrinkled sheets . . .
For a long time the ancient voice has been silenced.

The Nurse is so inured to solitude that she questions the reality of her own incantatory voice and doubts that the pleading anthem will rise even to paint an apocalypse. And she acknowledges for the modern poet that the potentially visible folded text dominates memories of a silenced ancient voice. It is only images of sibyls and prophets woven on a tapestry who serve as "témoins" to this apotheosis of the modern conversion of song into arcane, emblematic, self-reflexive visual images fit for an alchemist's manual ("grimoire").

In "Hérodiade," however, ironic variations upon Scripture not only define but also exorcise the limitations of writing. The "Ouverture" is composed of solitary autumnal reflections upon a violent past embodied by an absent, indifferent father. If a northern dawn is seen reflected as a "plumage héraldique" and Hérodiade wanders silently alone ("et sur ses ombres pas un ange accompagnant son indicible pas") in the North

> Son père ne sait pas cela, ni le glacier
> Farouche reflétant de ses armes l'acier
> Quand sur un tas gisant de cadavres sans coffre
> Odorant de résine, énigmatique, il offre
> Ses trompettes d'argent obscur aux vieux sapins!

> Her father does not know this, nor the fierce
> glacier reflecting the steel of armor and weapons,
> when on a felled heap of corpses without coffins
> odorous with resin, enigmatic, he offers
> his trumpets of black silver to the old pines!

Offering herself up to an impersonal ideal of absolute virginity, Hérodiade elaborates a travesty of the Scriptural obsession with identity performed by an Abraham to whom no angel provides a surrogate for his child. But just because Mallarmé so cruelly mocked the patriarchal Scriptural tradition, he defined the Old Testament's compensating stress upon communal cooperation as the standard by which we are to judge both the self-idolatry of a vision-obsessed Bride and the hermeticism of his own utterance.

Hérodiade begins the "Scène" by prophesying an emphatically vocal dawn: the death of a prophet of the incarnate Logos.

> et quel matin oublié des prophètes
> Verse, sur les lointains mourants, ses tristes fêtes?

> what morning
> forgotten by prophets pours, on the dying distance,
> its dreary festivals?

And it is by renewing the ancient mode of apostrophe that the poet's chief surrogate prepares a common verbal dancing place for herself and her male counterpart, St. Jean.

> Vous ayant reflétés, joyaux du mur natal,
> Armes, vases depuis ma solitaire enfance. (45)

> Vous le savez, jardins d'améthyste enfouis
> Sans fin dans de savants abîmes éblouis,
> Ors ignorés, gardant votre antique lumière
> Sous le sombre sommeil d'une terre première,
> Vous, pierres où mes yeux comme de purs bijoux
> Empruntent leur clarté mélodieuse, et vous
> Métaux qui donnez à ma jeune chevelure
> Une splendeur fatale et sa massive allure! (47)

> . . . of having reflected you, armor and vases,
> gems of my natal walls from my lonely childhood.

> You know that, amethystine gardens, hidden

without end in dazzling erudite abysses,
unknown golds, keeping your ancient light
under the somber sleep of primeval earth,
you stones from which my eyes like pure jewels
borrow their melodious clarity,
metals that give my young locks a fatal
splendor and their flowing massive charm!

When Hérodiade turns away from dialogue with the intimate single confidante ("tu") to apostrophize many groups of impersonal objects, she in effect anticipates the means by which the conflict between her desires for violation and integrity can be resolved. Many potential masculine or feminine readers may realize that she is parodying the other St. John's designation of the Bride Jerusalem as a bejewelled cube, and find in Mallarmé's intricate play with the elements of his medium the means of projecting a marriage of opposites as suggestive as the union of the Lamb and Jerusalem in Revelation.

Hérodiade anticipates the crossing and recrossing of genders in her male counterpart's orgasmic utterance, preparing us to read the "Cantique" as an authoritative challenge to modern intensifications of the obsession with exclusive patriarchal identity in Scripture.

    O miroir!
Eau froide par l'ennui dans ton cadre gelée
Que de fois et pendant des heures, désolée
Des songes et cherchant mes souvenirs qui sont
Comme des feuilles sous ta glace au trou profond
Je m'apparus en toi comme une ombre lointaine,
Mais, horreur! des soirs, dans ta sévère fontaine,
J'ai de mon rêve épars connu la nudité! (45)

Toi qui te meurs, toi qui brûles de chasteté
Nuit blanche de glaçons et de neige cruelle!
Et ta soeur solitaire, ô ma soeur éternelle
Mon rêve montera vers toi: telle déjà
Rare limpidité d'un coeur qui le songea,
Je me crois seule en ma monotone patrie
Et tout, autour de moi, vit dans l'idolâtrie
D'un miroir qui reflète en son calme dormant
Hérodiade au clair regard de diamant . . . (47–48)

    O mirror!
cold water frozen by ennui in your frame,
how many times and through what hours, distressed
by dreams and searching my memories, like leaves
under your ice in the deep hole, have I
appeared in you like a shadow far away,
but, horror! in the dusk, in your austere pool
I have known the nakedness of my scattered dreams!

you who die as yourself, who burn with chastity,
white night of icicles and cruel snow!

And your lonely sister, O my sister eternal
my dream will rise toward you: already such
rare limpidity of a heart that dreamed it,
I think I'm alone in my monotonous country,
and all, around me, lives in idolatry
of a mirror that reflects in its slumbering calm
Herodias with the lucid diamond look . . .

As Hérodiade addresses the mirror (masculine) as frozen water (feminine), she compares "souvenirs" (m) to "feuilles" (f), credits "mon rêve"
with "la nudité," announces that it will rise to the moon ("ta soeur"),
interprets her heart (m) as an emphatically feminine matrix ("telle déjà,
rare limpidité") of her masculine dream, and converts both identity-
assuring mirror and fatherland to instruments of matriarchal/naturalist
idolatry. This persistent tension between masculine and feminine beauti-
fully secularizes the Church's virginizing of the Mother in reinterpretations of the ancient nuptials of sun and moon.[3] It prepares us to observe
that still more self-reflexive St. Jean is a prophetic solar bridegroom as
violently challenging and *thus* restorative as the sun-like secretive/
revelatory Word in Revelation 19, a more radical version of the Psalmist's image of the Law.

When Hérodiade rejects the Nurse as interpreter, she dismisses the
ancient tradition of communal reading ("sibylles . . . Mages . . . une voix,
du passé longue évocation . . . prête à l'incantation" "la voix . . . sans acolyte aux versets demandeurs . . . la gorge ancienne . . ."). But Hérodiade
also thus creates an empty space which must be filled. And however much
she multiplies plural and more or less feminine images of her intensely
interpretive but basically solitary self ("pas/ Un ange accompagnant son
indicible pas") she cannot fill that void. The apostrophes "vous, joyaux,
armes, vases," "vous, jardins d'améthyste" "vous, pierres et vous/ Métaux"
merely symbolize her own self-reflexivity, and thus cannot answer the
"indicible question" which she asks them. Nor can either the feminized
masculine *miroir* or its partially masculinized feminine counterpart, the
moon ("ta soeur éternelle"), answer. Even more obviously than the jewels
and decorative metals, both are images of her self-idolatry. Hérodiade can
only be answered by a figure who is similar enough to sympathize with her
dilemma but different enough to place it in a larger context. The Baptist
provides the wider landscape so urgently demanded by Hérodiade's rejection of traditional mediation: he reads his own death in the terms of solar
rise and fall frequently used to represent continuity by the ancient writers
of the choral anthems which the Nurse lamented.

[3] See Hugo Rahner, "The Christian Mystery of Sun and Moon," in *Greek Myths and
Christian Mystery*, ed. E. O. James (New York, 1963).

Addressing her own lips, Hérodiade completes a parody of the Old Testament privileging of unique identity, and provokes a challenge in turn from a Messiah as violent as the Word in Revelation 19.

> Vous mentez, ô fleur nue
> De mes lèvres.
>   J'attends une chose inconnue
> Ou peut-être, ignorant le mystère et vos cris,
> Jetez-vous les sanglots suprêmes et meurtris
> D'une enfance sentant parmi les rêveries
> Se séparer enfin ses froides pierreries. (48)

>   O naked flower
> of my lips, you lie!
>   I await a thing unknown
> or perhaps, unaware of the mystery and your cries
> you give, lips, the supreme tortured moans
> of a childhood groping among its reveries
> to sort out finally its cold precious stones.

This climactic call for deconstruction of an outmoded concept of identity is apparently simultaneous with the soliloquy by the Baptist who announced the Logos' reconstruction of Old Testament prophecies of community. It therefore encourages us not only to read the decapitation which he vocalizes as a metaphor for the "castration" of the male in sexual intercourse, but also to read the correspondence of two brief odes to self-destruction as a metaphor for our exchange of intense self-criticism with the poet. Matching Hérodiade's articulation of her division between impulses toward masculine closure and feminine openness, the saint composes a common place to be occupied by those who have read reconstructive deconstructions of dialogue both in Scripture and in earlier European poetry derived from Scripture.

In the "Cantique" the forerunner of the Logos intones a song which the severed head of Milton's Orpheus might have sung while prefiguring a renaissance of poetry.

> (By the rout that made the hideous roar,
> His gory *visage* down the stream was sent,
> Down the swift Hebrus to the Lesbian shore.

> It was that fatal and perfidious bark
> Built in the eclipse, and rigged with curses dark,
> That sunk so low that sacred *head* of thine

> So sinks the day-star in the ocean bed,
> And yet anon repairs his drooping *head*,
> And tricks his beams, and with new spangled ore,
> Flames in the *forehead* of the morning sky.) [italics added]

> Le soleil que sa halte
> Surnaturelle exalte
> Aussitôt redescend
>   Incandescent

Je sens comme aux vertèbres
S'éployer des ténèbres
Toutes dans un frisson
    A l'unisson

Et ma tête surgie
Solitaire vigie
Dans les vols triomphaux
    De cette faux

Comme rupture franche
Plutôt refoule, ou tranche
Les anciens désaccords
    Avec le corps

Qu'elle de jeûnes ivre
S'opiniâtre à suivre
En quelque bond hagard
    Son pur regard

Là-haut où la froidure
Éternelle n'endure
Que vous le surpassiez
    Tous ô glaciers

Mais selon un baptême
Illuminée au même
Principe qui m'élut
    Penche un salut.

The sun that is exalted
by its supernatural halt
forthwith redescends
    incandescent

I feel how vertebrae
in the dark give way
all of them together
    in a shudder

And in lonely vigil
among flights triumphal
of this scythe's swings
    my head springs

as the downright rupture
represses or cuts rather
the primordial clash
    with the flesh

Drunken with abstinence
may it stubbornly advance
in some haggard flight
    its pure sight

up where the infinite
cold does not permit
that you be its surpassers
    O all glaciers

but, thanks to a baptism
shining from the chrism
of that consecration
    my head bows salutation.

Although it is very unlikely that Mallarmé wrote his lyric rendering of decapitation with one eye on Milton's, some analogies can be drawn between the cultural contexts of the two poems. By the end of the nineteenth century when Mallarmé was writing, the abuse of paternal authority which Milton attributed to the seventeenth-century Anglican bishops had become the rule of bourgeois colonialism. And at home, like the writers of free verse whom Mallarmé opposed in "Crise de Vers" ("quiconque avec son jeu ou son ouie individuels se peut composer un instrument"), every bourgeois individual had elected himself *chef d'orchestre*. Mallarmé thus could only prophesy a redemptive sunrise by presenting an erotic apocalypse which demands more from the reader than the unexpressive nuptial song of "Lycidas," more even than the dramatizations of writing and reading which prepare the marriage supper of the Lamb and Jerusalem in Revelation.

St. Jean interprets the rise, hesitation and fall of his severed head as a microcosmic imitation of the sun's course through high noon. But Mallarmé presented the virtual intercourse between the Baptist and Hérodiade as a provocative macrocosmic development of the tension between masculine and feminine articles and pronouns in French.

1. If the sun ("le soleil") is paradoxically exalted by its apparent hesitation at noon ("sa halte"), the male protagonist displaces his conflict with the female antagonist into a competition between his head (*"la* tête") and its gaze (*"le"* regard"): "ma tête surgie . . . qu'elle s'opiniâtre à suivre son pur regard."

2. The climactic address, "vous . . . Tous ô glaciers," rectifies this displacement; the masculine gaze, "son pur regard . . . le" competes with plural masculine "glaciers."

Là-haut où la froidure
Éternelle n'endure
Que vous le surpassiez
    Tous ô glaciers

3. Yet by calling attention to the femininity of "la froidure éternelle" when he anticipated the sound of the feminine article with "là-haut," Mallarmé established the tension between two masculine terms, singular and plural, "regard" and "glaciers," as a reflection of two other conflicts: between Hérodiade and St. Jean, between himself and us.

The one second-person pronoun (*"vous* le surpassiez") in the Baptist's soliloquy seems to be addressed to Hérodiade, the speaker of the preceding fragment. The "glaciers" to which St. Jean opposed the masculine gaze of this feminine head ("ma tête surgie") are Hérodiade's eyes—unnaturally multiplied because she has confused herself with a much reflected but non-reflective father ("son père ne sait pas cela, ni le glacier/ Farouche reflétant de ses armes l'acier").

The climactic address also activates exchange between writer and reader. Like the description of the Father in the "Scène" it invites us to acknowledge and thus perhaps resolve radical problems in conventional—patriarchal—priorities. Whereas Scripture invokes a paternal absolute, this text invokes a female arbiter of all its conflicts: "la froidure éternelle," a sterile anti-mother. Because the absolute which judges the competition between "regard" and "glaciers" is feminine, the second-person pronoun implicates the reader as collaborating interpreter. Because Mallarmé feminized the Absolute, we may find in the final word of the text an anti-traditional definition of salvation ("salut") as a mutual greeting ("salut") by similarly self-contradictory members of dialogue.

Grammatically feminine, the male's head has been exalted like a sun stopped midway in its course not by a Joshua's prayer to the absolute Father but by the grammatically feminine "halte" which should *result* from such a prayer. It thus hangs as a nuptial greeting to the self-obsessed daughter of a warrior—but only because its gesture towards an opening of intercourse is to be renewed as often as the poem is inter-preted by those who voluntarily assume the "feminine" role of reader.

The head's final pose is said to be authorized ("illuminée") by a mas-culine principle of identity ("au même/ Principe qui m'élut"). But we can appreciate its implications only if we recognize that the principle which defines one identical with oneself is a provocative transformation of the traditional masculine Principle, "là -haut . . . la froidure éternelle." Because the reference to the "même/Principe" further emphasizes the disconcerting displacement of Authority that it seems to correct, it provokes us to reevaluate the definitions and distinctions can-onized by patriarchal tradition.[4]

The severed head of St. Jean is thus a *chef d'orchestre* fit to replace the solar giant Victor Hugo in "Crise de Vers" and initiate the many exchanges of both challenge and nuptial greeting between poets and readers which that essay projects: "une immense concours pour le texte véridique . . . une disposition fragmentaire, avec alternance et vis-à-vis

---

[4] "In Principio erat verbum" which begins John the Evangelist's rewriting of Genesis 1 echoes in "au même/Principe qui m'élut." Austin Gill does not discuss "Hérodiade" in "Mallarmé's Use of Christian Imagery for Post-Christian Concepts" (in *Order and Adven-ture in Post-Romantic French Poetry* [Oxford, 1973]), but he does suggest that the cli-mactic "Anastase!" in "Prose, pour des Esseintes" refers to Christ's harrowing of hell "to figure the rescue of mankind from limbo by the post-Christian poet to come, the new Messiah" (p. 84).

concourant au rhythme total"; "an immense competition for the true text . . . a fragmentary disposition, with alternation and confrontations rivalling the total rhythm."[5]

For Mallarmé was dramatizing his vision of an equivalent to the jewel-encrusted new Jerusalem in Revelation: a community to be achieved in continual deconstruction of exclusive authorial identity. The text's apocalyptic imagery, rhetoric, and plot exaggerate the tendency to violate the implicit contract between writer and reader in such late derivatives of Romanticism as *symbolisme*—a tendency complementary to the authoritarianism which Milton personified in the Pilot. Precisely because "Hérodiade" provokes resistance from readers, it can help provide *salut* for modern culture in which we must continually challenge prescriptions of univocal authority if we are to approximate St. John's model of communal reciprocity.

Like "Lycidas," "Hérodiade" defines us as next in a line of solar agents who recognize that mutual challenge is the only ground for fertile marriages of heaven and earth, *nómos* and *phýsis*, convention and nature. It thus demonstrates that in the exchange between writer and reader both parties commit themselves more fully than they would to ordinary dialogue just because their text-mediated encounter never really takes place. As Pindar and the Psalmist and the writer of Revelation also prove, poetry can lead us to reevaluate cultural priorities because the very impossibility of completing our dialogue with a writer makes us intensely aware that all definitions require consensus—including those proposed by individuals whom the Atlantic separates from European tradition, and who feel as isolated as Celan did from his ancient heritage when he killed himself in Mallarmé's Paris.

Certainly it would be difficult to understand twentieth-century American poets' attempts to restore ancient dialogic definitions of identity without referring to their native model, Whitman. In the final sequence of this study, therefore, I will begin by reading Whitman's superb emulation of both "Lycidas" and Wordsworth's great Pindaric. But Mallarmé's more violent and provocative epithalamium will serve as a useful touchstone in the readings of Stevens, Eliot, Pound, Williams, Ashbery, and Ammons which follow.

---

[5] R. Champigny, "Mallarmé's Relations to Platonism and Romanticism," *Modern Language Review* LI (1956), 348–58, p. 350 identifies Mallarmé's maternal "other" as hazard, a version of the *khora* in the *Timaeus* ("a formless universal recipient which in the most dubious and scarcely explicable manner participates of an intelligible nature"). Mallarmé's essays, however, suggest that the recipient whom he requires is a more self-conscious presence, "une salle, il se célèbre, anonyme, dans le héros" (*O.C.*, p. 371): presence, reality, and identity come into being when an audience meets intense personifications of its desire for articulate identity. See also Jean-Pierre Richard, *L'univers imaginaire de Mallarmé* (Paris, 1961), chapter VII.

THREE
America

7

Poetic Dialogue in Whitman's America

i

Because the westward-moving New World of the nineteenth century established no common place for literary speculation, American poets have had to work very hard at demonstrating that the self-reflexive lyric can project unusually self-critical community. Few cultures could be less favorable to the development of a strong reciprocity between writers and readers than one which has still not outgrown its individualist obsession with frontiers. Just because of this, however, American poets have had everything to gain by insisting that we hear them.

Once again, recall how provocatively Wallace Stevens played apocalypse on his blue guitar.

> Ah, but to play man number one,
> To drive the dagger in his heart,
>
> To lay his brain upon the board
> And pick the acrid colors out,
>
> To nail his thought across the door,
> It wings spread wide to rain and snow . . .

The poet poses as an analyst of the consciousness which we share with him. But Steven's writing is authoritative when it respects the power of any particular imagination to match the sometimes quite violent questionings that it proposes. "Throw away the lights, the definitions . . . You as you are? You are yourself" tells the reader to destroy in turn the definitions sketched in "The Man with the Blue Guitar" as well as the conventions of European tradition.[1]

---

[1] See Wallace Stevens, "The Figure of the Youth as Virile Poet" in *The Necessary Angel* (New York, 1951), p. 45: "poetry is a process of the personality of the poet. This is the element, the force that keeps poetry a living thing, the modernising and ever-modern influence." See also Charles Molesworth, *The Fierce Embrace: A Study of Contemporary American Poetry* (Columbia, Missouri, 1979), pp. 8, 21:

> Again and again in American poetry the speaker will summon up some
> single figure to address, and my intuitive sense is that this occurs at least
> as often as the persona being allowed to speak on his or her own terms.
> This fretful struggle *just to be heard* dominates much of contemporary

Michel Benamou helps us read Stevens and many other Americans when he differentiates American "Adamism" from European equations of poetic dialogue with Orphic sacrifice.

> Orphism is the key to understanding the imagination of modern French poetry. The key unlocking Stevens' symbolic word is Adamism, which Roy Harvey Pearce rightly calls "the continuity of American poetry." The subject of Stevens' poetry is "man number one," Adam nailed like an eagle on display. The poetic act is not self-sacrifice but savage purification. The difference between French Orphism and American Adamism hinges on this question: who speaks? Both speak for man but one speaks as a young god, or angel, the other speaks as common man.[2]

Yet it is by no means a present, already defined common man who speaks through twentieth-century American poets. The savage signification in American poetry like "The Man with the Blue Guitar" does involve a self-sacrifice. However, it is a sacrifice not only of the writer but also of the reader and of his primary model: the writer as reader of many other poems besides his own. As we shall see, post-Miltonic Protestant Americans learned a great deal from the European Catholic, community-oriented poetics of sacrifice which Mallarmé dramatized in "Hérodiade." Both Stevens and Williams strictly qualified Whitman's characteristic naive use of metaphor to claim that the word presents the world's body. Yet each in his own way provided for an intensified, almost sacramental awareness of the capacity for innovation in *another* body: the "congregation"—as Stevens calls them in "The Auroras of Autumn"—summoned by a text which calls attention to its own conventionality.

Having explored several ancient and European representations of conflicts which animate literary genesis and performance, we can define a continuity in American poetry different from the Adamism studied by Pearce. We can see that American writing does not attempt to name the creatures of the New World as often as it attempts to build textual models for a still newer world. And we can appreciate more fully the definition of freedom with which D. H. Lawrence opposed American expansionism:

> Men are free when they are in a living homeland, not when they are straying and breaking away. Men are free when they are obeying some deep, inward voice of religious belief. Obeying from within. Men are free when they belong to a living, organic, *believing* community, active

---

poetry and thereby shapes its idiom . . . It only remains for contemporary poetry to find the audience it so deeply, though often confusingly, desires . . . It might be that a new awareness of whom to address . . . will be an important force in shaping the new idea of form.

2 Michel Benamou, *Wallace Stevens and the Symbolist Imagination* (Princeton, 1972), p. 101; Roy Harvey Pearce, *The Continuity of American Poetry* (Princeton, 1961). The classic study of references to the Adamic myth in American literature is R. W. B. Lewis, *The American Adam* (Chicago, 1955).

in fulfilling some unfulfilled, perhaps unrealized purpose. Not when
they are escaping to some wild west. The most unfree souls go west, and
shout of freedom.[3]

Much of what Lawrence called "classic American literature" asserts that
freedom is far from being the spontaneous or inherent energy assumed
by either the capitalist or the transcendentalist. The American literary
canon defines freedom as a never-to-be finished, interpersonal, and
indeed intercultural construction. Hawthorne, Melville, Dickinson, and,
as I will show, even the Whitman of "Out of the Cradle" opened European books to prove Lawrence's claim that men are free when they
belong to a living homeland and are fulfilling some "unfulfilled, perhaps
unrealized purpose" and not when they are escaping to some wild west.
However, unlike the community which Lawrence opposed to the anar-
chy of capitalist frontier individualism, the communities projected by
American writers are neither "organic" nor "believing." The poets to be
discussed here have established the authority of a non-organic, non-
believing interpretive imagination. Their texts thus recall the reconstructive critique of both materialism and transcendentalism in *Moby-Dick*,
Melville's rewriting of Job as well as Revelation.

   Melville made a supreme virtue of the major necessity facing American writers: the need to transform a mass of isolated individuals into a
community coherent enough to authorize definitions of a hero who is a
personal synecdoche of their common aspirations. Like his successors
Melville did so by explicitly acknowledging the difficulty of his task:
"they were nearly all Islanders in the Pequod, Isolatoes too, I call such,
not acknowledging the common continent of men, but each Isolato living on a separate continent of his own" (Chapter XXVII, "Knights and
Squires"). However, Tradition is the Book which Ahab and Ishmael have
to open as alternative figures of St. John's sacrificed Reader-Lamb.[4] And
it is by developing European projections of community that all strong
American writers have confronted the absence of a communal dimension

---

[3] D. H. Lawrence, *Studies in Classic American Literature* (New York, 1923), p. 9.
[4] Edgar A. Dryden, "Writer as Reader: An American Story," *Boundary 2* VIII (1979),
189–95, pp. 190–91:

> Reading . . . is no passive and parasitical activity, the pale complement
> of the original and glamorous act of creation itself. On the contrary, it is
> productive and active, associated with the practical researches of Egyp-
> tologists and archeologists who open up sites and descend into crypts in
> order to decipher and repeat the mystery of an original act of writ-
> ing. . . . For Melville . . . the writer is at first a reader. . . . The text of
> *Moby-Dick*, for example, is woven more from the threads of texts which
> fill Ishmael's library than it is from the lines and ropes of the whaling
> world. Indeed, Ishmael's relation to that world is that of a reader to a
> text, and he tries to organize and arrange it as he has previously done his
> library by establishing a bibliographical system.

in the ambition of American individualists—poets as well as business-men. Attentive to both native and foreign voices, the strongest American poets of this century have mocked their own narcissism. They have chal-lenged their impulse to identify with the Adam who names all creatures before he has met a bridal counterpart who not only welcomes his pre-scriptions but also questions them—like any alert reader of poetry.

Because each American writer has had to construct the Bride-City more or less on his own, it is on this side of the Atlantic that literature has most thoroughly developed St. John's revelation. Long after Melville, isolato-writers of diverse temperaments and ideologies have insisted that the new Jerusalem needs neither sun nor temple, neither maternal nature nor paternal Law. They have shown that it derives from mutual acknowledgment by those who give and take dictation that they are neither more nor less than images of a Reader who gives himself up to his responsibilities to both the text and other readers.

ii

In "Out of the Cradle Endlessly Rocking" Walt Whitman provided a dynamic model for later American poets' efforts to make energetic self-criticism project uncommonly vital communities. This idiosyncratic pas-toral elegy-ode reverses the rhetorical strategy of "Song of Myself," Whitman's most sustained attempt to proclaim himself the Pindaric genius of the American shore. Evoking arousal of "the fire, the sweet hell within/ The unknown want, the destiny of me," the text precisely sub-verts both the denial of future development and the fusion of opposites proclaimed in the longer work.

> Out of the dimness opposite equals advance—always substance and
>   increase, always sex;
> Always a knot of identity—always distinction—always a breed of
>   life.
>
> Lack one lacks both, and the unseen is proved by the seen,
> Till that becomes unseen, and receives proof in its turn.
>   "Song of Myself," section 52

Indeed "Out of the Cradle" proves the Heraclitean wisdom of "Song of Myself"—but it does so by opposite means. Rather than providing a dispassionate schema for the resolution of desire which knows "the perfect fitness and equanamity of things" (3), "Out of the Cradle" stimulates the reader's as well as the poet's desire for that which is *not* seen and not proved—thus in effect challenging Pindar's warning against what is not *pár podòs*. But in questioning his own bardic stance, Whitman also estab-lished a thoroughly Pindaric dialectical continuity between more recent European poetic tradition and the new American poetry. Not only does Whitman's provocative crossing of Virgilian pastoral elegy and Pindaric

Psalmist's solar imagery—in the Intimations Ode. It also translates Milton's "Lycidas" into terms appropriate for the New World. Precisely because Whitman lacked both the occasion and the context for writing that helped Milton transform elegy into ode in "Lycidas," in "Out of the Cradle" he elaborated the representations of dialogue in Milton's poem. It is pathetic when the bereft male mockingbird ends his song with "we two together no more," a counter-turn to the "we two together" which occurs three times in a nine-line ode to the sun by the two non-human pastoralists.

> *Shine! shine! shine!*
> *Pour down your warmth, great sun!*
> *While we bask, we two together.*
> *Two together! . . .*
> *Singing all time, minding no time,*
> *While we two keep together.*

But the loss of the bride-bird is a far less momentous occurrence than the drowning of Edward King, the other voice in the human pair who listened and sang through Milton's pastoral day "together both . . . both together." Milton wrote for a particular élite audience of learned friends and could thus demand that his readers collaborate actively in his reconstructive critique of the poetic profession ("what boots it with uncessant care/ To tend the homely slighted shepherd's trade . . ."). Whitman, however, had to conjure an audience from the vast expanses of a whole continent. Like Hölderlin who wrote at an earlier moment in the development of modern technology which shaped Whitman's America, the would-be bard could only attempt to compensate for the vagueness of this text's occasion and context by calling readers' attention to his isolation, inviting them to share it and thereby form a provisional community.[5]

Three surrogates of the male poet—mockingbird, boy, and man— compete as interpreters of the Mother Sea, the womb and tomb of all life. They thus form a bizarre latter-day version of Pindar's companies of rival mediators as well as of the solar Boy, Youth, and Man in Wordsworth's

---

[5] In *The American Adam* R. W. B. Lewis notes: "we respond far less willingly to Whitman's frontal assaults than we do to his dramatizations; when he is enacting his role rather than insisting upon it, we are open to persuasion" (p. 44).

Freudian readings of the poem claim that it does not resolve the conflicts which it evokes: this is because they do not observe that by multiplying personal figures of the text's mediatory function Whitman located the action in the exchange between poet and reader rather than in consciousness. See Neil Isaac, "The Auto-Erotic Metaphor," *Literature and Psychology* XV (1965); Stephen A. Black, *Whitman's Journey into Chaos: A Psychoanalytic Study of the Poetic Process* (Princeton, 1975). A refreshing contrast is offered by Edwin Fussell (*Lucifer in Harness: American Meter, Metaphor and Diction* [Princeton, 1973]) who reads "Out of the Cradle" as a poem about language, along with *Paterson* "the richest document in the philosophy of American poetic diction" (pp. 129–30).

mediators as well as of the solar Boy, Youth, and Man in Wordsworth's
great Pindaric elegy for spontaneity.

> Out of the cradle endlessly rocking,
> Out of the mocking-bird's throat, the musical shuttle,
> Out of the ninth-month midnight,
> Over the sterile sands and fields beyond,
>   where the child, leaving his bed, wander'd
>   alone, bareheaded, barefoot,
> Down from the shower'd halo,
> Up from the mystic play of shadows, twining and twisting
>   as if they were alive,
> Out from the patches of briers and blackberries,
> From the memories of the bird that chanted to me
> From your memories, sad brother—from the fitful
>   risings and fallings I heard . . .
> From the thousand responses of my heart, never to cease,
> From the myriad thence-aroused words
> From the word stronger and more delicious than any,
> From such, as now they start, the scene revisiting,
> As a flock, twittering, rising, or overhead passing,
> Borne thither—ere all eludes me, hurriedly,
> A man—yet by these tears a little boy again,
> Throwing myself on the sand, confronting the waves,
> I, chanter of pains and joys, uniter of here and
>   hereafter,
> Taking all hints to use them—but swiftly leaping
>   beyond them,
> A reminiscence sing.

This overture depicts the mature poet listening to all the voices, including his own, which will sound in his prophetic dramatization of poetic
genesis—with one very significant exception. He listens to "revisitations
of the scene" by the endlessly insinuating sea, the mockingbird, the
child, and his own innumerable responses. But omitted from this
catalogue is the voice of the mockingbird's mate—a surrogate for the
Mother Sea. There are two good reasons why the poet cannot depict
himself hearing her. If he were to "translate" (6) a fertile surrogate for
the untranslatable Mother he would assume a precocious resolution to
the problem which the whole complex interplay of interpreters is to
resolve: the absence of generative pastoral dialogue. He would thus less
effectively involve the reader, his actual partner.

The curious boy-translator, however, must overhear the bird's bridal
sun-song:

> I, with bare feet, a child, the wind wafting my hair,
> Listened long and long.
>
> Listened, to keep, to sing—now translating the notes,
> Following you, my brother. (6)

he is to persuade us to help the mature poet send sunrise out of himself—as the bard in "Song of Myself" boasts he can do. The solitary bird is a tiny surrogate for the mature bard; his failure serves as a foil to Whitman's potential success as the poet of pigmy size sets off Wordsworth's accomplishment in the Intimations Ode. But the bird also ratifies Milton's demonstration in "Lycidas" that a poet can only locate a mate by listening as much as he sings. He first characterizes his counterpart as a potential listener by addressing his own throat, "somewhere listening to catch you, must be the one I want," and then characterizes himself as a listener to the mate as well as the Mother: "and do you wait a moment, you husky-voiced sea/ From somewhere I believe I heard my mate responding to me/ So faint—I must be still, be still to listen." Certainly he tries to differentiate his voice from the myriad others which he hears:

> This gentle call is for you, my love, for you.
> Do not be decoy'd elsewhere!
>
> That is the whistle of the wind—it is not my voice;
> That is the fluttering, the fluttering of the spray;
> Those are the shadows of leaves. (7)

But if the bird is to continue to sing, he must listen to and even address his own gentle call—which mimes the sea's mutter even when declaring its independence: "yet I murmur, murmur on!/ O murmurs—you yourselves make me continue to sing."

The boy so passionately rivals the bird's stress upon the receptive moment in poetry that he in fact suddenly matures, radically shifting established distinctions between listener and speaker. He substitutes himself for the female mate:

> Demon or bird! (said the boy's soul)
> Is it indeed toward your mate you sing? or is it mostly to me?

But the man who has supposedly listened to the bird along with the boy suddenly takes over the outburst:

> The colloquy there—the trio—each uttering,
> The undertone—the savage old mother, incessantly crying,
> To the boy's soul's questions sullenly timing (8)
>
> O you singer, solitary, singing by yourself—projecting me;
> O solitary me, listening—never more shall I cease perpetuating you.
> Never more shall I escape, never more the reverberations,
> Never more the cries of unsatisfied love be absent from me,
> Never again leave me to be the peaceful child I was before what
>   there in the night,
> By the sea, under the yellow and sagging moon,
> The messenger arous'd—this fire, the sweet hell within,
> The unknown want, the destiny of me. (9)

If the listening man has in fact referred to the boy as a speaker before he has spoken, he now resumes the role of speaker—and thus rivals the boy's attempt to usurp the role of listener-mate.

This ironic complex of parallelism, differentiation, and identification of dialogic roles may even help convince us to complement the man's definition of a "trio" (8) of speakers. It may convince us to define the death-bearing Mother too as an intelligent listener to the man: one who can enter into quasi-erotic dialogue with him and thus ratify rather than drown his identity. It is only after all three male poet figures have defined listening as a matrix of potent articulateness that the sea's murmur is articulated as the meaningful word, "Death, Death, Death, Death, Death." As the bird has distinguished himself from the sea by listening to it as well as listening for his mate's potential response, the boy has identified himself as poet by insisting with equal passion that he has effectively replaced the missing female mate whom the bird summoned when he strategically assumed the listener's role. Similarly, when the man defines his listening to the sea as an effort to achieve mastery, he in effect asks that we authorize his project.

> A word then, (for I will conquer it)
> The word final, superior to all,
> Subtle, sent up—what is it?—I listen;
> Are you whispering it, and have been all the
>   time, you sea waves?
> Is that it from your liquid rims and wet sands?
> Death, Death, Death, Death, Death.

The poet has called up an answer from the sea by listening passionately to the bird's and the boy's descriptions of listening. We should be able to assign a strong identity to one who so respects the potential for intelligent attentiveness which we ourselves have actualized in following the twisting and twining of relationship among three poet-listeners.

Like "Hérodiade" Whitman's nuptial song is even more "unexpressive" than Milton's. "Lycidas" derives its authority to project a renewal of pastoral dialogue from continual reminders that the speaker's counterpart, the dead poet, will not answer him. Correspondingly, "Out of the Cradle" can project an endless generation of pastoral song because it dramatizes the failure of dialogue between the members of two odd couples: the mockingbird and his female mate, the mature poet and the Mother Sea who relentlessly announces death rather than rebirth. Yet "Out of the Cradle" also recalls more urgently how the apocalyptist defined correspondent, radically impure origins of vital community: his own translation of living experience into the dead letters of a text and the latter's consequent resistance to living readers. Certainly the stress of natural imagery and vocal discourse in "Out of the Cradle" contrasts with the stress of artifice and textual discourse in Revelation. But the poem reminds us how that series of mutually reflective visions across a "sea of glass" establishes the ultimately unbridgeable gap between any text and any reader as matrix of extraordinarily vivid mutual self-awareness. The Mother Sea's monotonous annunciation of radical discontinuity both counterpoints and motivates a potentially infinite series of variations upon our own effort to understand any provocative utterance, spoken or written.

> Out of the mocking-bird's throat . . .
> Out of the ninth-month midnight . . .
>   . . . where the child, leaving his bed,
>   wander'd alone . . .
> From the memories of the bird that chanted to me
> From your memories sad brother—from the fitful
>   risings and fallings I heard . . .
> From the thousand responses of my heart, never to cease,
> From the myriad thence-aroused words . . .

We recall that St. John initiated a steady proliferation of witnessings by displacing interest from unique, prescribed supernatural revelation to multiple readings. Here both the silence of the mockingbird's mate and the senselessness of the message from a natural Mother even more threatening than the maternal figures whom Milton's swain challenged identify self-conscious alienation as the ground of vital intercourse. Few texts since Revelation have so authoritatively defined the *coitus interruptus* between performer and interpreter as the matrix of marriage which is infinitely fertile in the challenges required to maintain both personal and communal identity. But Whitman's most attentive American readers have emulated his consummate renewal of Pindaric turning and counter-turning in longer poems which also rival Mallarmé's apocalypse.

8
Wallace Stevens and the Congregation

Stevens referred to Psalm 19 in a 1906 journal entry which expressed his ambivalent feelings about public worship.

> In the evening went to Christ Church. Full litany—sweet and melodious and welcome. They should have dark corners there. Impossible to be religious in a pew. One should have a great nave, quiet lights, a remote voice, a soft choir and solitude. . . . I wish that groves still *were* sacred—or, at least that something was: that there was still something free from doubt, that day unto day still uttered speech, and night unto night still showed wisdom. I grow tired of the want of faith—the instinct of faith. Self-consciousness convinces me of something, but whether it be something Past, Present or Future I do not know.[1]

It was by developing the tension between solitary self-consciousness and communal faith that Stevens gradually learned to make it seem that day still utters speech unto day and night unto night still shows wisdom. Not until the late long poem "An Ordinary Evening in New Haven" did he explicitly portray himself as an expert in comparative religion and comparative literature, "Professor Eucalyptus." But throughout his career Stevens analyzed literary and cultural history in order to establish intensely self-conscious poetry as a means of restoring the consensus once maintained by religious ritual.[2]

---

[1] *Letters of Wallace Stevens*, ed. Holly Stevens (New York, 1966), p. 86.

[2] *Souvenirs and Prophecies: The Young Wallace Stevens*, ed. Holly Stevens (New York, 1976), pp. 158–59. In his journal at least Stevens more often would counter solitude with concern for company:

> I want to see somebody, hear somebody speak to me, look at somebody, speak to somebody in turn, I want companions. I want more than my work, than the nods of acquaintance, than this little room. . . . As Marchbanks says in Act II of Shaw's *Candida*: "that is what all poets do: they talk to themselves out loud; and the world overhears them. But it's horribly lonely not to hear someone else talk sometimes." (*Ibid.*, pp. 128–29)

Adelaide Kirkby Morris, *Imagination and Faith* (Princeton, 1974) surveys Stevens' work with traditional Judeo-Christian forms but does not study his efforts to expand the private lyric and project definitions of personal identity in terms of communal response. The tendency to ignore Stevens' interest in communal forms of expression is strikingly exemplified by Diane Wood Middlebrook's discussion of Stevens' Whitmanian sun in *Walt*

i

Like Mallarmé's "Hérodiade," "Sunday Morning" (1915) defines modern poetry as a variant of ancient ritual sacrifice. Dramatizing tension between contrasted interpreters, it challenges us to achieve the marriage of opposites which it tantalizingly projects. As we have seen, "Hérodiade" renews the Messianic promise of Scriptural history by violently opposing a girl and a man who speak for identity and multiplicity, present and past. "Sunday Morning" subverts conventional distinctions by more subtly relating a woman and a narrator who seems to be a man.[3]

The first stanza of "Sunday Morning" does not define the primary speaker's sex but allows us to observe for ourselves that this narrator makes the claim to adequacy in interpretation characteristic of male authorities.

> Complacencies of the peignoir, and late
> Coffee and oranges in a sunny chair,
> And the green freedom of a cockatoo
> Upon a rug mingle to dissipate
> The holy hush of ancient sacrifice.
> She dreams a little, and she feels the dark
> Encroachment of that old catastrophe,
> As a calm darkens among water-lights.
> The pungent oranges and bright, green wings
> Seem things in some procession of the dead,
> Winding across wide water, without sound,
> The day is like wide water, without sound,
> Stilled for the passing of her dreaming feet
> Over the seas, to silent Palestine,
> Dominion of the blood and sepulchre.

The opening and closing phrases, "complacencies of the peignoir" and "dominion of the blood and sepulchre" evoke the secular present and

---

Whitman and Wallace Stevens (Ithaca, 1974): she continually translates "men" in Stevens' many evocations of corporate contest and concert as "man" (pp. 167–207).

[3] Stevens wrote that Hi Simon's article "Wallace Stevens and Mallarmé," *Modern Philology* XLVIII (1946), 235–59 made a great deal out of not very much:

> Mallarmé never in the world meant as much to me as all that in any
> direct way. Perhaps I absorbed more than I thought. Mallarmé was a
> good deal in the air when I was much younger. (*Letters*, pp. 635–36.)

But when Stevens thus disclaims a direct influence he does not discourage us from observing that his projections of a festival sphere are indeed considerably more like Mallarmé's prescriptions for "UNE CONSTELLATION" ("Un Coup de Dès") than Whitman's projections of "Myself." See also "Stevens and Mallarmé" in Benamou, *Wallace Stevens and the Symbolist Imagination*. In "Displacements of Parental Space in American Poetry and French Symbolism," *Boundary* 2 V (1977), 471–86, Benamou summarizes interpretations of Mallarmé by Jean-Francois Lyotard, Jacques Derrida, and Julia Kristeva as background for readings of Williams as well as Stevens that consider only the first moment in the swing between deconstruction and reconstruction which I have observed in Mallarmé.

sacred past which compete for the woman's attention. But they also emphasize the fact that this utterance is a narration even though it is in the present tense: such formulations are too striking not to express a distinctive point of view. Similarly, the parallelism of two third-person verb phrases, "she dreams . . . she feels," and a repetition in the account of her revery, "seem things . . . winding across wide water, without sound./ The day is like wide water, without sound," not only associate the speaker with the woman whose subjective experience he evokes but also differentiate one from the other. Both the parallel construction and the repetition at once mime the progressive development of the woman's revery and call attention to the presence of an observer.

The text plays six variations upon this introductory statement of tension between individual and community, present and past, protagonist and narrator. In the first the woman dominates, but the present tense is qualified by reference to the past.

> Why should she give her bounty to the dead?
> What is divinity if it can come
> Only in silent shadows and in dreams?
> Shall she not find in comforts of the sun,
> In pungent fruit and bright-green wings, or else
> In any balm or beauty of the earth,
> Things to be cherished like the thought of heaven?
> Divinity must live within herself:
> Passions of rain, or moods in falling snow;
> Grievings in loneliness, or unsubdued
> Elations when the forest blooms; gusty
> Emotions on wet roads on autumn nights;
> All pleasures and all pains, remembering
> The bough of summer and the winter branch.
> These are the measures destined for her soul.

Here the narrator speaks on behalf of the isolated woman, arguing in favor of her heterodoxy against the traditional use of the Sabbath. But when he prescribes an intensely personal program as a substitute for patriarchal Law, he becomes increasingly assertive. This ironic shift may remind us that the woman's post-Protestant, post-Romantic modernism in fact only brings up to date the exclusivity of the monotheist Old Testament.

The second variation turns our attention away from the solitary present in which the woman is to remember other privileged moments. Here the narrator explicitly reviews the curse of religious history and establishes the New Testament modification of the Law as model for a new community by repeating plural pronouns and future-tense verbs.

> Jove in the clouds had his inhuman birth.
> No mother suckled him, no sweet land gave
> Large-mannered motions to his mythy mind.
> He moved among us, as a muttering king,

Magnificent, would move among his hinds,
Until our blood, commingling, virginal,
With heaven, brought such requital to desire
The very hinds discerned it, in a star.
Shall our blood fail? Or shall it come to be
The blood of paradise? And shall the earth
Seem all of paradise that we shall know?
The sky will be much friendlier then than now,
A part of labor and a part of pain,
And next in glory to enduring love,
Not this dividing and indifferent blue.

The modern introspection prescribed in stanza II has restored the severe disjunction between divinity and nature which the iconoclast Old Testament brought about by deferring to a supreme patriarchal Authority ("Jove in the clouds"). But in secularizing and internalizing the Old Testament concern for the One, the woman has revealed how devotion to transcendent Identity can alienate one from many. We can thus value the Incarnation—"our blood commingling, virginal,/ With heaven"—as a fertile source of community rather than merely accept or reject it as a matter of prescribed faith.[4]

The third variation not only explicitly distinguishes the narrator from his subject by having her speak: it also reverses their positions.

She says, "I am content when wakened birds,
Before they fly, test the reality
Of misty fields, by their sweet questionings;
But when the birds are gone, and their warm fields
Return no more, where, then, is paradise?"
There is not any haunt of the grave,
Neither the golden underground, nor isle
Melodious, where spirits gat them home,
Nor visionary south, nor cloudy palm
Remote on heaven's hill, that has endured
As April's green endures; or will endure
Like her remembrance of awakened birds,
Or her desire for June and evening, tipped
By the consummation of the swallow's wings.

The woman speaks in the present tense but questions the validity of her attempt to find paradise now. The narrator meets her question by solemnly canonizing the memory which he prescribed for her in stanza II—and by adding to it the desire to which he there lightly alluded ("shall she not find in comforts of the sun . . ."). Memory and desire constitute a matrix for the paradise which he projected by questioning ("shall . . . ? shall . . . ? and shall . . . ?") his own account of the Incarnation.

---

[4] Robert Pinsky, *The Situation of Poetry* (Princeton, 1976) notes that this section "gives a kind of lightning-summary of the anthropological history of religion" (p. 145).

In the fourth variation the woman responds to the narrator's solemn refutation of her doubt ("but when the birds are gone . . . where, then is paradise?"); the narrator then both elaborates his argument *for* her untraditional association of femininity and introspection and begins to counter it.

> She says, "But in contentment I still feel
> The need of some imperishable bliss."
> Death is the mother of beauty; hence from her,
> Alone, shall come fulfillment to our dreams
> And our desires. Although she strews the leaves
> Of sure obliteration on our paths,
> The path sick sorrow took, the many paths
> Where triumph rang its brassy phrase, or love
> Whispered a little out of tenderness,
> She makes the willow shiver in the sun
> For maidens who were wont to sit and gaze
> Upon the grass, relinquished to their feet.
> She causes boys to pile new plums and pears
> On disregarded plate. The maidens taste
> And stray impassioned in the littering leaves.

Opposing the protagonist's objection with a litany of praise for a tradi-tional complex female figure, the narrator reminds us that when she has attempted to reject the Hebrew-Christian public tradition she has para-doxically exaggerated the Law's devotion to identity. But when he reminds her of maternal death he also begins to lead her out of the isola-tion induced by her rebellion against male prescription. When one link-ing of third-person female subject with present-tense verb is juxtaposed with another ("she says/ Death is . . .") a first-person plural pronoun hints that plurality and femininity may once more be associated and that both will be established as attributes of the future: "from her/ alone shall come fulfillment to our dreams,/ And our desires."

The fifth variation alludes to a text which is much better known to American readers than "Hérodiade" but anticipates its demonstration that art can make divorce and death generate marriage and life.

> Is there no change of death in paradise?
> Does ripe fruit never fall? Or do the boughs
> Hang always heavy in that perfect sky,
> Unchanging, yet so like our own that seek for seas
> They never find, the same receding shores
> That never touch with inarticulate pang?
> Why set the pear upon those river-banks
> Or spice the shores with odors of the plum?
> Alas, that they should wear our colors there,
> The silken weavings of our afternoons,
> And pick the strings of our insipid lutes!
> Death is the mother of beauty, mystical,

Within whose burning bosom we devise
Our earthly mothers waiting, sleeplessly.

This recalls "Ode on a Grecian Urn," in which Keats contemplates an artistic rendering of lovers who never quite embrace—their infinitely teasing and frustrating distance comparable to the distance between any artwork and its interpreters. Especially if we have noticed that Stevens echoes Keats' parable of art, stanza VI gives us a new perspective on the shining willow, new plums and pears, and littering leaves which encourage the virgins of stanza V to mimic the New Testament marriage of heaven and earth by "commingling" with their boys. These natural images now seem to represent poetry itself, which always approaches but never quite achieves the incarnation of ideas that it makes us desire— since its littered leaves are in fact not natural and organic like plums and pears but conventional and textual: silken weavings of afternoons as self-conscious and hermetic as the one evoked by Mallarmé in "Crise de Vers." Lamenting a generative relationship between model and imitation parallel to the one he presented as model for a perfect future in stanza III, the speaker defines exchange between writers and readers as the condition of paradisal "unchangingness." If the Incarnation made earth an image of heaven, the pears and plums on the riverbanks of poetry are merely images of our real afternoons. But because the speaker here so vigorously protests against his perverse celebration of death in stanza V, he may move us to oppose him as he has opposed his female alter ego.[5]

The choral song to the sun projected in the sixth variation is of course only another imitation of Romantic naturalism, but it can provoke generative reflection. For it too is a critical and self-critical imitation of another familiar text, Nietzsche's male supremacist *Thus Spake Zarathustra.*

Supple and turbulent, a ring of men
Shall chant in orgy on a summer morn
Their boisterous devotion to the sun,
Not as a god, but as a god might be,
Naked among them, like a savage source.
Their chant shall be a chant of paradise,
Out of their blood, returning to the sky;
And in their chant shall enter, voice by voice,
The windy lake wherein their lord delights,
The trees, like serafin, and echoing hills,
That choir among themselves long afterward.
They shall know well the heavenly fellowship

---

[5] Critics have noted allusions to another ode by Keats in the final section, but not, as far as I know, the more crucial parody of the "Ode to a Grecian Urn" here. See Helen Vendler, "Stevens and Keats' 'To Autumm'" in *Part of Nature, Part of Us: Modern American Poets* (Cambridge, Mass., 1980), pp. 22–23. George Bornstein, *Transformations of Romanticism in Yeats, Eliot and Stevens* (Chicago, 1976) compares Stevens' "The Anecdote of the Jar" to the "Grecian Urn."

Of men that perish and of summer morn.
And whence they came and whither they shall go
The dew upon their feet shall manifest.

Stevens himself supplied what remains the most helpful commentary on
stanza VII when he explained to Harriet Monroe of *Poetry* the words
"on disregarded plate" in stanza V ("Death causes boys to pile new
plums and pears/ On disregarded plate"):

> Plate is used in the sense of so-called family plate. Disregarded refers
> to the disuse into which things fall that have been possessed for a
> long time. I mean, therefore, that death releases and renews. What
> the old have come to disregard, the young inherit and make use of.[6]

Death is the mother of beauty because poets are men who know that
they perish but also know well the heavenly fellowship of literary history. The new plums and pears are new poems that boys like Stevens
pile on, and thereby renew, old poems which have been possessed and
thus disregarded for a long time—like the New Testament accounts of
the Incarnation.

In 1944 Stevens agreed with Hi Simon, who found in stanzas III and
VII proposals for a "naturalistic religion as a substitute for supernaturalism."[7] But if in stanza VI and his commentary on stanza V Stevens suggested that the love–death in question is literary, we may hear in both
stanza III and VII a note midway between naturalism and supernaturalism. It is a note sounded and developed solely by modulations of person,
number, and tense: the primary variables in language—which is neither
natural nor supernatural but historical.

Certainly the ring of men who will honor an image of their own
power to marry the dark Mother consummate the narcissism of the solitary modern woman who desires a June wedding ("her desire for June
and evening tipped by the consummation of the swallows' wings" IV).
But they also enact a compounding of self-reflexivity which can be productive: the virtual marriage of an isolated writer with future readers
whom he has courted by repeatedly subverting conventional distinctions
between identity and multiplicity, iconoclast scripture and iconophile
myth, individual talent and tradition, masculine and feminine.

In order to make us desire communion of the kind prophesied in
stanza VII, however, Stevens ended by recapitulating his initial statement of conflict.

She hears, upon that water without sound,
A voice that cries, "The tomb in Palestine
Is not the porch of spirits lingering.

---

[6] *Letters*, p. 183.
[7] *Ibid.*, p. 464.

It is the grave of Jesus, where he lay."
We live in an old chaos of the sun,
Or old dependency of day and night,
Or island solitude, unsponsored, free,
Of that wide water, inescapable.
Deer walk upon our mountains, and the quail
Whistle about us their spontaneous cries;
Sweet berries ripen in the wilderness;
And, in the isolation of the sky,
At evening, casual flocks of pigeons make
Ambiguous undulations as they sink,
Downward to darkness on extended wings.

The plural first-person pronoun in "we live" again opposes the singular third-person feminine in "she hears." But who are we—or, more to the point, *where* are we? We stand or sit in one of three places, each corresponding to a stage in the history of signification and interpretation to which the text has several times alluded: pre-Scriptural myth ("an old chaos of the sun"), Scripture in which day speaks unto day and night unto night ("old dependency of day and night"), or post-Romantic introspection ("island solitude"). And is our modern island deprived of guidance ("unsponsored"), positively liberated from divine Authority ("free") or an oppressive prison ("inescapable")? More concretely, do we live in a modern city circled by filthy pigeons whose casualness and multiplicity mock the purposiveness and singularity of the Pentecostal dove or in an ancient Biblical wilderness? ("Whence they came and whither they shall go/ The dew upon their feet shall manifest" is portentously Scriptural; if spontaneous and inspired John the Baptist was a voice crying in the wilderness, "the quail/ Whistle about us their spontaneous cries" also reminds us how in Exodus the Lord promised the Israelites in the wilderness food at evening: "and it came to pass, that at even the quails came up, and covered the camp" [16:13]). The first-person plural pronoun thus refers to no community more stable than the one which should have been provoked into existence by the dialectical play of contraries in Stevens' text. If the impossible but endlessly enticing crystalline City with no temple or sun in Revelation matches the seven-sealed Book of Life opened across a sea of glass, the only common place acknowledged by Stevens' reflections upon cultural and literary history is the gathering of mutually conflicting readings which it at once invites and resists.

"Sunday Morning" argues that Death is the mother of beauty in the sense that the dead letters of Scripture and literature release their potential for meaning when read by men and women who provisionally desert their prescribed cultural roles in order to confront paradoxes and ambiguities suppressed by modern, secular individualism. The early poem thus stands as a model for a career during which Stevens never asserted the truth of any religion or attempted to found an actual community, but built an alternative world of texts that require completion by living readers and can therefore illuminate our lives.

ii

Many years later Stevens projected a community grounded in continual self-questioning by analyzing Scriptural, literary, and cultural history more intensively than he had in "Sunday Morning." In "The Auroras of Autumn" (1947) he rivalled St. John's projection of a City by alluding to Psalm 19 and to two Shakespearean rewritings of Revelation. And in "An Ordinary Evening in New Haven" (1949) he more explicitly referred to both the Psalter and the last book of Scripture in order to build his own New Jerusalem as if in Connecticut.

> Is there an imagination that sits enthroned
> As grim as it is benevolent, the just
> And the unjust? . . .
>   And do these heavens adorn
> And proclaim it, the white creator of black, jetted
> By extinguishings, even of planets as may be,
>
> Even of earth, even of sight, in snow,
> Except as needed by way of majesty,
> In the sky, as crown and diamond cabala? (VII)

An ode to the Northern Lights, *aurora borealis*, "The Auroras of Autumn" questions the Psalmist's attempt to conflate naturalist myth and conventionalist scripture ("the sun is as a bridegroom . . . the Law of the Lord is perfect . . ."). And like "Sunday Morning" this text repeatedly contrasts attitudes toward signification: naturalist/matriarchal/comic on the one hand and supernaturalist/patriarchal/tragic on the other. But "The Auroras of Autumn" more compellingly shows how poetry can help reconcile severe ideological conflicts. For it not only alludes to particular texts as well as general cultural patterns, but also more elaborately represents the complex dynamics of exchange between writers and readers. As Stevens here associated the Northern Lights with recognizable figures from myth, Scripture, and Shakespearean drama, he also represented himself as a reader of the auroras who corresponds to the potential reader of "The Auroras." We can thus feel even more strongly called to acknowledge that alienation is the very condition of strong community than we do in "Sunday Morning."

Echoes of lines in Seneca's *Hercules furens* ("quis hic locus, quae regio, quae mundi plaga . . .") in "these fields, these hills, these tinted distances . . ." (I) establish a northern seascape as a theater appropriate for a masque of divinities far older than the Romantic imagination. The text presents the cosmic conflict between maternal nature and paternal Law strategically obscured both by the Psalmist's brilliant image of the

sun as a bridegroom/athlete and by the transformation of Tiamat, the
female sea-serpent in Babylonian myth, into the male Leviathan in Job.

> This is where the serpent lives, the bodiless.
> His head is air. Beneath his tip at night
> Eyes open and fix on us in every sky.
>
> Or is this another wriggling out of the egg,
> Another image at the end of the cave,
> Another bodiless for the body's slough?
>
> This is where the serpent lives. This is his nest.
> These fields, these hills, these tinted distances,
> And the pines above and along and beside the sea.
>
> This is form gulping after formlessness,
> Skin flashing to wished for disappearances,
> And the serpent body flashing without the skin. (I)

Reiterated demonstratives, "this is where . . . is this . . . this is where . . .
this is . . . this is" define the poet as a vigorously gesturing performer
who shares our space and time: "the eyes open and fix on us in every
sky."[8] But this confident demonstration is interrupted by another bid for
our participation. Alluding to Plato's allegory of the imagination in
Republic VII ("another image at the end of the cave"), the speaker questions his own location of the serpent in external reality. If the contrast
between the first two tercets compels us to assist both demonstration and
introspection, the stress upon ephemerality in both moments invites us to
read on in search of more specifics. And once we have followed the
twisting, flashing, serpentine progress of the text a bit further, we may
reread this provocative opening in terms of much more complex performances. We may recall that in *King Lear* villainous Edmund was
born under the dragon's tail (II ii 126) of the North Star which dominates the serpent-like Northern Lights, and that Lear defines both himself and his daughters (II iv 162) as descendents of the mythic female
sea-serpent whom the Law turned into Leviathan—alter ego of *both*
figures whom Lear imitates, the Lord and Job (Job 3, 7, 8, 18, 41).
Stevens' text does not send us to the reference shelves, however. Like
"Sunday Morning" it is authoritative in large part because Stevens was
profoundly receptive to tradition but did not flaunt his reading. Like St.
John he ate the Book, but digested it very well.[9]

Certainly "Auroras" later alludes to Prospero, Shakespeare's comic

---

[8] Vendler, *On Extended Wings* (Cambridge, Mass., 1969) notes: "The 'thisness' of "The
Auroras of Autumn" . . . is never allowed to lapse entirely. . . . The narrator remains
discreetly present in these recurrent demonstrative phrases." (p. 247).

[9] Vendler and Harold Bloom, *Poems of Our Climate* (Ithaca, 1977), both note that
stanza VII recalls the Pslams, but Bloom qualifies his acknowledgment by claiming that
this is "one of Stevens' rare Biblical echoes."

variant of Lear: a father who summons spectacles out of nothingness as
Stevens has in his initial presentation of the Northern Lights.

> The father fetches negresses to dance,
> Among the children, like curious ripenesses
> Of pattern in the dance's ripening . . .
> The father fetches pageants out of air,
> Scenes of the theatre, vistas and blocks of woods . . . (V)

The barely remembered mother is first opposed to the heavenly Serpent
whose form myth attributes to her; all members and moments of human
history are united in memories of her house:

> They are together, here, and it is warm . . .
> They are at ease in a shelter of the mind . . .
> And the house is of the mind and they and time,
> Together, all together. (III)

From this common inside the poet can only see the Northern Lights as
hostile: "boreal night/ Will be like frost as it approaches them." In contrast, the supernaturalist Mosaic father looks out of his Burning Bush "as
one that is strong in the bushes of his eyes" (IV). Indeed he is so strong
that—like Job and Lear—he can imitate his demonic opposite, the fiery
serpent: he leaps "from heaven to heaven more rapidly/ Than bad
angels leap from heaven to hell in flame" (IV).

Paradoxically composing a female snake-dance, the father in this
universal house attempts a grotesque, inchoate version of Stevens'
response to the serpentine midnight dawn: "the father fetches his un-
herded herds/ Of barbarous tongue, slavered and panting halves/ Of
breath" (V). But he thus establishes oral, choral "festival" as a positive
norm. Indeed it is the father who enables the isolated modern writer to
withstand the "poison" (I) of secular disbelief in wholeness that derives
from the supernaturalist Law's contempt for nature.

By hypothesizing a de-creative fatherly imagination whose colors are
those of the printed Law, black and white, Stevens was able to use
typography to reconstruct the New World as if from nothing and rival
the Psalmist's projection of universal eloquence.

> Is there an imagination that sits enthroned
> As grim as it is benevolent, the just
> And the unjust . . .
> And do these heavens adorn
> And proclaim it, the white creator of black? (VII)

But the modern poet cannot reproduce the Psalmist's tenuous reconciliation of Law and nature. If he did so, he would betray the basic strategy
of Psalm 19, more explicitly dramatized in Revelation: the displacement
of creative power from a static Author to many mobile interpreters.

Here imagination proves not to be enthroned in heaven or in any single consciousness; honoring both father and mother, both single-minded scripture and multiple nature, this text does not perpetuate the Judaic and Protestant obsessions with identity.

> It leaps through us, through all our heavens leaps,
> Extinguishing our planets, one by one,
> Leaving, of where we were and looked, of where
>
> We knew each other and of each other thought,
> A shivering residue, chilled and foregone,
> Except for that crown and mystical cabala. (VII)

Revealing the supposedly creative Romantic imagination itself as a destroyer of images, Stevens raised to a higher power the iconoclastic impulse in both Judaism and Protestantism. But his leaping, twisting iconoclasm does not destroy *all* images. As it leaves a "crown and mystical cabala," it projects a community of many interpreters who acknowledge their infallibility more consistently than those who gathered in the Temple at Jerusalem.

Indeed the cabalistic hermeticism of this sequence conjures its antithesis: a congregation like the one projected in the final stanza.

> Now solemnize the secretive syllables
>
> Read to the congregation, for today
> And for tomorrow, this extremity. (X)

Yet if secretiveness is to generate a community, the poet must not only present personae of himself and us, his readers, but must also personify the medium of our exchange. Allusions to Scripture and earlier literature suggest that the unstable, self-contradictory auroras of autumn represent the flashing, twisting words which compose "The Auroras of Autumn."

> It leaps through us, through all our heavens leaps,
> Extinguishing our planets, one by one . . .
> But it dare not leap by chance in its own dark. (VII)

What leaps and extinguishes natural light this way except the language of poetry? Literary discourse indeed "dare[s] not leap by chance in its own dark": like tragedy—which has been falsely etymologized as "goat-song"—it must question its own ambition and turn into the lesser goat-song, "caprice." As we have seen, however, the critique of exclusive identity or authority in "Sunday Morning" creates a leaping-place in which mutual interrogation by authority and interpreters can construct a new heaven and a new earth. Because continual self-criticism is the animating principle of Stevens' writing, both the auroras of autumn and their textual surrogate, "The Auroras of Autumn," can generate dialogue from duality.

But Stevens' speaker best convinces us to form a congregation when he admits in the final stanza that he is only a pale, endlessly contriving ghost of the solar Bridegroom.

> Read rabbi the phases of this difference . . .
> Now solemnize the secretive syllables
>
> Read to the congregation, for today
> And for tomorrow, this extremity,
> This contrivance of the spectre of the spheres,
>
> Contriving balance to contrive a whole . . . (X)

The speaker tells a priest of nature rather than Law to read to contemporary and future readers as if they were present in a new Temple his lunar ("phases"), self-reflecting ("secretive") reflections upon a natural/unnatural dawn at the year's end. In a secular age, however, the poet is only a "spectre of the spheres" and proclaims not his own glory but that of a yet uncreated genius who would speak for a congregation able to interpret three variations upon a phrase evoking conflict between mind and world.

> An unhappy people in a happy world—
> Read, rabbi, the phases of this difference.
> An unhappy people in an unhappy world—
>
> Here are too many mirrors for misery.
> A happy people in an unhappy world—
> It cannot be. There's nothing there to roll
>
> On the expressive tongue, the finding fang.
> A happy people in a happy world—
> Buffo! A ball, an opera, a bar.
>
> Turn back to where we were when we began:
> An unhappy people in a happy world.
> Now, solemnize the secretive syllables.
>
> The vital, the never-failing genius,
> Fulfilling his meditations, great and small . . .
>
> In these unhappy he meditates a whole,
> The full of fortune and the full of fate,
> As if he lived all lives, that he might know
>
>   . . . not hushful paradise. (X)

There are too many mirrors for misery in the second phase of this final difference "an unhappy people in an unhappy world": we cannot help but *know*, i.e., differ from the world. We even know we *must* know—but would not if the mind had the company of a world made in its unhappy image. Similarly, we have to reject the third phase of this difference, "a happy people in an unhappy world" because it obviates the need for the only reliable standard of reality in this poem about poetry: the finding of pleasure in mortal difference and contradiction. We must reject the fourth variant, "a happy people in a happy world," for the same reason. Like the alliteration with which Stevens describes it ("Buffo! a ball, an opera, a bar"), this denies distinctions we know and cannot forget. But if we turn back to the initial formula we can begin to find in knowledge and experience a satisfaction equal to the innocence which myth attributes to our origins. "An unhappy people in a happy world" most provocatively expresses our sense of difference and deprivation. It can thus set spinning an extreme contrivance: an infernal Miltonic machine for making a heaven of hell—a gift which serpentine Satan seems to have transmitted with his finding fang. The Fall may indeed be fortunate if we read Stevens' text as a common place in which many happy/unhappy people can meet and reflect upon the paradoxes of human existence.

If we turn back to "where we were when we began" this text, the phrase "an unhappy people in a happy world," we remember Eden: where we were when we began to live rather than to read. And that is precisely what we are to do: we are to replace the myth of primary innocence with experience of an intensely self-conscious text which imitates the serpentine movement of the Northern Lights.

But Stevens' homeopathic challenge to the serpent Nature is also a collaboration, a *con-trivance* for a congregation (from the medieval French *con-trover*, to find together). The "finding fang" that can rival and reverse the serpent's demonic reading of Creation can be found only in the mouths of many potentially articulate silent readers. By reading to a skeptical congregation the rabbi can complete the spectre's contrivance of a further double of his meditative self: the "never-failing genius" whose concern for balance and wholeness will fulfill his own meditations upon the ever-recurrent Fall. Stevens' alliteration "the full of fortune and the full of fate" reminds us that the genius will fulfill prophecies of redemption precisely because he compounds the Fall. He figures the perfection of a poetic mind which knows failure so well that it can transcend it by reflecting upon it. He will never fail because he represents both ever-failing common mortality and a potential community of readers who reflect upon the common lot along with the rabbinical writer.

Thus, by elaborating his dramatization of interplay between authorities and interpreters in "Sunday Morning," Stevens argued more authoritatively that the final unhappiness, death, is the mother of beauty if it is contemplated (from the Latin, *con-templum*) in a provisional common place between art and life: in the reading of such self-reflexive competitions with both nature and Law as Psalm 19, Revelation and "The Auroras of Autumn." Few modern poems so persuasively invite us to make a home of the no man's land in which we do in fact live: in a state of unending conflict between the mutually exclusive options proposed by culture and nature.

iii

The eye's plain version is a thing apart,
The vulgate of experience. Of this,
A few words, an and yet, and yet, and yet—

As part of the never-ending meditation,
Part of the question that is a giant himself:
Of what is this house composed if not of the sun,

These houses, these difficult objects, dilapidate
Appearances of what appearances,
Words, lines, not meanings, not communications,

Dark things without a double, after all,
Unless a second giant kills the first—
A recent imagining of reality,

Much like a new resemblance of the sun,
Down-pouring, up-springing and inevitable,
A larger poem for a larger audience,

As if the crude collops came together as one,
A mythological form, a festival sphere. (I)

Like "The Auroras of Autumn," "An Ordinary Evening in New Haven"
begins with a series of demonstrations and questions. But here we are not
asked to wonder whether a figure of the poet's endlessly self-
contradictory linguistic medium is real or imaginary ("or is this . . .
another image at the end of the cave"). Rather, we are involved in a
violent conflict between readings of visible reality by literary authorities
and their poet-readers. So that his Davidic text could be killed in turn by
that other Goliath, "a larger poem for a larger audience . . . a festival
sphere," Stevens "killed"—parodied—the giant sacred Text that ends
with Revelation. But ordinary morning and evening in the vulgate of
experience can only be like the promises kept in the Vulgate if the
speaker gathers many ordinary citizens ("crude collops") into a hypothetical community of interpreters that can rival Whitman's projection of
"Myself" as a synecdochic personification of the New World, "a mythological form, a festival sphere." This community can be cohesive *because*
it is grounded in common awareness that it is only hypothetical.

     This ordinary evening assigns us the privileged point of view of St.
John in Revelation.

Reality as a thing seen by the mind,
Not that which is but that which is apprehended,
A mirror, a lake of reflections in a room,
A glassy ocean lying at the door,

A great town hanging pendent in a shade,
An enormous nation happy in a style,
Everything as unreal as real can be,

In the inexquisite eye. (V)

Vendler says that this reduces "all of angular life" into the narrow circular compass of the secular eye, "the toy gazing globe in which the whole of Nature hangs pendent."[10] But the immediately following lines suggest that the speaker's eye is very large indeed and quite extraordinary. He sees as if he were St. John and saw historical actuality across a sea of glass (Revelation 4:6): upside down and backwards as if it were eternity, a bejewelled New Jerusalem/Judah replacing the common place of articulate festival, the Psalmist's Temple. "In the metaphysical streets of the physical town/ We remember the lion of Juda [Revelation 5:5] and we save the phrase" (XI).

Of course no secular modern writer can legitimately claim to represent historical reality as if in an eternal present: Stevens had to counter the solar Word's self-proclamation in John's Omega-book, "I am the Alpha and the Omega" (Revelation 22:13). But like the ancient writer of the apocalypse, the modern poet attributed strong personal identity to the reader when he personified elements of his own discourse. And if readers in the ordinary modern city recognize that the poet is contradicting Scripture, they in effect compose a self-conscious body of witnesses ("a festival sphere") like that generated by the Word's claim to join the beginning and the end of history.

> Reality is the beginning not the end,
> Naked Alpha, not the hierophant Omega,
> Of dense investiture, with luminous vassals.
>
> It is the infant A standing on infant legs,
> Not twisted, stooping, polymathic Z,
> He that kneels away on the edge of space
>
> In the pallid perceptions of its distances.
> Alpha fears men or else Omega's men
> Or else his prolongations of the human . . .
>
> Since both alike appoint themselves the choice
> Custodians of the glory of the scene.
> The immaculate interpreters of life.
>
> But that's the difference: in the end and the way
> To the end. Alpha continues to begin.
> Omega is refreshed at every end. (VI)

This sharply distinguishes between the plain vulgate of modern experience, naked Alpha, and the second giant, the figure of ancient pomp and circumstance who resembles the Psalmist's sun attended by the many other luminous heavens. But Stevens "killed" the final giant sun of the Vulgate in order to provoke a restorative counter-turn to his own parody of the

---

10 Vendler, p. 283.

ancient choral ode: a larger poem for a larger audience. Naked Alpha and hierophant Omega yield to "the infant A standing on infant legs" and "twisted stooping, polymathic Z." As the pompous "hierophantic" Greek is translated down to the naked vulgate—tragic goat-song into caprice—both initial and final letters are exposed as impotent. But this dense little dialectic ends by reconstructing a potent integrity worthy of St. John.

> Alpha continues to begin.
> Omega is refreshed at every end.

Like Revelation "An Ordinary Evening" authorizes its projection of a never-ending vocal liturgy by intensifying the dynamics of contradiction in ordinary speech. Because this last account of the relationship between Alpha and Omega requires us to reconsider both the initial sharp differentiation and the final identification, we can recognize each as one moment in a dialogue—which unlike simple polarity can be generative because it is open to variation and reinterpretation.

But ordinary evening and morning can seem like promises kept only because the text personifies and thus further encourages the interpretive efforts which it demands. The primal scene of literary intercourse is a *common* place of absence:

> These characters are around us in the scene.
> Since both alike appoint themselves the choice
> Custodians of the glory of the scene,
> The immaculate interpreters of life.

Letters ("characters") circle endlessly about us as twelve-times-twelve-to-the-nth-power witnesses circle the Reader across the sea of glass in Revelation ("a mirror, a lake of reflections in a room,/ A glassy ocean lying at the door"). And Stevens elaborately acknowledged that the new, transcribed New Haven is to be pendent in the eyes of many professors and students of comparative religious and literary history. He thus finally predicted that his text will be completed in being killed by a second giant: a poem which is as much larger than an ordinary evening as the ancient public lyric was larger than the modern private lyric—because it is for an audience which is in turn as much larger than the solitary modern reader as the ancient festival congregation was larger than each crude modern collop.

This, however, requires a portrayal of the author as explicit as St. John's self-portrait in Revelation. New Haven can provisionally stand as a new Jerusalem if many readers join "Professor Eucalyptus" (XXII) on an academic pilgrimage back through religious, political and literary history that emphasizes the deconstructive power of time.

The text provokes our attention by conflating two moments in cultural history, authoritarian and communist respectively. It must be a very windy night indeed when "the marble statues/ Are like newspapers blown by the wind" (XII). As section XXXI observes, marble statues are not at all like throwaway newspapers: the "general fidget" of modern history has replaced ancient "busts of Constantine"—imperial and imperious images of constancy ordered by the head of state—with newspaper photographs of the late President Blank, a meaningless synecdochic personification of the equally faceless commons. And twelve sections after the twelfth which perversely identifies marble statues and newspapers, Alpha and Z in the history of culture, Stevens explicitly described the apocalypse to be countered as well as commemorated by his "propounding of four seasons and twelve months" in which "Juda becomes New Haven or else must" (XI):

> . . . they blew up
> The statue of Jove among the boomy clouds.
> It took all day to quieten the sky
> And then to refill its emptiness again. (XXIV)

As "blew up" suggests hyperbole as well as revolution, "Professor Eucalyptus" defines history as a process of alternate deconstruction and reconstruction. He thus speaks from the vantage of the second giant, the larger poem for a larger audience. He describes as a day's work well done Stevens' still-pending task of filling the emptiness of the secular heavens with supreme fiction. But even while Stevens played professor of comparative religion and comparative literature, he could only end his transformation of the naked Alpha into the attended vision of the hierophant Omega by acknowledging that the emptiness is still to be filled, the ultimate Alpha/Omega poem still to be written. Even while retaining the dignified preterite, he characterized his "history" as prophecy:

> There was a clearing, a readiness for first bells,
> An opening for outpouring, the hand was raised:
> There was a willingness not yet composed. (XXIV)

If the familiar dry tone of the ironic commentator ("they blew up . . . it took all day") implicates us as co-conspirators on the long march of history, the flat objectivity of the narrative ("there was . . . the hand was raised. There was . . .") more strongly implies that we are co-composers of the "first bells." As Revelation asks us to imitate the Spirit and the Bride who invite us to the City without temple or sun, Stevens' apocalypse asks us to help build a city/temple that cannot be built: an all-inclusive enclosure in which instantaneous photographs take on the aura of constancy.

On the other hand, Professor Eucalyptus authorizes his cultural prophecy of regeneration with accurate literary history. It is by registering the vacillations of intellectual fashion that he challenges us to rebuild Jerusalem:

Professor Eucalyptus said, "The search
For reality is as momentous as
The search for god." It is the philospher's search

For an interior made exterior
And the poet's search for the same exterior made
Interior: breathless things broodingly abreath

With the inhalations of original cold
And of original earliness. Yet the sense
Of cold and earliness is a daily sense,

Not the predicate of bright origin.
Creation is not renewed by images
Of lone wanderers. To re-create, to use

The cold and earliness and bright origin
Is to search. Likewise to say of the evening star,
The most ancient light in the most ancient sky

That it is wholly an inner light, that it shines
From the sleepy bosom of the real, re-creates,
Searches a possible for its possibleness. (XXII)

These lines recall Milton's description of the Spirit ("darkness profound/
Covered th'abyss: but on the wat'ry calm/ His brooding wing the Spirit
of God outspread," *Paradise Lost*, VII, 234–35) and of Adam and Eve
("they hand in hand with wandering steps and slow/ Through Eden took
their solitary way," XII, 648–49). This parody is as parricidal as the
speaker has predicted that the larger poem is to be. But the speaker also
marks the distance between ancient and modern evaluations of language
by alluding to other intermediary texts. Anticipating Geoffrey Hartman,
this academic *pastor* in New Haven remembers that many English
imitators of Milton contemplated the ambiguity of the most ancient
light, the star which is Venus at evening and Lucifer at morning.[11]

But the text also repeatedly suggests that we are to regain paradise
by rejecting the merely singleminded parricide which Hartman's col-
league Harold Bloom finds in writing.[12] Stevens' guying of Milton
betrays not so much an anxiety of influence as a will to transcend the
"singleness . . . of will" involved in such attempts to kill—as he has put it
two sections earlier in a less particular recapitulation of cultural history.

The moon rose in the mind and each thing there
Picked up its radial aspect in the night
Prostrate below the singleness of its will.

That which was public green turned private grey.
At another time, the radial aspect came

[11] See "Evening Star and Evening Land" in *The Fate of Reading* (Chicago, 1975), pp.
147–48.
[12] See *The Anxiety of Influence* (New York, 1973); *A Map of Misreading* (New York,
1975).

From a different source. But there was always one:

A century in which everything was part
Of that century and of its aspect, a personage,
A man who was the axis of his time,

An image that begot its infantines,
Imaginary poles whose intelligence
Streamed over chaos their civilities.

What is the radial aspect of this place,
This present colony of a colony
Of colonies, a sense in the changing sense

Of things? A figure like Ecclesiast,
Rugged and luminous, chants in the dark
A text that is an answer, although obscure. (XIX)

Like Ecclesiastes, Stevens wrote an obscure but luminous answer to a question somewhat different from the one which Bloom attributes to him. "Professor Eucalyptus" does not speak so much as a David against a Goliath-precursor, but as if in full view of a corporate Goliath who is not yet fully composed. Future readers will inevitably "kill" the modern poet. But that deconstruction can construct a New Jerusalem by acknowledging collaborative, mutual self-criticism as the ground of community.

Because Stevens had a long memory and dared emulate poets of the public green such as the Psalmist and St. John, he could illuminate the private grey. Like the delicate dance between Alpha and Omega in section VI, the balancing of private and public modes of poetry in section XIX primarily asks how this non-place, this exclusive text can be common. "What is the radial aspect of this place?" The very asking of the question begins to define the negative integrity of both this century and this text as incentives for positive reconstruction. For the rhetorical gesture generates a community of analysts—even if their common denominator is private greyness. "There was always one/ A century in which everything was part of that century and of its aspect."

Yet the question is integrative because it is not answered. The final strict differentiation of photographs of the late president Mr. Blank from busts of Constantine (XXXI) acknowledges that even when authors blow up the statue of the Father among the booming clouds, they tend to remain on the side of imperial constancy: they articulate contemporary discontinuities in order to reconstruct traditions of continuity. Professor Eucalyptus acknowledges the current dominance of private grey and its literary counterpart, the self-reflexive lyric, and refuses to answer his question. We may thus not only respect his reluctance to be precocious in killing one giant of which this poem certainly tries to be a part, modern reality, but also resist his caution.

For as usual in good literary rhetoric, the phrasing of the momentous question stops just short of answering it. Though it in fact prescribes our answer, it leaves us the responsibility and privilege of formulating a response.

> What is the radial aspect of this place,
> This present colony of a colony
> Of colonies, a sense in the changing sense
>
> Of things?

This very strongly implies that the con-stancy of imperial Constantine can be substituted as standard for the isolation of one from many in daily vulgar parodies of our Augustan motto *e pluribus unum*: the isolation of one instant and one individual from another ("private grey") encouraged by the mass production of photographs of one faceless President Blank after another. But Stevens did not dictate: he did not violate, but finely developed the democratic concern for intelligent participation in presidential elections. If this place—this America as well as this emphatically American text—is a colony of colonies, we can easily turn back political and literary history far beyond Milton's predication of bright origins and lone wanderers. The new colony, whether American or Stevensian, remains attached to the old culture while being obviously apart from it. If Connecticut was previously a colony of England as England was a colony of the Romans, "An Ordinary Evening in New Haven" is a colony of "Sunday Morning" as "Sunday Morning" was itself a colony of colonies: derived from earlier writers' meditations upon art which in turn derived from promises in Scripture.

One and many, literary text and its historical contexts, each receives its due. Stevens prepared to close by explicitly describing the communal/individual vision to be achieved in many precarious balancings between the good citizen's acceptance of the general fidget from Constantine to President Blank and the good poet's rejection of it.

> A century in which everything was part
> Of that century and of its aspect, a personage,
> A man who was the axis of his time.
> . . . a bottomless sight,
> . . . a visibility of thought,
> In which hundreds of eyes, in one mind, see at once (XXX)

If in St. John's allegory the four living creatures full of eyes all around and within (Revelation 4:8) may represent the four Evangelists, in Stevens' allegory the hundreds of eyes which see at once represent centuries of readings of ordinary and colonial texts like "An Ordinary Evening." And we can credit this gathering of interpretive moments in a common non-place— any reading of this text—because "Professor Eucalyptus" has so thoroughly demonstrated his competence as cultural and literary historian. Each stage of the argument has been presented not only as an attitude of a single poet of this century, but also as a synecdochic part of a giant: an imagining of reality composed of constant mutual questioning by all poets and all readers from the beginning to the end of literary history.

And indeed Stevens was not alone in founding a colony of colonies. Of course like Williams and later American poets, he defined himself against T. S. Eliot.[13] In *Four Quartets*, however, Eliot had anticipated many of the strategies as well as some of the allusions and imagery in "The Auroras of Autumn" when he continued his early dialogue with Pound—a reader of both Whitman and Mallarmé radically unlike both Stevens and himself.

[13] *Letters*, p. 378:

> I regard [T. S. Eliot] as a negative rather than a positive force.

p. 67:

> After all, Eliot and I are dead opposites and I have been doing about everything that he would not be likely to do.

9

The Temple Buried:
Voices of Parody in *Four Quartets*

Le temple enseveli divulgue par la bouche
Sépulcrale d'égout bavant boue et rubis . . .
—Mallarmé, "Le Tombeau de Charles Baudelaire"

Wallace Stevens and T. S. Eliot were highly individual talents, but we can better appreciate their distinctiveness if we observe how they both established their texts as complex apostrophes to secular congregations. If in the essay "Tradition and the Individual Talent" Eliot claimed that the modern poet should sacrifice his personality to "the mind of Europe," in *Four Quartets* he elaborated the association of reading with both sacrifice and marriage in Revelation, "Lycidas," "Out of the Cradle," and "Hérodiade." Like Stevens' later works, the cycle of long poems demonstrates how a poet gains authority by acknowledging that he depends upon the attentiveness of an audience whom he can never be sure is there.[1]

---

[1] A. D. Moody, *Thomas Stearns Eliot, Poet* (Cambridge, 1979) notes that in *The Idea of a Christian Society* Eliot expressed an acute sense of his membership in a large community:

> The notion of communal responsibility, or the responsibility of every individual for the sins of the society to which he belongs, is one that needs to be more firmly apprehended; and if I share the guilt of my society in time of "peace," I do not see how I can absolve myself from it in time of war, by abstaining from the common action.

But, as Moody observes, the "Notes on War Poetry" strictly refuse to express the immediate consciousness of the people: the poet should write "not the expression of collaborative emotion/ Imperfectly reflected in the daily papers" but "the private experience at its greatest intensity/ Becoming universal." See also William H. Pritchard's characterization of Eliot as a gadfly in *Lives of the Modern Poets* (New York, 1980) esp. pp. 175 and 193:

> Eliot's poetry will continue to count as a living force insofar as we keep the poems open, prevent their hardening into meanings which make them easier to handle only because they are no longer fluid, problematic and alive.

> More than any other modern poem, *Four Quartets* causes us to think again about our deepest attitudes toward poetry—to question, in fact, whether we have such attitudes and if so how deep they are.

i

Mallarmé helped Eliot give the several voices of *Four Quartets* an erotic urgency even greater than that of Stevens' last speakers. Half a dozen years before the late long poems "The Auroras of Autumn" and "An Ordinary Evening in New Haven," Eliot reenacted on Anglo-American shores Mallarmé's strange versions of the marriage of the Lamb and Jerusalem.

Four Quartets alludes several times to Mallarmé's allegories of the sun. "Little Gidding" IV may recall the beginning of "Le Cantique de St. Jean," "le soleil . . . redescend/ Incandescent": "the dove descending breaks the air/ With flame of incandesent terror."[2] However, "garlic and sapphires in the mud/ Clot the bedded axle-tree" in "Burnt Norton" II clearly derives from two texts by Mallarmé, establishing the oxymoron of nuptial competition in Psalm 19—"the sun is as a bridegroom coming out of his chamber, and rejoiceth as a strong man to run a race"—as one model for the parodies in which Eliot reread literary history.

In "Le Tombeau de Charles Baudelaire" Mallarmé pictured the principal native influence on his writing as a brilliant, jewel-encrusted temple that has been buried and thoroughly desecrated.

> Le temple enseveli divulgue par la bouche
> Sépulcrale d'égout bavant boue et rubis . . .
> Quel feuillage séché dans les cités sans soir
> Votif pourra bénir comme elle se rasseoir
> Contre le marbre vainement de Baudelaire . . .
>
> (O.C. p. 70)
>
> The buried temple reveals by the sewer's dark
> sepulchral mouth slavering mud and rubies . . .
> What dried wreaths in cities without evening
> votively could bless as if could sit
> vainly against the marble of Baudelaire . . .

Mallarmé thus in effect prophesied how Eliot too would attempt to reconstruct the City which has no need of the sun—illuminated by many readers' encounters with the alienation, negation, and discontinuity that structure the Book of Life. Eliot too deferred to nature only by mocking the doctrine of universal continuity articulated in the Baudelaire sonnet which Mallarmé parodied.

> La Nature est un temple ou de vivants piliers
> Laissent parfois sortir de confuses paroles.
>
> Nature is a temple where living pillars sometimes
> let confused words emerge.
>
> "Correspondences"

---

[2] Edward J. H. Greene, *T. S. Eliot et la France* (Paris, 1951), pp. 138–41.

No more than Mallarmé could Eliot share the Psalmist's assumption that nature speaks, even in a confused manner. Like the master of the Rue du Rome, Eliot buried both the Temple and the jewel-covered City of Revelation in the mud of parody so that he could construct a community made up of truly living pillars: readers who at least momentarily define themselves in terms of scripture rather than nature.

The sonnet which is more clearly evoked by "garlic and sapphires in the mud/ Clot the bedded axle-tree" still better epitomizes Mallarmé's and Eliot's elaborations of the image of the Law as a solar bridegroom/ challenger in Psalm 19.

> M'introduire dans ton histoire
> C'est en héros effarouché . . .
> A des glaciers attentatoire
> Je ne sais le naïf péché
> Que tu n'auras pas empêché
> De rire très haut sa victoire
>
> Dis si je ne suis pas joyeux
> Tonnere et rubis aux moyeux.
>
> To bring myself into your tale
> is as a hero much afraid . . .
> Ravisher of glaciers I
> know no artless sin that after
> hindering you'll not deny
> its very loud victorious laughter
>
> And am I not joyous, say,
> thunder and rubies to the naves.

The tale into which Mallarmé introduced himself as mock-hero is much larger than either the story he had promised to write for his mistress Méry or her sexual organ, into which he habitually introduced himself in a more ordinary way.[3] In his translation of a treatise in English, *Les Dieux Antiques*, Mallarmé defined the movement of the solar chariot as model for all mythology and literature. And in *Four Quartets* Eliot elaborated Mallarmé's self-mocking erotic reduction of the history of symbolism to a mimesis of solar revolution.

This is perhaps most evident when Eliot's whole lyric drama climaxes with a translation of a more familiar line from Mallarmé's "Tombeau d'Edgar Poe." The French poet is a major component of the "familiar compound ghost" who speaks at dawn in "Little Gidding" II about having tried to purify the dialect of the tribe.

> Eux, comme un vil sursaut d'hydre oyant jadis l'ange
> Donner un sens plus pur aux mots de la tribu
> Proclamèrent très haut le sortilège bu

---

[3] Robert Greer Cohn, *Toward the Poems of Mallarmé* (Berkeley, 1965), p. 223.

Dans le flot sans honneur de quelque noir mélange . . .

Calme bloc ici-bas chu d'un désastre obscur,
Que ce granit du moins montre à jamais sa borne
Aux noirs vols du Blasphème épars dans le futur.

With a hydra-spasm, once hearing the angel endow
with a sense more pure the words of the tribe,
they loudly proclaimed the sortilege imbibed
from the dishonourable flood of some black brew . . .

calm block fallen down here from some dark
disaster, let this granite forever mark
bounds to dark flights of Blasphemy scarce in the future.

As we shall see, when in "Little Gidding" Eliot transposed to dawn a
dead poet's demonic triumph over the clouds at sunset, he rejected the
contempt for the crowd with which Mallarmé appropriately let himself
be possessed in order to honor Poe. Eliot did not take his stand under an
unchanging sculpture of wisdom, the "bust of Pallas" in "The Raven"—
indeed a "calme bloc ici-bas chu d'un désastre obscur." Rather, by countering the natural movement of the sun even more elaborately than Poe,
he criticized the cult of authority which Poe's demonism perpetuated.
He thereby developed the questioning of authorial identity in both
Mallarmé's weird celebration of noon in "Le Cantique de St. Jean" and
Whitman's rewriting of Poe's midnight exchange with the Raven in
"Out of the Cradle": "'Demon or bird' (said the boy's soul). . . ."

ii

Although each of the *Four Quartets* is named for a location on one
side of the Atlantic or the other, they in fact take place in the Anglo-
American poet's projection of recollective words into other minds.

What might have been and what has been
Point to one end, which is always present.
Footfalls echo in the memory
Down the passage which we did not take
Towards the door we never opened
Into the rose-garden. My words echo
Thus, in your mind.
                    But to what purpose
Disturbing the dust on a bowl of rose-leaves
I do not know.

The speaker of "Burnt Norton" I confidently describes two echoings
("footfalls echo in the memory," "my words echo/ Thus, in your mind")
but he declines the role of master: "to what purpose/ Disturbing . . . I do
not know." He can thus hear and invite us to hear a third echoing in still
another place:

                              Other echoes
Inhabit the garden. Shall we follow?
Quick, said the bird, find them, find them,
Round the corner. Through the first gate,
Into our first world, shall we follow
The deception of the thrush? Into our first world.
There they were, dignified, invisible,
Moving without pressure, over the dead leaves . . .
There they were as our guests, accepted and accepting.

This "we" is a "you and I" like those who are to go on an infernal journey at the beginning of "The Love Song of J. Alfred Prufrock" ("let us
go then, you and I, through certain half-deserted streets . . .").[4] And the
speaker elaborates his distinction between likes ("my words echo/ Thus
in your mind") when he differentiates both from a mediator-guide:
"shall we follow/ The deception of the thrush?" The thrush is another
personification of colloquy who calls attention to the fact that dialogue
differentiates its members more than it identifies them. The main voice
at first merges with the bird's, elaborating its directions: "round the corner. Through the first gate./ Into our first world, shall we follow. . . ."
But he qualifies his surrogate's authority when he refers to the "deception of the thrush." And indeed this thrush is more like the mockingbird
in "Out of the Cradle" than the thrush in "When Lilacs Last in the
Dooryard Bloomed": it helps project a mortal comradeship grounded in
alert, self-critical response rather than in assertion.

For who speaks next? An echo of the human speaker's phrase, "into
our first world," sounds like someone else's rumination and opposes the
choice implied in the phrase "the deception of the thrush." Could the
repetition not represent the echoing of "my words" in "your mind?" The
first-person plural possessive pronoun would thus be justified. In fact
only the response of *another* mind could open a place inhabited by
"other echoes." If it seems that someone else opposes the speaker's criticism of his alter ego, the thrush, we may credit a vision of the strange,
vague community that can be projected in the writing and reading of
poetry.

"There they were . . . accepted and accepting." Three parties are
"accepted": the speaker by the echoing of his words in another's mind—
even if it induces an exploration which he claims is futile; the reader by the
thrush who has twice voiced his curiosity; the other echoes by both speaker
and reader. Each is also "accepting" in turn: the speaker when he overcomes two statements of resistance, "to what purpose/ Disturbing . . . I do
not know" and "the deception of the thrush"; the reader when he echoes

---

[4] Balanchandra Rajan, *The Overwhelming Question* (Toronto, 1976) pp. 89–90 and
Bornstein (*op. cit.*, p. 130) differently compare the opening of "Burnt Norton" with the
opening of "Prufrock."

the speaker's tantalizing phrase "into our first world"; the other echoes when they move in a regular pattern, as memories may ("footfalls echo in the memory") but verse-feet certainly do. For this passage begins to suggest who—or what—the other echoes are. Countering the skepticism voiced in the third of the four opening phrases, "what might have been is an abstraction/ Remaining a perpetual possibility/ Only in a world of speculation," this sequence reminds us that the speculation expressed by self-reflexive poetic language can have different results from solitary mental reflection. Because writer and reader are *not* in fact present to each other, they can accept subversions of conventional definitions of presence and identity implied by vague figures whose very lack of definition—like that of Stevens' ever-shifting auroras of autumn—may remind us of poetic discourse more than anything else. For like the words of poetry, these echoes are "other" in that they are neither here nor there, neither exclusively "my words" nor "in your mind."[5]

Yet the most striking image in "Burnt Norton" suggests that the other echoes also correspond to writer and reader, both of whom have temporarily sacrificed their cultural and personal identities to the demands of their formally patterned exchange. A paradisal vision occurs because it is shared by three parties identified by pronouns, linguistic functions whose indeterminacy clearly shows how language transfers and transforms personal identities.

> So we moved, and they, in a formal pattern,
> Along the empty alley, into the box circle,
> To look down into the drained pool.
> Dry the pool, dry concrete, brown edged,
> And the pool was filled with water out of sunlight,
> And the lotos rose, quietly, quietly,
> The surface glittered out of heart of light,

---

[5] In *The Three Voices of Poetry* (New York, 1954), Eliot described the interconnectedness of three speech acts, the poet speaking to himself, to others and through others: "the voices are most often found together—the first and second . . . in non-dramatic poetry; and together with the third in dramatic poetry" (p. 32). In fact the poet does not ever talk with himself, but gradually and painfully finds out what it is that he has to say by engaging in protracted struggle with the medium before he eventually goes all the way out into it, adopting its maternal role:

> He does not know what he has to say until he has said it. He is oppressed by a burden which he must bring to birth in order to obtain relief. (pp. 30–31)

Developing his polemic against Romantic theories of selfhood in "Tradition and the Individual Talent," Eliot stressed delivery rather than conception:

> The final handing over, so to speak, of the poem to an unknown audience, for what the audience will make of it, seems . . . to me the consummation of the process begun in solitude because it marks the final separation of the poem from the author. (33)

Four Quartets continually emphasizes this productive form of alienation.

And they were behind us, reflected in the pool.
Then a cloud passed, and the pool was empty.

Although the circular pool is bright because it reflects the sun, it also
paradoxically mirrors the invisible "other echoes." Associating these eva-
nescent presences with the persons represented by the pronouns "I" and
"you" ("they were behind us"), the vision suggests that while we are
writing or reading we take on the ghostly, indeterminate nature of the
literary medium itself—and thus also its potential for revising prescribed
definitions of authority and identity.

This implication is supported by several reminders that discourse is
intersubjective. If the roses in the garden "had the look of flowers that
are looked at," it is the conjuring of an immanent circle of witnesses
which generates the unique lotos. If a bird calls in response to unheard
music, the speaker has called in anticipation of potential hearers'
response. And the ecstatic vision of wholeness is produced by several
proofs that we stand outside ourselves when we move with others who
accept and are accepted by language: every double moment of dialogue
challenges any notion of identity which the unaided mind can devise.
Thus, the lotos-sequence may persuade us to share the speaker's belief in
an inclusive community not because it evokes a transcendent divine
power but because it articulates interchange between moments and persons in literary history and performance.

But it is the sudden termination of the vision that most clearly establishes it as a specifically literary phenomenon.

Go, go, go, said the bird, for the leaves were full
    of children,
Hidden excitedly, containing laughter.
Go, go, go, said the bird: human kind
Cannot bear very much reality.

Assigning unseen children an inexhaustible potential for understanding
reality, Eliot may have been drawing upon Wordsworth's myth of child-
hood, most elaborately presented in the Intimations Ode: "though inland
far we be,/ Our souls have sight of that immortal sea . . . and see the Children sport upon the shore. . . ." But both the bowl of rose-leaves and the
rose-garden are certainly parodic diminutions of Dante's paradisal rose.
And if "the unseen eyebeam crossed" in the rosegarden sequences recalls
Donne's "Canonization," the pastiche of two Mallarmé lines, "garlic and
sapphires in the mud," follows in "Burnt Norton" II. So it is difficult not to
suspect that the "other echoes" stand for many previous literary interpretations of the Tradition which, as Eliot said in his essay, the individual talent
must accept if he is to be accepted by future readers as an authority in his
own right.

However, like the Nurse in "Hérodiade," Eliot composed places for shared contemplation by denying that any modern can really become a member of communities as vital as those celebrated in ancient choral song. Each of the *Quartets* can end by prophesying a renaissance of vital community because it begins by evoking a company of other echoes from which we are excluded—and which we may therefore desire all the more to join.

"East Coker" I defines a particular present place and time, but requires us to watch and hear from a distance:

> Now the light falls
> Across the open field, leaving the deep lane
> Shuttered with branches, dark in the afternoon,
> Where you lean against a bank while a van passes . . .
> In that open field
> If you do not come too close, if you do not come too close,
> On a summer midnight, you can hear the music
> Of the weak pipe and the little drum
> And see them dancing around the bonfire
> The association of man and woman
> In daunsinge, signifying matrimonie—
> A dignified and commodious sacrament.
> Two and two, necessarye coniunction,
> Holding eche other by the hand or the arm
> Which betokeneth concorde . . .

It is from a cautious distance that Thomas Stearns Eliot spoke through the persona of his ancestor Thomas Elyot ("in daunsynge signifying matrimonie . . .") and conjured a chorus of ghosts more vigorous than echoes in a rose garden. He also turned against his dead namesake, criticizing an old-fashioned lyric which he imitated:

> That was a way of putting it—not very satisfactory:
> A periphrastic study in a worn-out poetical fashion,
> Leaving one still with the intolerable wrestle
> With words and meanings . . .
> Had they deceived us
> Or deceived themselves, the quiet-voiced elders,
> Bequeathing us merely a receipt for deceit?

Commenting upon the uncertainty of relationships between signifiers and signifieds as well as between writers and readers, Eliot prepared us to assign his poetic syntax an extraordinary power to gather persons as well as historical and biographical moments.

"Dry Salvages" climaxes with a much more complex and and productive alienation of the primary voice: a reading of a distinctly foreign text.

> I sometimes wonder if that is what Krishna meant—
> Among other things—or one way of putting the same thing: . . .

> When the train starts, and the passengers are settled
> To fruit, periodicals and business letters
> (And those who saw them off have left the platform)
> Their faces relax from grief into relief
> To the sleepy rhythm of a hundred hours,
> Fare forward travellers! not escaping from the past
> Into different lives, or into any future;
> You are not the same people who left that station
> Or who will arrive at any terminus . . .
> And on the deck of the drumming liner
> Watching the furrow that widens behind you,
> You shall not think "the past is finished"
> Or "the future is before us."

Eliot's speaker relates to the dead sage of the *Bhagavad Gita* as tentatively as he has to the listeners in "Burnt Norton" I ("but to what purpose/ Disturbing the dust on a bowl of rose-leaves/ I do not know") and to the voices of Whitman's Mother Sea in "Dry Salvages" I: "I do not know much about gods, but I think. . . ." Yet he addresses the fictional passengers on train and boat as if *he* were Krishna.

Then something still more curious happens. When another voice speaks from the aerial, the main speaker joins us as passenger on the deck of the liner to hear a more extensive and significant echoing of his own words.

> At nightfall, in the rigging and the aerial,
> Is a voice descanting (though not to the ear,
> The murmuring shell of time, and not in any language)
> "Fare forward, you who think that you are voyaging;
> You are not those who saw the harbour
> Receding, or those who will disembark.

The unidentified voice assures the primary speaker and ourselves that we can appreciate another quotation set at two removes from our exchange:

> "At the moment which is not of action or inaction
> You can receive this: 'on whatever sphere of being
> The mind of a man may be intent
> At the time of death'—that is the one action.

At the close of the main quotation, Eliot's persona concisely defines reciprocity as the rubric of this text. Having revealed that it was the sage of the *Bhagavad Gita* speaking, "so Krishna, as when he admonished Arjuna," after a pause he repeats a phrase which "Krishna" has twice borrowed from him: "fare forward travellers!"[6]

---

[6] Referring to the recurrent apostrophe to voyagers and seamen, Harry Blamires (*Word Unheard*) p. 108 notes:
> The device is the poetic equivalent of repersonalizing one's conversation by breaking into one's own explanation, putting one's hand on to

As in "Burnt Norton" I, the interruption of a line represents the
passage of thought from one person to another.

> (My words echo
> Thus, in your mind.
>> But to what purpose
> Disturbing the dust on a bowl of rose-leaves
> I do not know.
>
>> Other echoes
> Inhabit the garden. Shall we follow?
> *Quick, said the bird.*)
>
> And do not think of the fruit of action.
> Fare forward.
>
>> O voyagers, O seamen,
> You who come to port, and you whose bodies
> Will suffer the trial and judgment of the sea
> Or whatever event, this is your real destination—
> So Krishna, as when he admonished Arjuna
> On the field of battle.
>
>> Not fare well,
> But fare forward, voyagers.
>> "Dry Salvages" III

"Krishna" ratifies the address with which the speaker interprets his doctrine ("I sometimes wonder if that is what Krishna meant . . . Fare forward, travellers! not escaping from the past/ Into different lives, or into
any future"). He also makes explicit the irony implied in that exclamation: "fare forward, you who think that you are voyaging." When the
usurping voice again varies the speaker's phrase, the pause which splits it
("fare forward/ /o voyagers") may suggest that "Krishna" is reflecting
upon his quotation of another's words (" ' 'on whatever sphere of
being . . .' ' "). As if sustained by the echoing of his words in another's
mind, he provokes us to collaborate in his challenge not only to linear
chronology but also to the patriarchal privileging of the inscribed past:
"the absolute paternal care/ That will not leave us, but prevents us
everywhere" ("East Coker" IV). But as Eliot progressed through *Four
Quartets* he presented more and more complex figures of himself and
his readers, notably the "familiar compound ghost" of "Little Gidding."

The calling of spectators to a dance in "East Coker" I is the primary
model for a final elaboration of "Burnt Norton" I in the first part of the
last poem.

> If you came this way,
> Taking the route you would be likely to take

---

the hearer's shoulders and claiming fresh attention by a warmer
approach. It establishes at least for a moment a sense of deepened
personal contact and intensified sincerity.

From the place you would be likely to come from,
If you came this way in may time, you would find the hedges
White again, in May, with voluptuary sweetness.

But if the speaker's words have presence and reality only if they echo in
another mind, the present moment of speculation is to be known only by
its power to project another. This evocation of the Anglican pastoral
community at Little Gidding yields to its demonic counterpart: "pentecostal fire" in the darkest time of the year.

The London Blitz, an apocalypse devised by the Nazis, is setting for
a variant of both the first encounter between Hamlet and the Ghost in
Shakespeare's tragedy and the meeting between "Dante" and his dead
master Brunetto Latini in the *Inferno*. In "Little Gidding" II Eliot's
speaker and a dead patriarch alternate as compassionate interpreter of
many violent impositions of authority; both speak for the Paraclete who
appeared in tongues of fire at Pentecost (Acts of the Apostles 2: 1–4)

> In the uncertain hour before the morning
> Near the ending of interminable night
> At the recurrent end of the unending
> After the dark dove with the flickering tongue
> Had passed below the horizon of his homing . . .
> I caught the sudden look of some dead master
> Whom I had known, forgotten, half recalled
> Both one and many; in the brown baked features
> The eyes of a familiar compound ghost
> Both intimate and unidentifiable.
> So I assumed a double part, and cried
> And heard another's voice cry: "What! are *you* here?"

Eliot assumed a double part in that he spoke not only as himself but also
as many other readers of Dante. The speaker meets a paternal spirit
compounded of many dead literary masters, one who like Mallarmé says
that "speech impelled us/ To purify the dialect of the tribe." But Eliot
also joined Whitman in defining "colloquy" a matrix alternative to the
Mother Sea to whom he deferred in "Dry Salvages." This climactic
sequence thus corroborates the text's many previous suggestions that
genuine authority derives from mutual acknowledgment of common
fallibility and duplicity.

iii

Four Quartets repeatedly demonstrate that the traditional respect
for both a unique divine Authority and individual human authorship
conceals—and can thus exacerbate—various kinds of division and alienation. And when Eliot turned the rigor of his analysis upon himself, he
emulated the Shakespeare of the tragedies as well as the Mallarmé of the
sacrificial mini-drama "Hérodiade." More strongly than Stevens in "The

Auroras of Autumn," he translated into the terms of the American modernist lyric the dramatic impulse which Mallarmé inherited from his own native precursor Racine but which poets writing in English can also learn from Shakespeare.

The first allusion to Mallarmé in *Four Quartets* mocks the tendency for both authors and paternal authorities to invoke prescriptive patterns.

> Garlic and sapphires in the mud
> Clot the bedded axle-tree . . .
> The dance along the artery
> The circulation of the lymph
> Are figured in the drift of stars . . .
> Below the boarhound and the boar
> Pursue their pattern as before
> But reconciled among the stars.
>   "Burnt Norton" II

Certainly this paraphrase of two poems by Mallarmé tempts us to want the mortal, physical round transfigured into an astral cycle. But Eliot also invited us to help construct a distinctively *literary* constellation when he observed that historical and astrological patterns are distinct: not among the eternal stars but "only in time can the moment in the rose-garden . . . be remembered." And the rest of the cycle shows that the time in question is indeed that of poetry rather than astrology. For Eliot the believer as well as for Stevens the agnostic, literary history continually upstaged religion.

Eliot's further allusions to astral time, however, develop the potential for projecting vital community in Scriptural criticisms of literature as well as of astrology. When the poet played Ecclesiastes in "East Coker" he summed up the intense skepticism about all writers and texts— including his own—that enabled him to project innovation by conjuring the other echoes which constitute Tradition.

> O dark, dark, dark. They all go into the dark,
> The vacant interstellar spaces, the vacant into the vacant,
> The captains, merchant bankers, eminent men of letters,
> The generous patrons of art, the statesmen and the rulers,
> And dark the Sun and Moon, and the Almanach de Gotha
> And the Stock Exchange Gazette, the Directory of Directors . . .
> So here I am, in the middle way, having had twenty years—
> Twenty years largely wasted, the years of *l'entre deux guerres*—
> Trying to learn to use words, and every attempt
> Is a wholly new start, and a different kind of failure
> Because one has only learnt to get the better of words
> For the thing one no longer has to say, or the way in which
> One is no longer disposed to say it.

Deconstructionist criticism has produced no more withering critique of the Romantic claim that a writer can achieve vatic power. But *Four*

Quartets also indicate how the modern poet can propose reconstructions of political as well as literary history. Recall, for example, how "Little Gidding" confronts us with three variations upon the more suggestive synonym of "pattern" in the Mallarméan "garlic and sapphires . . . light upon the *figured* leaf."

> And what you thought you came for
> Is only a shell, a husk of meaning
> From which the purpose breaks only when it is fulfilled
> If at all. Either you had no purpose
> Or the purpose is beyond the end you figured
> And is altered in fulfillment. (I)

> In the disfigured street
> He left me. (II)

> See, now they vanish,
> The faces and places, with the self, which, as
>   it could, loved them,
> To become renewed, transfigured, in another pattern. (III)

Here it is "you" who is to figure out the purpose: the text provokes us to make sense of what seemed to be the end of Western civilization, the Nazi blitz, by showing how historical actuality has disfigured projections of community in the figural, typological reading of Scripture which informs Mallarmé's best lyrics as well as Dante's epic. "The dark dove with the flickering tongue" presents the Nazi buzz-bomb as a hideous parody of the Pentecostal Dove-Spirit. Yet the purpose is beyond the end we figured, and transfigured in another pattern only because Eliot so relentlessly both allegorized and undermined his own ideas of order.

Like the Stevens of "The Auroras of Autumn" and "An Ordinary Evening in New Haven," though, Eliot more often analyzed literary rather than Scriptural history—including debts to both Milton and Shakespeare which he shared with Stevens. "Little Gidding" III refers to three men who died on the scaffold—Charles I, Laud and Stafford—because they upheld the royalist translation of Scriptural deference to unique Authority. This allusion permitted Eliot to speak with compassion of "one who died 'blind and quiet'": Milton, an opponent he shared with the three seventeenth-century royalists. As Milton criticized absolute monarchy but opposed to it an equally absolute faith in the individual conscience, he served Eliot as a literary authority against whom to rebel in turn. But Eliot's reminiscence of the old quarrel between Catholics and Protestants also recalls major images with which Shakespeare rendered tensions between naturalism and supernaturalism in *King Lear*, one of the several texts reflected in the shifting verbal mirrors of "The Auroras of Autumn."

> If you came this way in *may time*, you would find the hedges
> White again, in *May*, with *voluptuary* sweetness.
> It would be the same at the end of the journey,

If you came at night *like a broken king*,
If you came by day not knowing what you came for,
It would be the same, when you leave the rough road
And turn behind the *pig-sty* to the *dull facade*
And the tombstone . . .
                        There are other places
Which also are the world's end, some *at the sea jaws*,
Or over a *dark lake* . . . [italics added]

Ancestress of Shakespeare's Marina as well as of Miranda, Cordelia is a
transitory "May" who addresses the avatar of the sea-god Lir and the
counterpart of the voluptuary Gloucester as a prodigal son: "and wast
thou fain, poor father,/ To hovel thee with swine . . ./ In short and
musty straw?" (IV vii 38). And "Poor Tom" sings about Nero, angler in
the lake of darkness (III iv 6) and Child Roland (III v 186) whose sister is
possessed by a demon because she goes round a church widershins:
against the course of the sun. But it is not only the imagery of "Little
Gidding" which recalls Shakespeare's tragedy; the rhetoric of the whole
lyric cycle attempts to generate a community-in-alienation like that projected by Shakespeare's portrait of broken, prodigal Lear.

At one moment in each of the four poems Eliot praised the humility
of old men in preaching that is as intransigently negative as Lear's to
Gloucester ("thou know'st the first time that we smell the air/ We wawl
and cry. I will preach to thee . . . When we are born we cry that we are
come/ To this great stage of fools" [IV vi 176]).

Do not let me hear
Of the wisdom of old men, but rather of their folly . . .
The only wisdom we can hope to acquire
Is the wisdom of humility.
                        "East Coker" II

For example, the speaker of "Burnt Norton" III demands a sacrifice far
more inclusive than that which Eliot prescribes in "Tradition and the
Individual Talent":

'Descend lower, descend only
Into the world of perpetual solitude,
World not world, but that which is not world.'
Internal darkness, deprivation
And destitution of all property . . .

As if inspired by the Spirit-less tawdry wind that sweeps parts of the
disaffected contemporary city—"Hampstead and Clearkenwell, Camden
and Putney, Highgate, Primrose and Ludgate"—this preacher reveals
the tendency toward absolutism in traditional negative theology. However, like Shakespeare, Eliot deconstructed traditional thought and discourse in order to project new forms of community.

In "East Coker" III a more extensive and absolute prescription of the ascesis that moves *King Lear* more clearly designates the secular text as a non-place in which authority and interpreters can transform mutual resistance into communion.

> You say I am repeating
> Something I have said before. I shall say it again.
> Shall I say it again? In order to arrive there,
> To arrive where you are, to get from where you are not,
>   You must go by a way wherein there is no ecstasy.
> In order to arrive at what you do not know
>   You must go by a way which is the way of ignorance. . . .
> And what you do not know is the only thing you know
> And what you own is what you do not own
> And where you are is where you are not.

Varying Whitman's "do I contradict myself? Very well, then, I contradict myself" in "Song of Myself" section 51, Eliot attributed an objection to the reader but simply overrode it. He then intensified this disregard for potential criticism by asking our permission to repeat himself, but continued on his singleminded way without a pause. This has something like the effect of the concluding scene in Shakespeare's earlier tragedy to which Eliot also alluded in "Little Gidding" II. As Hamlet emphatically identifies himself to Laertes by repeatedly denying that he has any effective identity, even his paradox is not his own but derives from a sequence in St. Paul's letter to the Romans ("for that which I do I allow not: for what I would, that do I not; but what I hate, that do I . . . Now if I do that I would not, it is no more I that do it, but sin that dwelleth in me" Romans 7:15, 20).

> If Hamlet from himself be ta'en away,
> And when he's not himself does wrong Laertes,
> Then Hamlet does it not, Hamlet denies it.
> Who does it then? His madness.
>   (*Hamlet* V i 223)

When Eliot's speaker denies us any effective relationship with our experience, he intones "you" seventeen times and thus in fact attributes strong potential to us. He makes this explicit in using the first-person plural pronoun to define an equivalent of "madness" as a homeopathic means of achieving sanity:

> The wounded surgeon plies the steel
> That questions the distempered part;
> Beneath the bleeding hands we feel
> The sharp compassion of the healer's art . . .
> Our only health is the disease . . .
> . . . to be restored, our sickness must grow worse.

If Hamlet claims that he must be cruel in order to be kind, in *Four Quartets* the healer's compassion is indeed sharp.

When in "Dry Salvages" Eliot again referred to his own previous utterance, he used the first-person plural to name a community-in-exile achieved by the tragic agon of *King Lear* and projected by the sermons of "Burnt Norton" and "East Coker."

> I have said before
> That the past experience revived in the meaning
> Is not the experience of one life only
> But of many generations—not forgetting
> Something that is probably quite ineffable:
> The backward look behind the assurance
> Of recorded history, the backward half-look
> Over the shoulder, towards the primitive terror.
> Now, we come to discover that the moments of agony . . .
> . . . are likewise permanent
> With such permanence as time has. We appreciate this better
> In the agony of others, nearly experienced
> Involving ourselves, than in our own. "Dry Salvages" III

Eliot has scared us with many recollections of primitive, pre-Scriptural terror associated with many voices which come up from Whitman's Mother Sea. We are to join the chorus of anxious worried women lying awake trying to "unweave, unravel and piece together the past and future" with Gloucester fishermen who continually reenact the primal combat between hero and sea-serpent which Shakespeare elaborated in his saga of another Gloucester. We may thus be seduced into helping mourn anonymous dead mates even more effectively than we are by the protests of the uncouth swain in "Lycidas" and the mockingbird in "Out of the Cradle," both earlier attempts to assign ironic pastoral some of the resonance of tragedy.

Yet it is Eliot's climactic parody of both the beginning and the end of *Hamlet* that invites us most urgently to recognize the agony of others as a reflection of our own—and thus begin to redeem both. "Little Gidding" II concisely dramatizes the whole cycle's projection of an inclusive community grounded in criticism of exclusive definitions of identity: "the absolute paternal care/ That will not leave us, but prevents us everywhere" ("East Coker" IV). Before the anonymous compound master fades "on the blowing of the horn," a debased, mechanical equivalent of the crowing of the cock which frightens away the Ghost in *Hamlet*, he outdoes the absolutism of the father whose delivery of a commandment for revenge parodies the Lord's giving of the Law to Moses: "my tables: meet it is I set it down . . ." (*Hamlet* I v 107). However, if in *Hamlet* the initial mockery of the exchange on Sinai eventually causes Hamlet to parody St. Paul's provocative statement of the New Testament law of love, "Little Gidding" II reverses this sequence. The final harshness of the paternal "compound ghost" serves as foil to his opening bid for fraternal forgiveness:

> These things have served their purpose: let them be.
> So with your own, and pray they be forgiven
>   By others, as I pray you to forgive
>   Both bad and good . . .
> Let me disclose the gifts reserved for age
>   To set a crown upon your lifetime's effort.
>   First the cold friction of expiring sense
> Without enchantment, offering no promise
>   But bitter tastelessness of shadow fruit
>   As body and soul begin to fall asunder.
> Second, the conscious impotence of rage
>   At human folly, and the laceration
>   Of laughter at what ceases to amuse . . .

As the primary speaker has subverted conventional distinctions ("both one and many . . . I assumed a double part"), we may want to contradict in turn the ghost's contradiction of his earlier bid for charity—and thus complete Eliot's critique of exclusive deference to authority. When the poem dramatizes various alienations inherent in writing and reading, it tells us that we ourselves are ultimately responsible for assuring both the text's integrity and its relationship with many earlier and later utterances. But it also invites us to derive a stronger sense of our own integrity and relatedness to many other past, present, and future interpreters by confronting the fact that disintegration and division are constants in mortal life.

If we have wanted to challenge the compound ghost's final deconstruction of life as a prologue to death, we can applaud when Eliot's speaker challenges the whole cycle's emphasis upon alienation:

> We die with the dying:
> See, they depart, and we go with them.
>   "Little Gidding" V

All four poems have insisted that the sufferings which they represent are as alien, "the agony of others," as the textual fragments, "other echoes," which evoke them. But this final stress upon the commonness of mortality invites us to project a community of self-conscious interpreters like the men who perish but sing to the sun in "Sunday Morning"—and thus to ratify Eliot's final repetitions of the prefix which Stevens also favored when he summoned a company in "The Auroras of Autumn."

> An easy *com*merce of the old and the new,
> The *common* word exact without vulgarity,
> The formal word precise but not pedantic,
> The *com*plete *con*sort dancing together.

As the "other echoes" in "Burnt Norton" I can most easily be seen as vague figures of literary tradition, the community which Eliot affirmed most explicitly is his own text. *Four Quartets* is both old and new, celebrates commonness without being vulgar, formal and precise but too critical of antiquarianism to be pedantic: a complex—Pindaric—unity constituted by incessant dynamic ("dancing") contradiction. Yet the cycle consummately develops the implication ("and they were behind us, reflected in the pool") that the other echoes in "Burnt Norton" correspond not only to the textual moments which compose Tradition but also to their authors and interpreters: individual talents who voluntarily sacrifice their prescribed identities for the duration of their exchange. We can thus read ourselves into Eliot's final description of his textual cycle as a choral dance like Pindar's. We may even discover in this further statement of a negative poetics something like the potency which Stevens attributed to his circle of men in the sun.

Like Stevens, Eliot refused to designate any common place for revelation other than the utopia of interchange between writer and reader. Despite his Anglo-Catholicism, Eliot buried his temple in literary and Scriptural parody as provocatively as Stevens, who would never feel as much at ease in any church. Both stay-at-home Stevens and expatriate Eliot devised effective challenges to the solipsism proposed as the spirit of American poetry in "Song of Myself" by elaborating Whitman's use of transatlantic models in "Out of the Cradle" to criticize his own assertions of authority. But we can more clearly observe common denominators in the work of these very different writers if we compare their late long poems with Pound's *Cantos*.

10
Templum Aedificans, Not Yet Marble: Dictation in the *Cantos*

> Templum aedificans, not yet marble
> Canto C
> This morning Pound came up with a remark like this,
> over the Jewish question: "it's too bad, and just when I
> had plans to rebuild the Temple in Jerusalem for them."
> Charles Olson, "Cantos 1946–8"

Distinguishing himself from Whitman in a 1909 essay, Ezra Pound showed how much more he owed to the absolutist author of "Song of Myself" than to the self-critical author of "Out of the Cradle."

> Like Dante [Whitman] wrote in the "vulgar tongue," in a new metric. The first great man to write in the language of his people. Et ego Petrarca in lingua vetera scribo, and in a tongue my people understand not.[1]

As Pound often quoted texts written in Latin, he wrote English as if it were a dead, scriptural language whose definitions are not to be disputed. Although Eliot dedicated *The Waste Land* to Pound as "il miglior fabbro [del parlar materno]" (*Purgatorio* XXVI), Pound never did court the vulgar mother tongue.[2] And as we shall see in examining his variations upon lines from both "Out of the Cradle" and a Mallarmé sonnet, unlike Eliot he never seriously questioned the motives or methods of his attempt to establish his own poetic authority. Finally, when he tried to rebuild the Temple he failed to take his cue from the Psalmist who made up for the destruction of the Temple with a text that praises the Text but also incorporates pre-Scriptural devotion to nature.

---

[1] Herbert Bergman, "Ezra Pound and Walt Whitman," *American Literature* XXVII (1955), pp. 56–61, p. 60.

[2] Pound said the same of Milton:

> Milton undoubtedly built up the sonority of the blank verse paragraph in our language. But he did this at the cost of his idiom. He tried to turn English into Latin, to use an uninflected language as if it were an inflected one, neglecting the genius of English, distorting its fibrous manner.

> (*Literary Essays* [London, 1954], p. 237)

i

The beginning of the *Cantos* contrasts with the end of *The Waste Land* in ways that anticipate more striking differences between Eliot's and Pound's later responses to Mallarmé and Whitman.

If in *The Waste Land* Tiresias impersonates the alternations of role in dialogue when he throbs between the two lives of man and woman, he/she finally makes the Thunder sound as if it were soliciting intelligent and sympathetic response rather than imposing authority:

> DA
> *Damyata*: The boat responded
> Gaily, to the hand expert with sail and oar
> The sea was calm, your heart would have responded
> Gaily, when invited, beating obedient
> To controlling hands.

Although Tiresias sits alone on dry land rather than in a responsive boat along with other interpreters ("you"), he quotes Dante's description of Arnaut Daniel, with whom Eliot identified Pound in his dedication: "Poi s'ascose nel foco che gli affina . . ." (*Purgatorio* XXVI). Eliot thus reminded us that his gathering of textual fragments advances a dialogue between brother-poets.

In contrast, Pound's first Canto suppresses several representations of fraternal dialogue in a single old text, Andreas Divus' Latin translation of *Odyssey* XI: "I sat to keep off the impetuous impotent Dead/ Till I should hear Tiresias."[3] Whereas Eliot took the role of Tiresias and thereby acknowledged that he was as impotent if not as impetuous as the many shades whom he met in an underworld, Pound took the role of an Odysseus who is a unique patriarchal authority, strictly distinguished from the unfortunates whom he meets. Correspondingly, he had Tiresias predict a total destruction of community. In Divus' Homer, Tiresias gives Odysseus a choice, predicting that he will return home alone *if* he and his companions steal the oxen of the sun; in Canto I Tiresias gives Odysseus no alternative: "Odysseus/ Shalt return through spiteful Neptune, over dark seas, lose all companions." Thus Tiresias merely reflects the scriptural absolutism which Pound expressed by alliterating two Latinate words, "impetuous impotent," to define his own superiority over the shades.

Two encounters between Odysseus and his mother Anticlea more clearly show how ruthlessly Pound restricted the dialogic impulse in *parlar materno*. In both Homer and Divus, Odysseus is deeply moved by his mother's first apparition and must control his eagerness to speak with her in order to hear Tiresias' prophecy, "hanc quidem ego lachrymatus

---

[3] *The Cantos of Ezra Pound* (London, 1964).

sum videns miseratusque sum animo. . . ." Pound's Odysseus, however, simply notes "and Anticlea came, whom I beat off, and then Tiresias Theban." And whereas the Odysseus in the Greek and Latin texts speaks at great length with his mother when she appears for the second time, Pound's Odysseus only notes "then Anticlea came" and propitiates his textual authority by citing its title page: "Lay quiet Divus. I mean, that is Andreas Divus/ In Officina, Wecheli, 1538, out of Homer."[4]

Finally, whereas in *The Waste Land* Eliot used Frazer's *Golden Bough* to invite the reader to share "the awful daring of a moment's surrender," in Canto I Pound referred twice to a golden bough in a way that prefigures many aggressive uses of a phallic pen in the *Cantos*. This Aphrodite bears "the golden bough of Argicida." Having misread the Homeric Hymn to Aphrodite printed at the end of Divus' *Odyssey*,[5] Pound assigned to her instead of Hermes a masculine instrument similar to the golden staff which Homer/Divus assigned sexually ambiguous Tiresias. As Pound greatly restricted the mediatory role of Tiresias, he attributed the symbol of mediation to a single stable image of perfection whom he substituted for the many companions who challenge Odysseus to define and defend his project.[6]

Certainly Stevens and Eliot too defined the poetic text as the primary dancing-place of revelation. But unlike these two other American modernists, Pound did not modify his sanctification of textual architecture by repeatedly insisting that the text is only a mediatory space where incarnate, more-than-textual subjects—writer and reader—can meet. Correspondingly, although Pound sometimes cast himself as the reader of Tradition as he did in playing Odysseus and interrogating Tiresias, more often he played the writer of absolutely authoritative, uniquely potent texts. But whether he was attributing universal power to his text or to himself, Pound lacked the taste for mediation which led Stevens to associate poetry with the ever-changing aurora borealis and Eliot to define it as a dance: metaphors which are more faithful to St. John's dramatization of reading in Revelation than any of Pound's apocalypses.

---

[4] See Pound, *Make it New* (London, 1934), p. 140. Pound did not observe that his translation of the Anticlea episode is among his "few abbreviations" of Divus.

[5] Hugh Kenner, *The Pound Era* (Berkeley, 1971), pp. 427–30.

[6] The way in which an unburied companion of Odysseus requests a tomb inscription also privileges individual scriptural authority over dialogue. Asking to be designated as "'a man of no fortune with a name to come'" Elpenor quotes the epigraph which Pound had devised ten years earlier for a preface to a posthumous edition of poems by his dead friend Lionel Johnson, but which was appropriate for himself (see Kenner, p. 360). Secondly, in saying "heap up mine arms, be tomb by sea-bord" Elpenor recalls the style of Pound's attempt to duplicate the sonorities of Anglo-Saxon texts in "The Seafarer," an earlier "translation."

ii

After Pound broadcast for Mussolini, however, he was forced for a brief time to play Tiresias. When the American Army of Occupation confined him to a cage in Pisa, he himself was surrounded with a trench like the one which imprisons Homer's shades: "they digged a ditch around about me" (455). He then adopted as non-patriarchal standard the "natural" circulation of funds by a bank in Siena, the Monte dei Paschi, and wrote a series of pastoral elegies which qualify the lack of respect for dialogue in his earlier parodies of Homer's epic.[7]

Throughout the Pisan Cantos Pound addressed Eliot as a brother *daimon* equivalent both to Lycidas and to the bird in "Out of the Cradle." Although he reaffirmed his earlier concern for non-dialogic writing, he did so by challenging Eliot and thus projected a kind of dialogue with the poet who had called him a *miglior fabbro*. Canto LXXIV opposes a definitive apocalypse to Eliot's ambiguous mock-prophecy in "The Hollow Men" that the world would end "not with a bang but a whimper":

> yet say this to the Possum: a bang, not a whimper,
>   with a bang not a whimper
> To build the city of Dioce whose terraces are the
>   color of stars. (451)

And in Canto LXXVII Pound continued a debate with Eliot, characteristically asserting the superiority of scripture over dialogue but to some extent imitating that more dynamic, open-ended use of language.

>   mouth, is the sun that is god's mouth
> or in another connection (periplum)
> the studio on the Regent's canal
> Theodora asleep on the sofa, the young
> Damio's "tailor's bill"
> or Grishkin's photo refound years after
>   with the feeling that Mr. Eliot may have
> missed something, after all, in composing his vignette periplum

Certainly when Pound had reproduced in his printed text the Chinese ideogram for mouth and identified it with the sun, he developed only the

---

7 M. L. Rosenthal (*Sailing into the Unknown* [New York, 1978]):
    The protagonist regains his full authority after being brought down.
    He endures the symbolic death that has always been on his mind and
    accepts disastrous isolation and deprivation in a new way, while echo-
    ing his earlier self enough to make the new perspectives absolutely
    continuous with his memory and his enduring preoccupations. (p. 98).
I would argue that this sequence like moments in "Lycidas" and *Four Quartets* could be said to have tragic resonance because Pound at least to some extent realized the potential in pastoral elegy for demanding emotional and intellectual commitment from the reader by defining dialogue ("together both . . . both together") the standard model for interpretation.

literal message of Psalm 19: praise of the unique solar Text. He continued to ignore the Psalmist's compensating acknowledgment of both multiple nature and non-textual, vocal communion. And he summoned two kinds of graphic evidence, Damio's "tailor's bill" and Grishkin's "photo" in order to counter Tiresias' vocal presentation of a sordid vignette in *The Waste Land*: "the typist home at teatime . . . the young man carbuncular arrives . . . Exploring hands encounter no defense . . . (And I Tiresias have foresuffered all/ Enacted on this same divan or bed)." According to Pound, Eliot was too easily seduced by *parlar materno* and missed the eros in intercourse. But even when Pound referred to graphic documentation, he was reopening dialogue with his former friend.

Similarly, Canto LXXX suggests that Eliot might enhance his dialogic prophicies by reading translations of hieroglyphs:

> There is according to some authors a partial
>   resurrection of corpses
> on all souls day in Cairo
>   or perhaps all over Egypt
>   in identity but not atom for atom
> but the Sadduces hardly give credence
> to Mr. Eliot's version
> Partial resurrection in Cairo . . .
> centuries hoarded
> to pull up a mass of algae
>   (and pearls)
> or the odour of eucalyptus or sea wrack
>   cat-faced, croce di Malta, figura del sol
>   to each tree its own mouth and savour (531)

Pound would have none of Eliot's Christian resurrection, but here he supplied Eliot with a reference that would support such purely literary resurrections as a recurrent quotation from *The Tempest* in *The Waste Land*: "(and pearls)" recalls "those are pearls that were his eyes." And although Pound again referred to the sun as an image of clear individuality rather than circulation, "figura del sol, to each . . . its own mouth," he did so in the context of interchange with his erstwhile friend.

Two variations upon elements of Canto I elaborate this minimal acknowledgment of fraternity. If in Canto I Pound referred to Circe as a benign mistress, "Circe's this craft, the trim-coifed goddess," in Canto LXXIV he stressed her maleficence: "ac ego in harum./ so lay men in Circe's swine-sty; ivi in harum ego ac vidi cadaveres animae." Pound thus acknowledged that he had been betrayed by Circe along with his companions. And this use of the written language, Latin, paradoxically confirms a benign transformation of the narcissistic emphasis upon writing in Canto I: "Elpenor can count the shingle under Zoagli" (LXXX). In Canto I Elpenor's corpse was to lie beneath an inscription on an unidentified shore, sterile counterpart to an Odysseus who would lose all companions. But here in Canto LXXX he is resurrected as a positive image of the reader: as a capable interpreter of many pebbles on the beach near Rapallo where Pound/Odysseus was arrested.

During his solitary confinement Pound read the New Testament and came to agree with at least part of St. Paul's call for communal prophesying in 1 Corinthians 13–14, "and the greatest is charity" (461):

> to have friends come from far countries
>   is not that pleasure
> nor to care that we are untrumpeted?
>   filial, fraternal affection is the root of humaneness
>   the root of the process

He affectionately recalled particular companions whom he had lost: Ford, Yeats, and Joyce.

> Lordly men are to earth o'er given
>   these the companions:
> Fordie that wrote of giants
>   and William who dreamed of nobility
>   and Jim the comedian singing
>   "Blarney castel me darlin" (459
>
>   and for all that old Ford's conversation was better,
> consisting in *res* non *verba*
>   despite William's anecdotes, in that Fordie
>   never dented an idea for a phrase's sake
> and had more humanitas (560)

These passages give Pound's old friends the intense particularity which Canto LXXVII claimed Grishkin's photo gave Theodora. And Pound here was using the language of the Vulgate to mark a shift in allegiance from fixed inscription in photographs and hieroglyphics to conversation in the mother tongue.

Pound also paid homage to the Mother by quoting the mockingbird in "Out of the Cradle":

> meaning Whitman, exotic, still suspect
> four miles from Camden
> "O troubled reflection
>   O throat, O throbbing heart"
> How drawn, O GEA TERRA,
>   what draws as thou drawest
>   till one sink into thee by an arm's width
>
>   embracing thee, Drawest
>   truly thou drawest (56)
>
>   connubium terrae
>   mysterium . . .
>
>   three solemn half notes
>   their white downy chests black rimmed

on the middle wire
    periplum (561–62)

Here the Latin "connubium terrae" universalizes Whitman's courtship of the mother vernacular as well as nature. It is striking, however, that Pound quoted the self-obsessed bird in "Out of the Cradle" rather than the listening boy: he thereby ignored the emphasis upon exchange with which Whitman curbed his own tendency to upstage any other speaker or listener. Interpolating the characters of a second foreign script, Greek after Chinese, Pound only returned to the major Circean theme ("periplum") by reducing Whitman's bird to one of three bird-like notes on a musical score. Noman/Odysseus even acknowledges the probable result of his preference for unmouthed, hypostatized words: "But I will come out of this knowing no one/ neither they me."[8]

iii

Pound also prescribed his ultimate failure to rebuild the Temple of Jerusalem by repeatedly misreading a phrase in Mallarmé's response to alien architecture, the sonnet "Remémoration d'amis belges."

A des heures et sans que tel souffle l'émeuve
Toute la vétusté presque couleur encens
Comme furtive d'elle et visible je sens
Que se dévêt pli selon pli la pierre veuve

Flotte ou semble par soi n'apporter une preuve
Sinon d'épandre pour baume antique le temps
Nous immémoriaux quelques-uns si contents
Sur la soudaineté de notre amitié neuve

O très cheres rencontres en le jamais banal
Bruges multipliant l'aube au défunt canal

---

[8] Roy Harvey Pearce, (*The Continuity of American Poetry*) analyzes the echoes of Whitman in Canto LXXXII as evidence of Pound's "identification" with Whitman (pp. 4–8): he does not observe how Pound indicated severe *dis*continuities in American poetry by making Whitman write in Latin. Even when Pound presented a baby wasp as intermediary in another infernal conversation with Tiresias, he stressed the two strictly defined poles of the exchange: the writing/seeing I/eye and the single sun-like object of vision and writing—Aphrodite with a golden bough in Canto I.
              The infant has descended . . .
                  [to] have speech with Tiresias, Thebae
                      Cristo Re, Dio Sole . . .
              and that day I wrote no further.
This projection of *connubium terrae* misinterprets the mediatory sun/Son as a unique, exclusive patriarchal writer, and as Pound transferred the golden bough from the potently ambiguous mediator Hermes to the univocal object of reverence Aphrodite here he assigned to himself, an isolated male writer, a comment which the female member of a famous couple in Dante, Paolo and Francesca, makes about their mutual reading: "e quel giorno più non vi leggemo avante."

Avec la promenade éparse de maint cygne . . .

Sometimes and without such a rousing puff
all the decrepitude (almost color of incense
as furtively and visibly I sense
how fold by fold the widowed stone strips off)

wavers or seems in itself without evidence
except to spread, like healing balm, the time
when we immemorial someones (were) so content
with the suddenness of our new friendship's prime

O very dear ones met in this never banal
Bruges multiplying the dawn on the defunct canal
with the scattered promenade of many swans . . .

Mallarmé's sonnet pictures the decaying city of Bruges as a solemn temple
or cathedral ("la vétusté presque couleur encens . . . solennellement . . .")
in which many articulate counterparts of the new Psalmist prophesy an
ongoing conspiracy between a lecturer and an audience to regenerate the
Spirit. None of Pound's rewritings of Mallarmé's phrase "pli selon pli (fold
by fold)" offer such a complex, vital sense of interplay among many
moments in time and many persons in literary performance.

Pound modelled many passages on "pli selon pli" but each renders
an obsessive interest in repetition that is strictly opposed to the concern
for variation which Stevens and Eliot recognized in Mallarmé and developed in their turn. A passage in Canto IV sets the tone for the long series
of variations upon an unacknowledged original.

the light rains. . . .
e lo soleils plovil
The liquid rushing crystal
beneath the knees of the gods.
Ply over ply, thin glitter of waters . . .

Ply over ply
The shallow eddying fluid
Beneath the knees of the gods (19)

This does not evoke potentially alert participants in a common reflection
upon many sunrises and sunsets, the subject of Mallarmé's sonnet. It
refers rather to divine figures who are inscribed in an eternity as exclusively consistent as unmoving stone.

In Canto II an allusion to the sea-god whom Shakespeare's Lear
identifies as his prototype, "sleek head, daughter of Lir," introduces a
transformation of the natural sea into a sea of glass: "ship stuck fast in
sea-swirl"; in Canto XVII a similar transformation derives from several
variants of "pli selon pli," the phrase with which Mallarmé evoked a
genesis of renovative light from stone.

The light now, not of the sun.
Chrysoprase,

And the water green clear, and blue clear;
On, to the great cliffs of amber.
No gull-cry, no sound of porpoise,
Sand as of malachite, and no cold there
    the light not of the sun
        a boat came,
One man holding her sail,
Guiding her with oar caught over gunwale, saying:
"   There, in the forest of marble,
"   the stone trees—out of water—
"   the arbours of stone—
"   marble *leaf, over leaf*
"   silver, *steel over steel,*
"   silver beaks rising and crossing,
"   *prow set against prow,*
"   stone, *ply over ply,*
"   the gilt beams flare of an evening"
Borso, Cammagnola, the men of craft,
Thither, at one time, time after time, . . .
And the white forest of marble, bent *bough over bough,*
The bleached arbour of stone. (pp. 80–81) [italics added]

As the chrysoprase-decorated Bride Jerusalem in Revelation is a negative mirror-image of any mortal city—"and I saw no temple in the city . . . and the city has no need of sun or moon" (Revelation 21:22–3)—Pound's Venice rises from an exclusively graphic interior sea very different from the many-voiced waters of "Dry Salvages." In the *Cantos* light comes from an imagination more radically singular than that figured in Revelation by the sea of glass across which the solitary St. John hears a choral liturgy: "one man holding her sail . . . one eye for the sea, through that peek-hole." For Pound continually imitated the unhumbled, foolish stony-hearted Lear's mockery of creation *ex nihilo* in Genesis, "nothing will come of nothing" (*King Lear* I i 89). Pound's temple could only be constructed by an imagination as exclusive as that of Lear's dictatorial reincarnation of the sea god at the beginning of the tragedy ("come not between the dragon and his wrath . . ."; "ingratitude . . . more hideous . . . than the sea-monster").

The variations upon "pli selon pli" in Canto XXVII even more clearly and insistently define Pound's Venusberg/Venice as an anti-populist, totalitarian paradise:

And Tovarisch lay in the wind
And the sun lay over the wind,
And three forms became in the air . . .

      Nothing I build

Where as the wall of Eblis
At Ventadour, there now are the bees,
And in that court, wild grass for their pleasure
That they carry back to the crevice

> Where loose *stone hangs upon stone.*
> I sailed never with Cadmus,
>   lifted never *stone above stone.*" . . .
> "Baked and eaten, tovarisch my boy,
> "That is your story. And up again,
> "Up and at 'em. Laid never *stone upon stone.*" (p. 137)

Of course the three graces appear in vain to the comrade who builds nothing from nothing: the passage so thoroughly mocks a figure of the Russian masses that it justifies William Carlos Williams' description of Pound as a dictator made to Lenin's measure.[9]

The next variation on "pli selon pli" develops the initial rejection of the Mother which differentiates Pound from Eliot in Canto I.

> She is submarine, she is an octopus, she is
> A biological process.
> So Arnaut turned there
> Above him the wave pattern cut in the stone
> Spire-top alevel the well-curb
> And the tower with cut stone above that, saying:
>   "I am afraid of the life after death."
>
> and I, "but this beats me,
> Beats me, I mean that I do not understand it;
> "This love of death that is in them."
>
> The tower, ivory, the clear sky
> Ivory rigid in sunlight

Like Lear—"O! how this mother swells up . . . down . . . thy element's below" (II ii 54)—Pound challenged the natural matrix which Eliot ("Arnaut") courted as ultimately redemptive death by water.

Miming the destruction of the Albigensian ivory tower Mon Segur where Pound set his defiance of Arnaut/Eliot in Canto XXXIX, the variations upon "pli selon pli" in Canto XLVIII to some extent acknowledge limitations in Pound's emphasis of prescribed polarity.

> Falling Mars in the air
> *bough to bough,* to the stone bench
> Then the towers, high over chateau—
>
> Fell with *stroke after stroke*, jet avenger
> bent, rolled, severed, and then swallowed *limb after limb* (p. 253)

But this violently iconoclastic account of destruction in fact reinforces the idolatry of monumental fixed architecture which dominates Pound's efforts to rebuild a radically exclusive textual Temple.

In Canto XL Pound made a map for the Temple by using "ply" in another way while reiterating the familiar pattern. The Carthaginian Hanno is an Odysseus precisely opposed to the Roman Aeneas upon

---

[9] Donald Davie, *Ezra Pound: Poet as Sculptor* (New York, 1964) p. 131.

whom Dante modelled himself when he wrote in his *parlar materno*:

> that he *ply* beyond the pillars of Herakles
> 60 ships of armada to lay out Phoenician cities
>
> And by day we saw only forest
>   by night their fires
> With sound of *pipe against pipe*
> The sound *ply over ply*; *cymbal beat against cymbal*,
> The drum, wood, leather, beat, beat noise to make terror . . .
>
> One pillar of light above others
> Scorched at the sky and stars . . .
>
> Out of which things seeking an exit
> To the high air, to the stratosphere, to the imperial
> calm, to the empyrean, to the baily of the four towers
>   the ineffable crystal:
> Krxedonian Basileos
>   hung this with his map in their temple. (207–8)

Here "ply" is a verb: to voyage out beyond the pillars of Hercules—and indeed to make an exodus worthy of the Temple. Although it is sound which is ply over ply ("pipe against pipe"), the one-eyed tower of the Lir-Canto and the ivory tower of the polemic against Eliot return in the form of one Mosaic pillar of fire. All Pound's variations upon the circular *Odyssey* seek an exit from disorderly mortal experience into a transcendent temple ruled by a Platonic *Nous* as abstract as the iconoclastic Father in Scripture. The plying of this Odysseus out of the Mediterranean paradoxically imitates the exodus of Moses to which Pound opposed his attempt to rebuild Mediterranean culture. It also exaggerates the exclusionist tendencies of Hebrew iconoclasm. The "things" from which Hanno/Pound seeks an exit are manifestations of the submarine biological Mother rejected in two previous variations upon Mallarmé's "pli selon pli," the one directed against Marx (Canto XXVII), the other against Christian Eliot (Canto XXIX). "We did not take any man, but three of their women . . . we took three women/ who but snatched wd not follow their takers killed flayed, brought back their pelts into Carthage" (209). This is a horrific parody of the ineffectual apparition of the three graces to Tovarisch ("nothing I build"), but also expresses the violence of Pound the fanatical architect who challenged all manifestations of the Mother.

In yet another refolding of Mallarmé's phrase, three decadent aristocratic ladies—Italian, English, and Austrian—replace the Graces in Canto XXVII and show how the democracies imitate Hanno the rapist.

> "Sure they want war, said Bill Yeats,
> "they want all the young gals for themselves."
> That lovely unconscious world
>   *slop over slop*, and blue ribbons (213)

Mussolini challenged the democracies, "drained the muck in Vada" (210), and then caught the point of the *Cantos* "before the aesthetes had got there" (210). He thus emerges as the ideal reader of the *Cantos*, definitive alter ego to Pound, who rejected "kikery" in the most repulsive and revealing variation on Mallarmé's phrase: a variation which also indicates most clearly why Pound's foldings of text upon text do not project generative intercourse among readers.

> Democracies electing their sewage
>   till there is no clear thought about holiness
> a dung flow from 1913
> and, in this, their kikery functioned, Marx, Freud
>   and the american beaneries
>   *Filth under filth* (647)

Pound was blind to the fact that the two heirs of Moses whom he mentions, Marx and Freud—"kikery"—, tried to lead both gentiles and Jews into the same promised land of freedom from exclusive Authority which he himself had been prophesying throughout his career. And when Pound contrasted filth under filth to light over light he lost a chance to learn from Marx and Freud as well as the Jew who wrote Psalm 19 to suspect his own devotion to univocal Authority.

This eruption of filthy-minded bigotry spectacularly violates even the decorum of the most flexible literary mode. Parody permitted Eliot to confirm Mallarmé's burying of the Baudelairean sapphire-encrusted temple of correspondences in the mud, in "dung and death." But it broke under the strain which Pound imposed on it in trying to divorce light over light from filth under filth. Pound failed to become the new Whitman not because he was an anti-semite, but because his anti-semitism manifested a taste for simple dualism fatal to dialogue between poet and readers.

Since Pound developed neither the radical self-questioning of "Out of the Cradle" nor the self-sacrifice of "Hérodiade," his reiterations of binary conflict cannot successfully rival *Four Quartets*, in which Eliot demonstrated that authority must be continually regenerated by dialogue among self-critical interpreters. Pound left his challenger William Carlos Williams the task of trying to out-do Eliot in projecting a New Jerusalem with neither temple nor sun.

11

William Carlos Williams and Europe

> He claims American birth, but I strongly suspect that he emerged on
> shipboard just off Bedloe's Island and that his dark and serious eyes
> gazed up in their first sober contemplation at the Statue and its bra-
> zen and monstrous nightshirt. . . . One might accuse him of being,
> blessedly, the observant foreigner, perceiving American vegetation
> and landscape quite directly, as something put there for him to look
> at.[1]

Paterson amply justifies Pound's claim that William Carlos Williams was
always the intruding tourist. As a poet, Williams was no more exclusively
American than Eliot or Pound were European. He only learned to dramatize a distinctively American concern for dialogue between writers
and readers by achieving something like the mastery of foreign languages which he attributed to Poe.

> If there ever had been another American to use his Greek, Sanscrit,
> Hebrew, Latin, French, German, Italian and Spanish—in the text—
> with anything like the unspoiled mastery of Poe, we should have
> known, long since, what it meant to have a literature of our own.[2]

Certainly Williams announced *Paterson* as a "reply to Greek and Latin
with the bare hands" and mocked the disregard for communication in
poetry written with an eye to European tradition.

> And so about a generation ago, when under the influence of Whit-
> man the prevalent verse forms had gone to the free-verse pole, the
> countering cry of Order! Order! rewakened. That was the time of the
> new Anglo-Catholicism . . . Nothing can be simply beautiful, it must
> be so beautiful that no one can understand it *except* by the assistance
> of the cult. It must be a "mystery."[3]

But this passage from the 1929 essay "Against the Weather: A Study of
the Art" follows a criticism of Whitman in which Williams corroborated
Mallarmé's critique of free verse.

[1] Pound, "Dr. Williams' Position," first published in *The Dial*, 1928; republished in
Literary Essays, pp. 390–91.
[2] *In the American Grain* (first published, 1925) New York, 1956, p. 230.
[3] *Selected Essays of William Carlos Williams* (New York, 1954), p. 212.

Verse is measure, there is no free verse. . . . Whitman was never able
fully to realize the significance of his structural innovations. As a
result he fell back to the overstuffed catalogues of his later poems
and a sort of looseness that was not freedom but lack of measure.
Selection, structural selection was lacking.[4]

Even though Williams sometimes became strident in his Americanism
and claimed that the French were superficial readers of Poe, he followed
Mallarmé in choosing Poe as a model for rigorous self-criticism in
poetry. And, as we shall see, he ended *Paterson* by speaking French as
well as Eliot did when he punctuated *Four Quartets* with echoes of
Mallarmé more accurate and productive than Pound's variants of "pli
selon pli."[5]

Paterson bears comparison with Stevens' and Eliot's long poems.
While it sometimes justifies Poe's doubts about the long poem, many of
its dramatizations of interchange between poet and reader are strong
enough to set beside the best sequences in *Four Quartets* and "An Ordinary Evening in New Haven." For they bring the dialectic structure of
Pindar's odes up to date and reply to Greek and Latin with hands that
are far from bare.

i

Early in Book of *Paterson* Williams addressed himself: "say it!/ No
ideas but in things."[6] Most readers of *Paterson* stress the message "no
ideas but in things": a denial of the idealist distinction between mind
and matter which has characterized Western thought since Plato and
Aristotle.[7] But the *form* of Williams' subversion—"say it!"—is just as
interesting. When the poet emphatically commanded himself to deny
that there is any binary conflict to mediate, he called attention to his
linguistic medium and acknowledged that this abrupt negation is a
moment in a dialogue with readers. In *Paterson* "ideas" are generated
from complex stagings of the potential encounter between the common
reader and disparate texts ("things").

Louis Martz, an outstanding exegete of the poetry of meditation,
locates *Paterson* in Williams' mind:

---

[4] *Ibid.*, p. 212.

[5] Rosenthal, *op. cit.*, pp. 212–13: "Williams—especially in *Paterson* . . . —had far more
in common with the poetics of Eliot than with those of Pound and Yeats as well, than he
or many of his followers would ordinarily recognize."

[6] William Carlos Williams, *Paterson* (New York, 1963).

[7] See J. Hillis Miller, *Poets of Reality* (Cambridge, Mass., 1965).

> To give up the ego means to give up also those dramas of the inter-
> change of subject and object, self and world which have long been
> central in Western philosophy and literature. The poet's resignation
> puts him beyond romanticism. (p. 287)

Book V suggests that we might read *Paterson* as a kind of tapestry, woven out of memories and observations, composed by one man's imagination but written in part by his friends, whose letters are scattered throughout, by his patients, whose words are remembered throughout, and by all the milling populace of Paterson, past and present, including that unicorn in the center of the field: the King-self, within whose mind these thoughts assemble like "a flight of birds all together, seeking their nests in the season."[8]

But Williams' tapestry is woven more than in part by "patients." It continually requires that readers help reassemble the bird-thoughts of a fallen king—who is himself only insofar as he is a synecdochic personification of a large community. By presenting many aspirants to the role of mediatory Word who are still more obviously inadequate than Whitman's mockingbird, *Paterson* provokes us to counter a general lack of communication ("the language is missing them/ they die also/ incommunicado . . .").

Williams' alter ego is not articulate. Words fail N. F. Paterson ("Sam Patch") when he expects to rise like Milton's Lycidas but without the "dear might of him who walked the waves":

On the day the crowds were gathered on all sides. He appeared and made a short speech as he was wont to do. A speech! What could he say that he must leap so desperately to complete it? And plunged toward the stream below. But instead of descending with a plummet-like fall his body wavered in the air—speech had failed him. He was confused. The word had been drained of its meaning. There's no mistake in Sam Patch. He struck the water on his side and disappeared. A great silence followed as the crowd stood spellbound. (27)

The long poem can eventually project resurrection, however, because it provides for a secular equivalent of the intense recreative dialogue between the Word and his witnesses in Scripture. As Williams had the grotesque Sam Patch double his role of show-off, he had an equally bizarre minister's wife impersonate the reader.

Having ascended the flight of stairs (the Hundred Steps) Mr. and Mrs. Cummings walked over the solid ledge to the vicinity of the cataract, charmed with the wonderful prospect . . . where thousands have stood before, and where there is a fine view of the sublime curiosities of the place. When they had enjoyed the luxury of the scene for a considerable length of time, Mr. Cummings said, "My dear, I believe it is time for us to set our face homeward"; and at the same moment, turned round in order to lead the way. He instantly heard the voice of distress, looked back and his wife was gone! (24)

The text later implies a marriage-in-death between these self-destructive figures who represent the extremes of extroversion and introversion bred

8 *The Poem of the Mind: Essays on Poetry of England and America* (New York, 1966), p. 161.

by a society which derives identity from exclusive ownership.

> Patch leaped but Mrs. Cummings shrieked
> and fell—unseen— . . .
> :a body found next spring
> frozen in an ice-cake; or a body
> fished next day from the muddy swirl— (31)

We may see this tentative association of male and female bodies respectively yielded and held by the river as a prefiguration of our exchange with Williams. As readers we join him in voluntarily giving ourselves up alternately to the endless flow of the idiom and to our common urge to freeze time into crystalline significance. When the performer's and the spectator's bodies are both joined and separated, the mix of alienation and intimacy in the relationship between writers and readers is as emphatically defined the focus of interest as it is in St. John's account of the Lamb's self-sacrificial union with the crystalline Bride Jerusalem.[9]

Williams authorized his projections of a *Liebstod* between weird figures of himself and his readers by acknowledging that his experiment in secular apocalypse was inspired by a series of non-Scriptural variations upon the tense relationships between performers and audiences in Revelation. The speaker calls for inspiration that will save him from writing dead letters: "stale as a whale's breath: Breath! Breath!" (31). But as an interpolated prose-fragment notes, "the artist is an Ishmael" (40). It is in fact a whale's breath which saves *Paterson* from being stale: the long poem is structured by variations upon the domestication of Shakespearean tragedy in *Moby-Dick*. If we recognize that Williams took turns playing the indiscriminately responsive Ishmael and the compulsive show-off Ahab, we are more likely to help him rearticulate literary history and moderate Mrs. Cummings' obsession with fluid multiplicity.

Unlike the author of *Moby-Dick*, however, Williams could not expect his readers to recognize many Biblical allusions. In order to project an equivalent intensity of relationship between authority and interpreters, he had to represent both its violent and its erotic aspects more explicitly than Melville did. The dialogue of an anonymous couple provides a concentrated model for garrulous *Paterson*:

> we sit and talk
> I wish to be with you abed, we two
> as if the bed were the bed of a stream
> —I have much to say to you
>
> We sit and talk (35)

---

[9] Mary Benetta Quinn, *The Metamorphic Tradition in Modern Poetry* (New York, 1955), p. 99 notes that contemporary accounts of the accident looked forward to the "resurrection" of Patch.

Yet a poet can only compensate for the lack of generative dialogue in modern culture if he repeatedly acknowledges that poetic communication is a *coitus interruptus.* In making love with the Park upon the rock, "female to the city/ —upon whose body Paterson instructs his thoughts" (57), Paterson imitates the brash, lordly Whitman of "Song of Myself." But he is often interrupted by a female disciple who complains that he has not adequately transmitted his poetic genius to her: "the outcome of my failure with you has been the complete damming up of all my creative capacities . . ." (131). Similarly, an anonymous follower of undetermined sex, the reader, is to reanimate the tradition of erotic poetry by witnessing an apocalyptic destruction of a library which paradoxically assures its continuity:

> (breathing the books in)
> the acrid fumes
> for what they could decipher
> warping the sense to detect the norm, to break
> through the skull of custom

As in the Scriptural apocalypse which burns up the old world and its texts, "ideas" occur in the *destruction* of "things": in interchange between interpreters who challenge as much as they desire each other. But several more provocative replays of the grotesque mystic marriage of Patch and Mrs. Cummings more urgently invite us to help reconstruct a cohesive community of times and persons.

In an idyll set on a distinctly Lesbian shore, a female Corydon (the Virgilian counterpart of Thyrsis, model for Milton's uncouth swain in "Lycidas") tries in vain to make an eternal POEM with Phyllis—who also sports in the shade with Paterson.

> Here it is. This is what I've been leading up to It's called, *Corydon,*
> *A Pastoral.* We'll skip the first part, about the rocks and sheep, begin
> with the helicopter. You remember that?:
>   . . . drives the gulls up in a cloud
> Um . . . no more woods and fields. Therefore
> present, forever present (190)

The artificial controlled present of a colloquial pastoral only exposes the absurd recurrence of death, incarnated in a corpse also of indeterminate sex: "some student come/ waterlogged to the surface following/ last night's thunderstorm" (196). However, a letter from a homosexual male poet, Allen Ginsberg, ratifies the mock-marriage between "Corydon" and "Phyllis" and suggests that literary genesis does not follow the rhythms of nature but those of dialogue. As the new Lycidas' sex is uncertain, Paterson's counterpart writes exclusively neither as a son nor as a father—

> in the style of those courteous sages of yore who recognized one
> another across the generations as brotherly children of the muses. In

> Pierre and the Confidence Man my literary liking is Melville and in
> my own generation, one Jack Kerouac whose first book came out this
> year. (204)

Quoting Ginsberg's deference to one of his own primary authorities and
then his praise for a fraternal *miglior fabbro*, Williams defined reversible
exchange between poet-readers as the primary matrix of his utterance.

This definition is further established when another female image of
the reader replaces Mrs. Cummings: a "compact black bitch" greets the
godly father-son as the resurrected image of both Sam Patch and the
Lycidas-like drowned student. Williams domesticated the ancient
impulse to represent exchange between authors and interpreters even
more systematically than Melville, a literary authority he shared with
Ginsberg.

> She looks to sea, cocking her ears and,
> restless, walks to the water's edge where
> she sits down, half in the water
>> Climbing the
> bank, after a few tries, he picked
> some beach plums from a low bush and
> sampled one of them, spitting the seed out,
> then headed inland, followed by the dog (237)

Through interplay between a performer and an attentive witness, a prophetic dissemination ("spitting the seed out") challenges the alienations
of individual persons and moments prescribed by modern secular variants of Scriptural patriarchy. Unlikely Nausicaa to an Odysseus whom
Williams was trying to save from the bookshelves to which Pound's
imitations of Andreas Divus condemned him, the humble dog helps
bring home to the American shore the concern for reciprocal exchange
which animates the European literary tradition from Homer and Pindar
to Mallarmé and Celan.

Although Williams advertised the reunion of swimmer and dog as
"the eternal close of the spiral/ . . . the end," he later added two more
turns of the screw. Offering his text to two female interpreters, he more
authoritatively located himself in the European tradition—and vice-
versa. If Eliot's Tiresias throbs between the two lives of man and woman,
in *Paterson* a man/woman lives on still another Lesbian shore.

> There is a woman in our town
> walks rapidly, flat bellied
> in work slacks upon the street
> where I saw her
>> neither short
> nor tall, nor old nor young
> her
>> face would attract no
>> adolescent.

An inconspicuous decoration
made of sombre cloth, meant
I think to be a flower, was
pinned flat to her
                right
breast—any woman might have
done the same to
say she was a woman and warn
us of her mood. Otherwise
she was dressed in male attire,
as much as to say to hell
with you

I'll speak to you, alas
too late! ask
What are you doing on the
streets of Paterson? a
thousand questions:
Are you married? . . .
have you read anything that I have written?
It is all for you. (255)

Assigning the role of sexually ambiguous Tiresias to a figure of his prospective readers rather than to himself, Williams intensified Eliot's suggestion in *The Waste Land* that it is readers who are ultimately responsible for generating reconstructive dialogue from the duplicities of modern urban experience.

We are even better prepared to mediate conflicts between one and other prescribed by patriarchal Scripture when "Paterson" plays spectator to a more disturbing incarnation of ambiguity: a virgin/whore-spectator in the Unicorn tapestries at the Cloisters Museum in Manhattan.

—a fragment of the tapestry
preserved on an end wall
        presents a young woman
        with rounded brow
lost in the woods (or hiding)
        announced . . .
            (that is, the presentation)
by the blowing of a hunter's horn where he stands
        all but completely hid
        in the leaves. She
interests me by her singularity,
        her courtly dress
            among the leaves, listening!

The expression of her face,
        where she stands removed from the others
—the virgn and the whore
        an identity,
            both for sale
to the highest bidder!

>   and who bids higher
>   than a lover? Come
>   out of it if you call yourself a woman. (276)

The pictured virgin/whore is a more provocative emblem of a mutual exchange of performer- and spectator- roles than the three other sexually ambiguous figures: "Corydon," the drowned student, and the woman on the streets of Paterson. Because the girl in the tapestry is an interpreter who cannot herself be interpreted, she provokes the poet to challenge her in turn; he dares her to step out of the tapestry into the hermeneutic space which his verbal work projects. But if she is to step out of the tapestry through the text into the space in which we read it, we are to step into the textual weave and help remake modern Paterson in the image of an unorthodox medieval wedding-festival.

>   A flight of birds, all together
>   seeking their nests in the season
>   a flock before dawn, small birds
>   "that slepen al the night with open ye,"
>   moved by desire, passionately, they
>   have come a long way, commonly . . .
>   . . . the old man's mind is stirred . . .
>   Their presence in the air again
>   calms him. Though he is approaching
>   death he is possessed by many poems . . .
>   They draw him imperiously
>   to witness them . . .
>   to refresh himself
>   at the sight direct from the 12th
>   century what the old women or the young
>   or men or boys wielding their needles . . .
>   together as the cartoon has plotted it
>   for them. All together, working together,
>   all the birds together. (269)

This description of picturing and pictured groups of both sexes recalls the General Prologue of Chaucer's *Canterbury Tales*, the most familiar medieval representation of communal art. But the modern poet must exaggerate the medieval poet's interest in the interplay between the subjects and objects of interpretation if he is to establish the Unicorn tapestries as images of both Paterson and *Paterson* that can help us mediate conflicts which threaten their respective integrities.

By displacing interest from the unique performer, the Unicorn, to an ambiguous spectator, the virgin/whore, Williams to some extent legitimized his prophecy of renewed communal dialogue. Reading a medieval image of community produced *by* a community, Williams' speaker sees in one figure complementary aspects of the obsession with ownership which has corrupted Paterson and could flaw the text named for the city: the virginal ideal of individual self-sufficiency and the whorish mutual exploitation. In the virgin/whore who stands removed from the others, Williams represented the ambiguities of modern life more provocatively than he did in pairing the exhibitionist Sam Patch and the introspective Mrs. Cummings. And he thus more urgently challenged us to help transform sterile opposition into productive dialogue. If we too applaud the "working together, all together" pictured in two mutually reflecting negative images of the modern city, the Unicorn tapestries and *Paterson*, we in fact already constitute a community equivalent to the one projected by the many double negations and reversals in Revelation. When Williams used the exchange between performer and witness in a European tapestry as model for the many tensions between writer and readers which animate *Paterson*, he made it clear that the place of reconstruction is not Paterson itself and not even the poem named for the city. He located renaissance in conflict between text and readers which *Paterson* generates not only by calling attention to differences between geo-history and literature but also by representing several attempts to bridge the gaps between original and image.

Book V acknowledges that *Paterson* is as much a "world of speculation" as any of Eliot's reflections upon geographic places in *Four Quartets*. The last completed book of the poem holds up a dark allegorical mirror to the four earlier books' attempts to "say it! no ideas but in things."

> —the hunt of
>   the Unicorn and
>   the god of love
>   of virgin birth
> —shall we speak of love
>   seen only in a mirror
>   —no replica?
> reflecting only her impalpable spirit
>   which is she whom I see
>   and not touch her flesh? (272)

Eliot began his exploration of mortal temporality by acknowledging that poetry is generated in the no man's land between text and reader: "my words echo thus in your mind" ("Burnt Norton" I). Williams ended his attempt to transform Paterson into a new Jerusalem by acknowledging that an apocalyptic wedding can seem to take place *because* the artist—like the Unicorn—has "no mate . . . no peer" (246) except the reader whom he sees in the mirror of his self-reflexive text.

"Shall we speak of love/ seen only in a mirror?" In poetry we can *only* speak of love seen in a mirror: love seen but never to be touched. Williams therefore could achieve a reply to Greek and Latin with the bare hands by betraying the mission of the American bard as proclaimed in "Song of Myself": by using twelfth-century European artworks as mirrors of both Paterson and *Paterson* and defining the Unicorn as an apotheosis of "Paterson" (Sam Patch) who resembles Mallarmé's St. John far more than the King-self Walt Whitman.

The reality to which *Paterson* finally points is alien to the American marketplace and *thus* capable of finding ideas in its things.

> A WORLD OF ART
> THAT THROUGH THE YEARS HAS
> SURVIVED!
> —the museum become real
> *The Cloisters*
> on its rock
> casting its shadow—
> "la réalité! la réalité!
> la réa, la réa, la réalité!" (244)

As the Unicorn is French—French or Flemish, says Williams (274), trying to interweave the Unicorn-crucifixion with the Breughel *Nativity*— "*the Cloisters*/ on its rock/ casting its shadow" becomes real only in the form of a self-echoing exclamation in French. Similarly, Williams domesticated the regal foreign Unicorn by reporting that it has been seen on the American plains by a regal French explorer/artist:

> Audubon (Au-du-bon), (the lost Dauphin)
> left the boat
> downstream
> below the falls of the Ohio at Louisville
> to follow
> a trail through the woods
> across three states
> northward of Kentucky
> He saw buffalo
> and more
> a horned beast among the trees
> in the moonlight
> following small birds
> the chicadee
> in a field crowded with small flowers
> its neck
> circled by a crown!
> from a regal tapestry of
> stars! (246–47)

Like all early travellers in the New World, an aristocratic Frenchman would naturally make the wilderness his mirror and translate American nature into the civilized terms of traditional fables—thus anticipating in reverse Eliot's prescription of interplay between each American individual talent and the Mind of Europe. Williams had to stress the fact that vision is intersubjective in order to construct a "temple" which is not threatened but animated by the continual loss of sense in the fall and flow of language as well as time.

> that the poem the most perfect rock and temple, the high-
> est falls, in clouds of gauzy spray, should be so rivaled . . . that the
> poet in disgrace, should borrow from erudition (to unslave the mind):
> railing at the vocabulary (borrowing from those he hates, to his own
> disenfranchisement) (99)

It is because Williams consistently looked to Tradition for paradoxical readings of loss as gain that he could rival the complex idea of a reconciliation of form and flux which he found in the things of Paterson, its architecture, and its falls.

Williams finally countered the fact that what passes for common sense in America is a mechanical recycling of worn-out conventions—"the ignorant sun/ rising in the slot/ of hollow suns risen" (12)—by having his speaker read a medieval visual narrative of apocalyptic challenge and marriage as model for the genesis of community from violent questionings of individual identity. Associating himself with the obviously artificial, non-American museum-Unicorn, "Paterson" can make the fundamental problem of the American artist the ground of its resolution:

> Here
> is not there,
>   and will never be.
>   The Unicorn
> has no match
>   or mate   the artist
>   has no peer
> Death
>   has no peer:
> wandering in the woods,
>   a field crowded with small flowers
> in which the wounded beast lies down to rest
>
>   We shall not get to the bottom:
>   death is a hole
>   in which we are all buried
>   Gentile and Jew.
>
>   The flower dies down
>   and rots away
>   But there is a hole
>   in the bottom of the bag
>
>   It is the imagination
>   which cannot be fathomed.
>   It is through this hole
>   we escape
>
> So through art alone, male and female, a field of
> flowers, a tapestry, spring flowers unequaled
> in loveliness

> Through this hole
> at the bottom of the cavern
> of death, the imagination
> escapes intact.
>
> he bears a collar round his neck
> hid in bristling hair (246–47)

"Divorce is/ the sign of knowledge in our time,/ divorce! divorce!" (28). There is really no way of marrying here and there, Paterson and the Cloisters, America and Europe, life and art, life and death—readers and poet. Yet as we are all to be buried in death, both Gentile and Jew ("Gentile or Jew . . . consider Phlebas, who was once handsome and tall as you," *The Waste Land* IV), Williams' catalogue of divorces may project a common immortality even more authoritatively than Stevens' evocation of a ring of men who perish but sing to the sun. "There is a hole in the bottom of the bag . . . it is through this hole we escape. . . ." For Williams, imagination is not the constructive, esemplastic power it is for Coleridge: it is negative and *dis*integrative. As we have seen, Book V of *Paterson* mirrors both the city Paterson and itself in the tapestries that hang in a building which is in turn mirrored by the Hudson if seen from the New Jersey—the Paterson—side of the river, and reality becomes no more than shadows of images articulated in a foreign language: "la réa, la réa, la réalité." But if the Unicorn's impotent solitude reminds us that Williams' attempt to build a New Jerusalem will inevitably fail, we can redefine our common mortality—of which the immortalizing museum is the lifeless counterpart—as the principle of true community.[10]

A macabre visualization of the conflict evoked by the phrase "Gentile and Jew" helps us reflect upon a bewildering series of mirrorings in ways that project an equivalent of the templeless City in Revelation. The speaker remembers a distinctly untraditional avatar of the self-sacrificing Lamb-Unicorn "Paterson": one whom no temple, museum or library can fully domesticate.

---

[10] In *The Inverted Bell: Modernism and the Counterpoetics of William Carlos Williams* (Baton Rouge, 1974) Joseph Riddell deconstructs *Paterson* as an anticipation of Jacques Derrida's *De la Grammatologie* and reads the Cloisters tapestries according to Georges Bataille:

> As marriage is a ceremonial violation of the taboo against sexuality, and this but another example of religion as the ritualized violation of sacred laws, so are the tapestries disclosures of marriage as a transgression. (p. 286)

Williams certainly did prove that man "lives a pattern of desire that must violate its object" (p. 278) and found intercourse between reader and text no exception to the rule. But because *Paterson* continually acknowledges absurdity and represents it in terms of the mutual challenge between members of the performance, it can project a "gathering up . . . a celebration."

```
I . . .                laughed
recalling the Jew
     in the pit
        among his fellows
when the indifferent gun
        was spraying the heap
he had not yet been hit
but smiled
comforting his companions
     comforting
        his companions (26)
```

The gently smiling Unicorn matches the anonymous dying Jew, and both match not only the *Paterson*-poet and "Paterson," his chief persona, but also—potentially—Paterson itself. Initiating endless interplay among these correspondences, the text challenges us to make the museum real and to make the Spirit and the Bride Jerusalem invite us all to a wedding-supper—just as "Little Gidding" challenges us to conspire with the poet in renewing Pentecost by outrageously equating the Nazi dive-bomber with the Spirit ("the dark dove with the flickering tongue . . . the dove descending breaks the air/ With flame of incandescent terror").

Literary art can never be adequately defined because like "la réalité" it is both intertextual and intersubjective.

```
A flight of birds, all together,
seeking their nests in the season
a flock before dawn, small birds
"That slepen al the night with open ye,"
moved by desire, passionately, they
have come a long way, commonly.
Now they separate and go by pairs
each to his appointed mating. The
colors of their plumage are undecipherable
in the sun's glare against the sky
but the old man's mind is stirred
by the white, the yellow, the black
as if he could see them there. (269)
```

Isolated subjectivity can animate intersubjective community, however, if mental reflection ("the mind is the demon/ drives us" [272]) is matched by self-reflexive representations of itself: by works such as *Paterson* and the Unicorn tapestries which associate art and the communal scattering of identity in ritual sacrifice.

Certainly art imitates our possession by demonic dreams.

```
Dreams possess me
        and the dance
            of my thoughts
involving animals
        the blameless beasts (261)
```

> Though he is approaching
> death he is possessed by many poems. (269)

But artistic play differs from the dream-work in that it occurs *between* subjects—"my words echo thus in your mind" Eliot said—and is composed not of ideas but things: words, paint, threads. The Unicorn-like pure reality which can cure the corruption of Paterson, N.J., comes from the materials of art, not from some transcendent Platonic realm of ideas.

> Pollock's blobs of paint squeezed out
> with design!
> pure from the tube. Nothing else
> is real (248–49)

> The Unicorn roams the forest of all true
> lovers' minds. They hunt it down. Bow wow!
> sing hey the green holly!

> —every married man carries in his head
> the beloved and sacred image
> of a virgin
> whom he has whored
> but the living fiction
> a tapestry
> silk and wool shot with silver threads
> a milk-white one-horned beast (272)

Of course the Unicorn is an image reflected in as many minds as are activated by desire ("roams the forest of all true lovers' minds"). But that desire is to be articulated by objective, material prefigurations of wholeness ("the living fiction/ a tapestry/ silk and wool shot with silver threads").

Yet such an objective prefiguration of mental reflection can allow the museum to become real only because it is an image *of* witnessing. "In a field with small flowers/ its neck circled by a crown/ from a regal tapestry of stars" the Unicorn is chiefly characterized by his own visible gentle eye, as regal as the "Dauphin" Audubon, witness to a New World:

> lying wounded on his belly
> legs folded under him
> the bearded head held
> regally aloft (246)

As the four living creatures seen across the sea of glass in Revelation prefigure the perfect, foursquare City because they have eyes within and all around, the silver, silk and wool Unicorn in the Cloisters tapestries reflects his counterpart across the actual sea in the Musée de Cluny: the beast who is captured by the Lady when he is reflected in her mirror.

> —shall we speak of love
> seen only in a mirror

> —no replica?
> reflecting only her impalpable spirit?
>   which is she whom I see
>   and not touch her flesh? (272)

"Paterson's" totemic image thus generates not only recollection of intensely visible destruction—in effect a blinding—but also of a thrusting *counter*-sign to his fallen horn.

> silk and wool shot with silver threads
>   a milk-white one horned beast
>   I, Paterson, the King-self
> saw the lady
>   through the rough woods
>   outside the palace walls
> among the stench of sweating horses
>   and gored hounds
>   yelping with pain
> the heavy breathing pack
>   to see the dead beast
>   brought in at last
> across the saddlebow
>   among the oak trees.
>   Paterson,
>   keep your pecker up
>   whatever the detail! (272–73)

The elaborate display of the Unicorn's regal impotence makes regal "Paterson" potent. For like *Paterson* as well as the highly concentrated first-person account of sacrifice in Mallarmé's "Cantique de St. Jean" it makes its interpreters undergo the potentially creative alienation of self-criticism. And as I will observe in a final essay, at least one contemporary American interpreter of European tradition—not only verbal but also visual—has elaborated Williams' last strategy of talking about himself by analyzing an exquisitely crafted image of self-contemplation so intense that it recalls the Lamb's self-sacrifice.

12

The Reader is the Medium:
Ashbery and Ammons

> The reader is the medium by which one
> work of art judges another.
> —A. R. Ammons, *Sphere*

Both first published in 1974, "Self-Portrait in a Convex Mirror" by John Ashbery and *Sphere* by A. R. Ammons develop Stevens' attempt to construct an apocalyptic "festival sphere" in "An Ordinary Evening in New Haven." Both poems project secular equivalents of the New Jerusalem in Revelation. But whereas Ashbery primarily develops elements in Stevens which the latter shares with Mallarmé, Ammons emulates Stevens' other master, Whitman—unfortunately more the braggart bard of "Song of Myself" than the reflective elegist of "Out of the Cradle."[1]

Like Mallarmé, Ashbery continually acknowledges that he performs on this side of the dark mirror evoked by St. John's great precursor in letter-writing, St. Paul: "for now we see through a glass, darkly; but then face to face." In contrast, like the Whitman of "Song of Myself," Ammons claims to achieve transcendent face-to-face meetings. As Williams contradicted his announced intention of replying to Greek and Latin with bare hands when he completed *Paterson* by reading a visual equivalent of Revelation, the apocalyptic Unicorn tapestries, Ashbery contemplates a half-sphere made by the late Renaissance painter Parmigianino. He invites his readers to complete a full revolution of time and language by continually reflecting upon the *im*perfection of both visual original and textual parody. Ammons keeps his hands bare, however, and challenges his readers to help him break the textual mirror and

---

[1] This is to qualify Harold Bloom's reading of Ashbery—along with Stevens—as exclusively American. In "The Breaking of Form" in *Deconstruction and Criticism* Bloom calls Ashbery "like Stevens a profoundly Whitmanian poet, frequently despite appearances." Both Stevens and Whitman are ancestral presences in "Self Portrait." And in "John Ashbery: the Charity of the Hard Moments" in *Contemporary Poetry in America* ed. Robert Boyers (New York, 1974) Bloom declares that "Ashbery goes back through Stevens to Whitman" (p. 110) but that Ammons descends from Emerson. Indeed he states that Ashbery is "in temperament, more like Whitman than Stevens . . . even the French poet he truly resembles is the curiously Whitmanian Apollinaire" (p. 112).

achieve a "united/capable nation and a united nations" without making sustained reference to another work of art or subjecting his own aspirations to very rigorous critical analysis.

Both Ashbery and Ammons have been accused of making texts which are "fabrics of solipsism" in which "self-consciousness substitutes for subject matter."[2] But at least in "Self-Portrait" and quite often in *Sphere* these poets construct common places for recreative criticism of common sense. Certainly they explore what Roger Shattuck has mocked as an "Einsteinbergian" (Einstein & Saul Steinberg) universe of poetic reflections upon poetry.[3] And some of their other works may be vulnerable to the charge of willful obscurantism. "Self-Portrait" and much of *Sphere*, however, invite us to help reexamine clichés of perception and expression in ways that show how limited and limiting their denigrators' positions can be.[4]

Yet when Ashbery reflects upon a painting of a reflection, like Williams he draws upon a major resource which Ammons rejects to his own disadvantage. Like Revelation, "Self-Portrait" attempts to control the "shananigans . . . in the lingo" (*Sphere*, section 154) by referring to visual constructions which not only call attention to the fact that a text is a visual object but also define this as ground for intersubjective exchange.

i

Earlier long poems by Ashbery and Ammons, *Three Poems* and "Hibernaculum" anticipate the contrasting dramatizations of reading in "Self-Portrait" and *Sphere*.

In "The New Spirit," the first of the *Three Poems* (New York, 1972), Ashbery projects an unconventional order of governance and definition.

---

[2] John Romano, "The New Laureates" *Commentary* LX (1975), 54–58.

[3] "Poet in the Wings," (review of *Houseboat Days*) *New York Review of Books* March 23, 1978. Shattuck cites approvingly two attacks upon the self-enclosure of contemporary poetry already mentioned in the notes to Chapter One: Wendell Berry, "The Specialization of Poetry," *Hudson Review* (1975) and Christopher Clausen, "The Decline of Anglo-American Poetry," *Virginia Quarterly Review* LIV (1978), 73–86.

[4] In "The Prophetic Ashbery," *Beyond Amazement: New Essays on John Ashbery* ed. David Lehman (Ithaca, 1980), Douglas Crase defends Ashbery from the charge of narcissism, characterizing him as a critic of the narcissism that sustains American public discourse.

> The difficulty with Ashbery is that his poetry is *so* public, so accurately a picture of the world we live in, that it scarcely resembles anything we have ever known. . . . Of the poets I know, Ashbery is the most ruthlessly available to the present. . . . The poet [is] at work on an attitude that in fact diminishes the scope of the American self. How to get loose from our narrow predicament? Why, one need only style the self as the exiguous facture it truly is. (pp. 30, 32, 64)

> Do these things between people partake of
> themselves, or are they a subtler kind of
> translucent matter carrying each to a compromise
> distance painfully outside the rings of authority? (p. 10)

Ashbery would violate his sustaining respect for the potential in dialogue
if he asserted it other than in a question. For he depends upon readers'
resistance to cultural, linguistic and literary syntax.

> I as I seem to you, you as you are to me, an
> endless game in which the abraided memories
> are replaced progressively by the new empty-
> headed forms of greeting. Even as I say this
> I seem to hear you and see you wishing me well,
> your eyes taking in some rapid lateral development . . .
>   . . . reading without comprehension
> and always taken up in the reel of what is
> happening in the wings. Which becomes a medium
> through which we address one another, the
> independent life we were hoping to create. (pp. 12–13)

Now that drama ("wings") has largely given way to film ("takes up on
the reel . . ."), collaborative creation can take place if each of us
acknowledges not only that his reading excludes others ("I as I seem to
you, you as you are to me"), but also that in an advanced technological
culture all attempts to create "independent life" must reckon with the
fact that discourse is increasingly controlled by impersonal mechanical
and electronic systems.

But the poem named for the apparent enemy of creative independence, "The System," defines the Scriptural concern for individual identity as an equal and opposite danger.

> No, what was wanted and was precisely lacking
> in this gay salubrious desert was an end to
> the "end" theory whereby each man was both an
> idol and the humblest of idolaters, in other
> words the antipodes of his own universe,
> his own redemption or his own damnation,
> with the rest of the world as a painted back-
> drop to his own monodrama of becoming of
> which he was the lone impassioned spectator. (p. 64)

The poet can challenge the tendency for solipsism in the private reading
which Luther and Calvin taught Americans to value if he repeatedly
observes that any system of signification at once determines individual
utterances and is continually modified in dialogue.

> The person sitting opposite you who asked you
> a question is still waiting for the answer;
> he has not yet found your hesitation unusual,
> but it is up to you to grasp it with both

hands, wrenching it from the web of connectives
to rub off the grime that has obscured its
brilliance so as to restore to him, that pause
which is the answer you have both been
expecting. (p. 97)

And because Ashbery defines poetry as uncompleted mutual questioning, he can end the third poem, "The Recital," by imitating the Prospero-Stevens who addresses a congregation at the end of "The Auroras of Autumn."

The performance had ended, the audience streamed
out: the applause still echoed in the empty
hall. But the idea of the spectacle as something
to be acted out and absorbed still hung in
the air long after the last spectator had
gone home to sleep. (p. 118)

This reconciliation of objective system and intersubjective reading precisely contrasts with one in Ammons' rehearsal for *Sphere*.

Near the end of "Hibernaculum," Ammons gives away one of the best kept secrets of his attempts to project universal openness. He falls prey to the kind of melancholy which Ashbery regularly accepts as vivifying ground of both writing and reading.

The world seems to me a show closed down,
a circus left standing: the ropes slack,
the loose tent bellies and whomps in the wind
like a scared gigantic jellyfish: some stragglers
are around but they are turned inward on their
purposelessness: they make up directions that
go nowhere: they turn missing corners:

the clown's paint has worn off: his rags have become
rags: his half-bald wig has become his head,
        his falls
have become his tricks: he now clowns to the universe.
                              (*Selected Longer Poems*, p. 93)

Although Ammons makes many extravagant gestures to his readers, when he clowns to the universe he most often seems absolutely alone in the midst of endless multiplicity. Like Pound, he frequently fails to acknowledge that he depends upon at least the ghostly echo of an audience's applause.

ii

"Self-Portrait in a Convex Mirror" contemplates a half-sphere which the Mannerist painter Parmigianino had made to counterfeit his reflection in a convex mirror.

As Parmigianino did it, the right hand
Bigger than the head, thrust at the viewer
And swerving easily away, as though to protect
What it advertises.
              Vasari says, "Francesco one day set himself
To take his own portrait, looking at himself
              for that purpose
In a convex mirror, such as is used by barbers . . .
He accordingly caused a ball of wood to be made
By a turner, and having divided it in half and
Brought it to the size of the mirror he set himself
With great art to copy all that he saw in the glass,"
Chiefly his own reflection, of which the portrait
Is the reflection once removed.
The glass chose to reflect only what he saw
Which was enough for his purpose: his image
Glazed, embalmed, projected at a 180° angle. (69)

If Parmigianino's self-portrait in a convex mirror makes the viewer stand
in for the artist who took the viewer's role in relation to himself, as
viewer of the Parmigianino Ashbery stands in for all of us who read his
various attempts to see himself in another convex self-portrait. But each
analogy in this complex system has its corresponding antithesis. Ashbery
can engage in productive dialogue with Parmigianino only because he
resists the temptation fully to identify with him. And the reader must
avoid trying to identify with Ashbery if he wishes to open productive
dialogue with his text.

As the distortions in the painted image call attention to the surface
on which it is painted, Ashbery's text in turn calls attention to its own
problematic surface.

But your eyes proclaim
That everything is surface. The surface is what's there
And nothing can exist except what's there. (70)

The Moebius-strip world that Ashbery shares with Einstein (and, indeed,
Steinberg) refuses distinctions which animate both Cartesian rationality
and Romantic efforts to subvert it: distinctions between core and surface,
inner and outer, one and many, then and now, here and there. But
Ashbery authorizes a positive reading of that subversion by taking dialogue as model, standard, and origin of reality.

And just as there are no words for the surface, that is,
No words to say what it really is, that it is not
Superficial but a visible core, then there is
No way out of the problem of pathos vs. experience.
Your gesture which is neither embrace nor warning
But which holds something of both in pure
Affirmation that doesn't affirm anything. (70)

When we either speak with another human subject or interpret an art
object we cannot clearly separate our own experience from intimations
we have of another's experience ("pathos"). And in such exchanges the
major poles are not "yes" and "no" but "you" and "I": deciders rather
than decisions.

Ashbery is no Romantic: he does not look at himself in a mirror in
order to explore inner depths. Rather, "*the glass* chose to reflect" (68):
"what is novel is the extreme care in rendering/ The velleities of the
rounded reflecting surface" (74). And the text imitates an ironic, joking
identification of *another* artist with a viewer which calls more attention
to the interface between artist and viewer than to either pole of the
intersubjective exchange: the primary subject of the convex self-portrait
in Vienna is its imitation of a mirror. As Sydney Freedberg notes in his
Parmigianino (Cambridge, Mass., 1950), the painting lacks the scientific
detachment of unreflective, impersonal mimesis.

> this man who
> "dabbled in alchemy, but whose wish
> Here was not to examine the subtleties of art
> In a detached, scientific spirit: he wished through them
> To impart the sense of novelty and amazement to
>   the spectator"
> (Freedberg)   (74)

Correspondingly, the subject of the new convex self-portrait is its imitation
of that imitation of a mimetic medium. But the shifting of focus away from
individual persons to objective interpersonal medium serves warm intersubjective play rather than cold analysis. Imparting a sense of novelty and
amazement, it communicates a virtuoso's delight in showing off.[5]

---

[5] Although I thoroughly agree with David Kalstone (*Five Temperaments*, New York,
1977) that "in the distorting self-portrait of Parmigianino Ashbery found the perfect mirror and the perfect antagonist—a totem of art and the past caught in the act of trying to
escape from itself," I question his definition of the mind as the "place" privileged in
Ashbery's poem.

> The blurring of personal pronouns, their often indeterminate refer-
> ence, the clouding of landscapes and crystal balls, are all ways of
> trying to be true not only to the mind's confusions but also to its resis-
> tance to stiffening formulations. (p. 183)

"Self-Portrait in a Convex Mirror" presents itself as taking place in the midst of heavily
mediated intercourse among several minds, notably those of Parmigianino, Ashbery and
the reader. Indeed Alan Holder, *A. R. Ammons* (New York, 1978) attributes to *Sphere* an
attitude which—with a small but significant emendation—might be applied to "Self-
Portrait."

> It can be said that as the poem unfolds, we find Ammons like Milton's
> Satan, praising the power of mind to create its own place. But at the
> same time, Ammons feels something deeply wrong about thus dismiss-
> ing creation as it exists, a given, a thing independent of mind's
> liquifying and arsonous acts. (151–52)

Indeed, Ashbery's isolation of artistic self-reflexiveness from common life serves to show up the *lack* of potential for charity and community in the naive mimesis to which his challengers would have poetry return.

> you could be fooled for a moment
> Before you realize the reflection
> Isn't yours. You feel then like one of those
> Hoffmann characters who have been deprived
> Of a reflection, except that the whole of me
> Is seen to be supplanted by the strict
> Otherness of the painter in his
> Other room. We have surprised him
> At work, but no, he has surprised us
> As he works. (74)

Addressing the reader as "Parmigianino" addresses the viewer, "Ashbery" alludes to literary tradition (". . . one of those Hoffmann characters") to register negative, privative, and divisive aspects of the visual rhetoric which his text elaborates ("you feel like one of those . . . who have been deprived of a reflection"). He honors that strategy's positive, unifying power, however, by substituting "the whole of *me*" for the "you" deprived of a reflection. And he confirms this implicit inclusion of readers in a positive community by continuing the meditation in the first-person plural. Yet even in offering an external analogue to the reciprocity which he supposedly enjoys with readers ("we have surprised him . . . he has surprised us") he presents the relationships "Parmigianino"-ourselves and "Ashbery"-ourselves as not only analogous but also competing: "except that. . . ." Such provocative turns and counter-turns ensure that this intensively self-referential text can challenge the narcissism concealed in conventional formulations of identity.

But like Milton's uncouth elegist, Ashbery's speaker effectively gestures toward his potential readers by having his speaker address an angel-like—"rather angel than man [Vasari]" (73)—figure of their shared obligation to interpret elusive signs.

Ashbery too refers to a creation independent of the mind's water and fire, but a creation which is artistic rather than natural: Parmigianino's self-portrait, the perfect antagonist indeed. In a review of *Houseboat Days* more sympathetic than Shattuck's, Calvin Bedient nicely explains why "Self-Portrait" saves Ashbery from his characteristic pitfalls, "at one extreme a programmatically empty manner, at the other, a flatteringly explicit interest in his manner as the matter of the poem":

> Ashbery is precisely a poet of "otherness." Few objects ever in the
> world could be so well calculated to release his divinatory powers as
> this particular painting. Where else would he find equal exterior
> provocation? ("The Tactfully Folded-Over Bill" in *Parnassus* VI [fall/
> winter, 1977], 161–69, pp. 163–64, 165)

I am arguing, however, that the much-needed "exterior provocation" of the Parmigianino is strong enough to organize the whole poem, not only the first ninety-nine lines which Bedient singles out for praise.

Whose curved hand controls,
Francesco, the turning seasons and the thoughts
That peel off and fly away at breathless speeds
Like the last stubborn leaves ripped
From wet brenches? I see in this only the chaos
Of your round mirror which organizes everything . . .
I feel the carousel starting slowly
And going faster and faster: desk, paper, books,
Photographs of friends, the window and the trees
Merging in one neutral band that surrounds
Me on all sides, everywhere I look. (71)

As we have seen, it is because Parmigianino was more interested in the rounded reflecting surface than in his own punctual identity that it has enough *will* of its own to have "velleities": if in the beginning "the glass chose," "it is your round mirror which organizes everything around the polestar of your eyes." The virtuoso Parmigianino has hyperbolically honored the medium of his art by thrusting the painted imitation of a reflective surface at the viewer even more aggressively than the image of the hand that transferred the whole image from a glass half-sphere to wood turned for counterfeiting. *Consequently* the modern counter-counterfeiter can attribute to his and our alter ego an organizational, syntactic power which can make provisional sense of time—the only medium of human existence of which we are all more continually aware than we are of language. Pretending to take literally the painting's transformation of the viewer into "Parmigianino," the several-centuries-younger artist takes its spatial form as model for a corroboration of Einstein's theory that space and time are relative because space is curved—variously, irregularly, depending upon point of view. But the speaker later acknowledges that the distance between himself as viewer and Parmigianino as viewed by *him*self is not what it first appears, a "straight way out" (71) of the isolation to which each is condemned by his dependence upon ocular globes that distort relative dimensions.

The speaker still more urgently invites us—Parmigianino's alternative doubles—to help make a verbal translation of the picture in Vienna when he challenges the painter to survive further turns and counter-turns of artistic development.

But something new is on the way, a new preciosity
In the wind. Can you stand it,
Francesco? Are you strong enough for it?
This wind brings what it knows not, is
Self-propelled, blind, has no motion
Of itself. (75)

Acknowledging that the history of art and literature is as influential a medium of exchange between interpreters as the painted or printed surface,

the speaker prepares to intensify his strategy of reconstructing communi-
cative identity by deconstructing common-sense definitions. The blindness
of time is its "negative side" but

> its positive side is
> Making you notice life and the stresses
> That only seemed to go away, but now,
> As this new mode questions, are seen to be
> Hastening out of style. (75–76)

Yet still more insistent acknowledgment of temporal relativity is required
to establish Parmigianino's meta-painting as a prophetic metaphor for
modern space/time.

> Your argument, Francesco,
> Had begun to grow stale as no answer
> Or answers were forthcoming. If it dissolves now
> Into dust, that only means its time had come
> Some time ago but look now, and listen:
> It may be that another life is stocked there
> In recesses no one knew of; that it,
> Not we, are the change; that we are in fact it
> If we could get back to it, relive some of the way
> It looked, turn our faces to the globe as it sets
> And still be coming out all right:
> Nerves normal, breath normal. Since it is a metaphor
> Made to include us, we are a part of it and
> Can live in it as in fact we have done,
> Only leaving our minds bare for questioning
> We now see will not take place at random
> But in an orderly way that means to menace
> Nobody—the normal way things are done,
> Like the concentric growing up of days.
> Around a life: correctly, if you think about it. (76)

The Vienna picture stands as an authoritative metaphor for the reflexivities
of consciousness and signification because Ashbery in turn has made a metaphor to include it and us as well as himself. "If you think about it."
According to this text, the reading of poetry is far more than overhearing
someone else reflect upon his own experience. It is not even listening to
someone else reflect upon yet another person's experience ("pathos") and
helping him convert it into his own. Rather, it is listening to someone else
reflect upon another person's failure to subject his medium to his own will
and helping him read that failure as an opportunity to prove that diverse
moments and persons can form vital communities if each continually demonstrates that he or it is both like and unlike all the others.

    As we have seen, Stevens' "New Haven" hangs pendent in a dis-
affected eye like the new Jerusalem seen across a sea of glass in Revelation ("not that which is but that which is apprehended,/ A mirror, a lake

of reflections in a room,/ A glassy ocean lying at the door," "An Ordinary Evening in New Haven" V). Ashbery, however, does not project the regaining of a natural paradise but the construction of a shadow-city of interpretation whose otherness and self-reflexivity can inspire self-criticism and compassion in any real city.

> The shadow of the city injects its own
> Urgency! Rome where Francesco
> Was at work during the Sack: his inventions
> Amazed the soldiers who burst in on him;
> They decided to spare his life, but he left soon after;
> Vienna where the painting is today, where
> I saw it with Pierre in the summer of 1959; New York
> Where I am now, which is a logarithm
> Of other cities. Our landscape
> Is alive with filiations, shuttlings;
> Business is carried on by look, gesture,
> Hearsay. It is another life to the city,
> The backing of the looking glass of the
> Unidentified but precisely sketched studio. It wants
> To siphen off the life of the studio, deflate
> Its mapped space to enactments, island it.
> That operation has been temporarily stalled
> But something new is on the way, a new preciosity
> In the wind. Can you stand it,
> Francesco? (75)

Another life to the city which presses in upon the self-isolating artefact, the "landscape" of interpretation threatens the object's integrity. But because the luminous half-sphere is doubly challenged—by various time/places of viewing as well as by the violent Sack of Rome which its calm originally opposed—it can achieve the conjugal force of alternative Scriptural symbols of community: the bridegroom-sun in Psalm 19 and the Bride-City in Revelation. (Ashbery of course makes no direct allusion to either moment in Scripture, but the complex meditation upon relations between art object and various communities which dominates the last two-thirds of the poem would seem to derive from Stevens' reconstructive parodies of Revelation in "An Ordinary Evening in New Haven.")

Because the only room for Parmigianino's soul is "our moment of attention" (69)—wherever, whenever, whoever we are—the bright Parmigianino-like "Ashbery" can make room in his merely provisional hemisphere for all kinds of time/places. These are defined by varying degrees of commonness and uncommonness, receptivity and challenge: as disorderly as Rome where Parmigianino painted, as neatly catalogued as museum-Vienna where Ashbery and a friend viewed the painting, and as supremely integrative as logarithm-New York where Ashbery attempted to write us into his text. "Self-Portrait" does not primarily portray Ashbery or even his poem but the potential for any painting or any text to provoke comparisons of persons, moments, and places— comparisons so subversive of conventions of identity that they imply an apocalyptic or utopian City of Mutual Discourse like that which Geoffrey Hartman finds projected by various new approaches to reading.[6] Our landscape is "alive . . . another life to the city" *because* it is made up of continual interdependent subjective transformations and reinterpretations. *Because* its filiations and shuttlings are animated by fallible, inauthentic looks, gestures and hearsay they can stand the test of time. No single artist—neither Parmigianino nor Ashbery—can stand and be strong enough for the continual challenge of future reading and counter-reading; only a text as continually irreverent of exclusive defini- tions of readers as well as of authors can meet this challenge.

Of course Ashbery is lucid and precise when he collaborates in the filiations and shuttlings of interpretation which want to "island" and "deflate" any studio. His definition of New York as a logarithm of *other* cities is an exact mirror-inversion of his definition of multiple response to the work of art as *another* life to *the* city. If we really "think about it," if we contemplate the otherness of art with sufficient intensity to find life in it, we not only serve—to use Ammons' terms—as the medium by which one work of art judges another. Allowing the New York poem to judge the Vienna painting, we can also better confront and even challenge the domi- nance of impersonal prescriptive system over individual freedom in New York or any of the actual cities for which it can serve as exponential stan- dard ("logarithm"). For in mediating between original and very free imita- tion, we develop a strong awareness that even widely separated times and persons can engage in mutually transforming dialogue.

The penultimate allusion to "the city" in "Self-Portrait" more strongly suggests that by locating any particular work in a much wider landscape of interpretation we can project an equivalent of the New Jerusalem which St. John on his island of Patmos saw descend from heaven.

> it is certain that
> What is beautiful seems so only in relation to a
> specific
> Life, experienced or not, channeled into some form
> Steeped in the nostalgia of a collective past.
> The light sinks today with an enthusiasm
> I have known elsewhere, and known why
> It seemed meaningful, that others felt this way
> Years ago. (77)
> the look
> Some wear as a sign makes one want to
> Push forward ignoring the apparent

---

6 Hartman, *The Fate of Reading*, p. 13.

Naïveté of the attempt, not caring
That no one is listening, since the light
Has been lit once and for all in their eyes
And is present, unimpaired, a permanent anomaly,
Awake and silent. On the surface of it
There seems no special reason why that light
Should be focused by love, or why
The city falling with its beautiful suburbs
Into space always less clear, less defined,
Should read as support of its progress. (77–78)

If Ashbery's reflections upon the velleities of the rounded surface ("on the surface of it") make us want to go out of ourselves enough to greet an individual figure of the collective past such as "Parmigianino," the very lack of definition of many *other* cities which shadow the painted studio/island can look like the beautiful Bride-City descending from heaven in Revelation—a city which focuses and supports the development of love.[7]

But Ashbery can authorize this reading of tradition as a City of Mutual Discourse only if he develops St. John's strategy of parodic reflection. As several grotesque mockeries of the bridegroom—including a beast who has horns like a lamb but speaks like a dragon—establish the authority of the Lamb-Reader, the contemporary John establishes his own authority as a reader/writer of complex images by mocking his own quietly mocking iconoclasm.

"Play" is something else;
It exists, in a society specifically
Organized as a demonstration of itself.
There is no other way, and those assholes
Who would confuse everything with their mirror games
Which seem to multiply stakes and possibilities, or
At least confuse issues by means of an investing
Aura that would corrode the architecture

---

[7] Laurence Lieberman, "Unassigned Frequencies: Whispers out of Time," *American Poetry Review*, 1977, reprinted in *Unassigned Frequencies* (Urbana, 1977) quotes "business is carried on . . ." out of context in order to advance his reading of the poem as an affirmation of the poet's power to wrail against a commercial society—an opposition so simple that it entirely ignores the complex relationship which the passage sets up among venerable art objects, cities primarily associated with different historical moments, and the interpreters and modes of interpretation associated with each city.

> In every age, the city has been hostile to the artist, as well as to the dream-life of which he is the overseer and caretaker. The modern city is worse. Not only does it try to squelch the artist, and thereby to starve the roots of its own dream-life: it would also ignore the great past—its weapon, total cultural amnesia. The business life in its obsession with speed and efficiency, muffles the living nuance, the surviving residues—shades, hues, accents, tones—of other best lives that transpired in this topography. (p. 41)

Of the whole in a haze of suppressed mockery,
Are beside the point. They are out of the game,
Which doesn't exist until they are out of it. (79–80)

One of those "assholes" of self-reflexive, apparently auto-erotic literature,
Ashbery invites us to reinvest aura by helping him do "something else." We
are to help build a city by the measure of an estranged, architecture-
corroding *angelos*: a man who not only has no identity except as a transmitter of messages but also distorts all the messages he transmits. The "city"
to be constructed is a profane new New York rather than a new Jerusalem,
made in the lunatic image of a self-deforming poet who finally mocks his
alter ego "Parmigianino" as an insect no less demonic and divided than
Kafka's metamorphosed Gregor Samsa.

Parmigianino has appeared "rather angel than man (Vasari)" (73)
but he is finally only an insect-eye in a convex mirror:

Therefore I beseech you, withdraw that hand,
Offer it no longer as shield or greeting,
The shield of a greeting, Francesco:
There is room for one bullet in the chamber:
Our looking through the wrong end
Of the telescope as you fall back at a speed
Faster than that of light to flatten ultimately
Among the features of the room . . .
We have seen the city; it is the gibbous
Mirrored eye of an insect. (82–3)

The shadowing of the global room/city in the Vienna "self-portrait" in
three stages of interpretation—by Parmigianino in Rome, by Ashbery
and Pierre in Vienna, by "Ashbery" and the reader in "New York"—has
indeed made the painted Parmigianino recede faster than light, Einstein's measure of energy and time. Because the text thoroughly mocks
the painter as well as his poet-imitator, along with its author we are
finally free to reject the relative confinement of even this extraordinarily
spacious convex self-portrait.

How is it, after all, that the Vienna painting and the New York
poem themselves become logarithms of *other* cities whose "forms retain
a strong measure of ideal beauty" (73)? Ashbery has already told us that
it is because "they forage in secret on our idea of distortion" (73). Only
because the textual self-portrait so consistently calls attention to the distorting effects of art as well as consciousness can it move us "out of the
dream and into its codification" (73): out of the unexamined illusion of
life and into thoroughly examined illusions of art.

iii

In *Sphere* Ammons mocks Ashbery's identification of New York as a
"logarithm of other cities" and his taste for "mirrorments."

most of our writers live in New York City
densely: there in the abstractions of squares and glassy
floors they cut up and parcel out the nothingness they

think America is. (38)

but the mirrorments, astonishments of mind,
what are they to the natural phenomena, the gross
          destructions
that give life, we cooling here and growing on a
          far outswing

of the galaxy, the soaring, roaring sun in its thin-cool
texture allowing us . . . (45)

If Ashbery's allegories contemplate a man-made, visual imitation/reflection of a man-made reflective hemisphere, Ammons' mimesis celebrates both the great globe itself and its primary mediator, mind.

if one follows the western
littoral of Africa northward, one moves up past
          Walvis Bay
to Sorris and, rounding out westward and turning back

again, to Beguela and Lobito and then way on up,
          swerving
out again slightly westward . . .
one turns into the other side of the world . . .

          mind, many-sided, globe-like,
rich whith specification and contrariety, is secure from
slogans, fads, starved truths, and propaganda—
          defeats itself,
meanwhile shoring itself up with sight and insight:
          how to
devise a means that assimilates small inspirations into a

large space, network, reticulation complex (almost
          misleading)
but moved forward by a controlling motion, design,
          symmetry,
suasion, so that harmony can be recognized in the
          highest

ambience of diversity

If Ashbery calls up Leviathan as the singularly rendered hand of a single dead artist—

Francesco, your hand is big enough
To wreck the sphere, and too big . . .
(Big, but not coarse, merely on another scale,
Like a dozing whale on the sea bottom . . . (70)

Ammons multiplies Leviathan as if he were the Ishmael of "A Squeeze of the Hand" in *Moby-Dick*, or the Whitman of "The Sleepers."

all the people asleep with
me in sleep, melted down, mindlessly interchangible
resting with a hugeness of whales dozing (43)

Indeed Ammons baldly declares his large intention: "I want, like Whitman, to found a federation of loveship" (66).

Yet *Sphere* is moved by many self-qualifying reflections upon art
like those which shape Ashbery's half-sphere—and Whitman's own un-
typically self-critical "Out of the Cradle." Having dismissed "mirrorments" in favor of "the soaring, roaring sun," for instance, Ammons'
speaker may assure us that we can throw sunrise out of ourselves like
Whitman's "Myself": "we are as in a/ cone of ages: each of us stands in
the peak and center/ of perception" (47). But he authorizes this assur-
ance by qualifying it as carefully as Ashbery would.

but then
the base widens dropping back and down in time through

the spinal stars of spirals and deepens broadening into
the core of our configuration with its ghostly other side:
and then gulfs and deepenings begin and fall away

through glassy darkness and shadowy mind. (47–48)

Like the *con*trivance by the "spectre of the spheres" in Stevens' "Auroras of
Autumn," *Sphere* is thrown out as *"our* configuration." If Ashbery celebrates "another life to the city/ The backing of the looking glass" (75), Ammons' sphere is the "ghostly other side" of many turns and counter-turns
toward and away from a long literary tradition of figuring the reading as
well as the writing of poetry. Indeed, *Sphere* can appear a solar orb
because it is primarily moved by invitations and challenges to a large
potential readership.

Early and late, *Sphere* recalls the Psalmist's claim that the heavens
declare the glory of God in order to declare itself an experiment in "religion" (*re-ligere*, to bind).

around us, in the immediate area of recent
events, the planets make quickly-delivered news
and the sun
acquaints us of its plumes eight minutes old (47)

but all movements are religious: inside
where motions making up and rising turn about and
proceed,
node and come to pass, prayer is the working in
the currents,

hallelujahs dive and sculp the mud, mazes of mud
melting away
from the slurpy lifting loads: when the mob
goes wild and thrashes

> a bit copulating, shaking the bushes, it is moving
>   in service. (53–54)

But as Ashbery convinces us that in reading his half-spherical gibbous convex mirror "we have seen the city" because he exaggerates Parmigianino's concern for the viewer, Ammons establishes his poem (and, by derivation, himself) as a whole solar orb by addressing us much more carefully than Ashbery does.

>   this measure moves
>   to attract and hold attention: when one is not holding on,
>   that is a way of holding: dip in anywhere, go on until the
>
>   attractions fail: I angle for the self in you that
>   can be
>   held, had in a thorough understanding: not to
>   persuade you,
>   enlighten you, not necessarily to delight you.
>   but to hold
>
> you.   (44)

And "the self in you that can be/ held" eventually proves to be one less neutral and moderate than it appears in this early sequence. As in Ashbery, it is an interpreter who is to challenge the poet and to join him in conjugal exchange only after being gently challenged in turn.

>   I can't understand my readers:
>   they complain of my abstractions as if the United
>   States of America
>   were a form of vanity: they ask why I'm so big on the
>
>   one: many problem, they never saw one: my readers:
>   what do they
>   expect from a man born and raised in a country
>   whose motto is *E*
>   *pluribus unum*:   (122)
>
>   my readers are baffling and
>   uncommunicative (if actual) and I don't know what
>   to make of
>
>   or for them: I prize them, in a sense, for that:
>   recalcitrance: (124)

Ammons seems to see the good of non-acceptance as much as Ashbery: with one gesture he both contradicts the egoistical sublime of "Myself" and exposes the sterility of Whitman's primarily auto- and homo-erotic pose.

>   I didn't mean to talk about my poem but
>   to tell others how to be poets: I'm interested
>   in you, and
>   I want you to be a poet: I want, like Whitman, to found

a federation of loveship, not of queers but of
    poets, where
there's a difference: that is, come on and be
    a poet, queer
or straight, adman or cowboy, librarian or dope
    fiend,
housewife or hussy: (I see in one of the monthlies
    an astronaut
is writing poems—that's what I mean, guys): (120)

We can entertain this climactic claim of altruism towards a loveship/
readership because—again like queer, gibbous-eyed "Ashbery"—the
straight/queer speaker of *Sphere* has sacrificed his ordinary egocentrism in
order to contemplate the alternative solar system of literary symbolism.

        (when an image or
item is raised into a class representative or
        cluster, clump,
or set, its boundaries are overinvested, the
        supercharge is
explosive, so that the burden of energy overwhelms
        the matter,
and aura, or glow, or spirituality results, a kind of
        pitchblende,
radium, sun-like: and when the item is moved
        beyond class
into symbol or paradigmatic item, matter is a mere
        seed
afloat in radiance (64–65)

Approximately halfway through the poem this analysis of synecdoche
quite convincingly locates the divinity that shapes our ends in vibrations
between single signifier and multiple signified—vibrations which urgently demand interpretation. As each of the facets of Ashbery's mirror-
text has its own authority because it reflects the whole, this comparison
of literary generativity with Einsteinian relativity is convincing because
it exemplifies the primary strategies of *Sphere*.

Ammons offers us only one truly sun-like symbol: *Sphere* itself. We
recognize our own solar system as radiantly itself because we know that
it has billions of counterparted macro- and micro-counterparts, other
galaxies and systems of particles which constitute the moment/space of
our experience. Similarly, Ammons' text can project a City of Mutual
Discourse because it is moved by many miniature apocalyptic reflections
of itself like this comparison of the rhetorical figure of synedoche to the
sun. Far from destroying the aura of either part or whole, our awareness
of their emphatically *literary*—both highly structured and deconstructive—interrelationship can intensify the spirit which the letter only at
first seems to kill.

Indeed Ammons prepares to end his projection of endless literary revolution by deconstructing his pivotal celebration of symbolism as solar construction.

> from other planets,
> as with other planets from here, we rise and set,
> our presence,
> reduced to light, noticeable in the dark when the sun is
>
> away: reduced and distanced into light, our brotherhood
> constituted into shining, our landforms, seas, colors
> subsumed to bright announcement: we are alone in a
> sea that
>
> shows itself nowhere in a falling surf but if it
> does not
> go on forever folds back into a further motion of
> itself:
> the plenitude of nothingness! (149–50)

As Einstein considered solar energy measureable only in terms of the point/moment of interpretation, Ammons suggests that the sun-like energy of literary signification is measureable only in terms of the reader's response. If from the earth we see other planets rise and set, from other planets—as from Parmigianino's half-sphere "if we could get back to it"—*we* could be seen to rise and set as radiant, spirited seeds.

But Ammons most effectively authorizes his claim to perform the religious function of linking diverse persons as well as concepts, objects and moments when he elaborates his unorthodox displacement of spirit into letters ("when an image or/ item is raised into a class representative . . . aura, glow or spirituality results . . . sun-like . . .").

> I found this
> word *repodepo* in the newspaper only to find it,
> apparently,
> a mischance of machinery: I could not myself have
> invented
>
> a nonexistence so probable, insignificance so well
> made: let
> it stand for a made nothing, a pointer with no point: or
> for anything about which the meaning is insecure: a
> heavy
>
> registration: a cluster of empty pods, or a special
> phonetic
> depot, or something that repods pseudopods: a leaf
> cannot
> appear upon or fall from the branch except via total
> involvement of the universe: you and I cannot
> walk the street
> or rise to the occasion except via the sum total
> of effect

and possibility of the universe. (74)

The writer can proclaim the universe an integral community because he is acutely aware of "shananigans in the lingo" (37) more obviously unnatural than the gathering of items and images into a class-symbol to which he has attributed radiant power. Here a non-symbol, a typographical error, generates an aura of significance. The reader-poet justifies his religious vision of universal participation and linkage by imitating Creation *ex nihilo*, creating from nothing three alternative microcosms:

> a cluster of empty pods, or a special phonetic
> depot, or something that repods pseudopods

But Ammons makes it clear that his poem derives not from nature but from implied comparisons between Scripture and newsprint which recall Stevens' mocking allusions to Psalm 19 and Revelation in "An Ordinary Evening." As he later observes, "the imagination can dwell in nothingness"—can create something from a nothing like "repodepo"—because it is "the memory or imagined memory of shapes" (108). The contemporary poet can establish the literary symbol as a sun if he and his readers recall that the Psalmist interpreted the Law, a textual gathering of religious symbols, as a sun. *Sphere* legitimizes its Emersonian wedding of Mind and Nature by often corroborating Ashbery's provocative critique of transcendentalism, his concentration on the literary surface and its power to provoke *inter*subjective collaboration.

If imitative/self-reflexive *Sphere* is to respect its own principle of relativity, it cannot finally resolve the tensions which move it—especially the conflict between open nature and closed cultural convention. A truly critical poem must leave a lot to do for the critic who lurks in any reader.

> the most open suasion:
> a darkness in the method, a puzzling, obfuscating
> > surface,
> is the quick (and easy) declaration of mystery,
> > with the risk,
> though, that should the method come plain, be
> > made out, the
> mystery, surficial, its elements jumbled, would
> > disappear,
> unless, of course, under the quick establishment
> > of difficult
> method the true mystery survived: (50)

As Ashbery displaces authority and potency from the self-reflexive artwork to shuttlings and filiations which locate it in a landscape of interpretation, Ammons attempts to relocate paradox and ambiguity *outside* the work and thus reverse the New Critical assumption that the poem is a well-wrought urn. But if the easiest and most open method of imitating and celebrating the mystery of nature is to make the poem difficult and self-enclosed, such surface mimesis risks being merely superficial—not a generative interface like the prominent surface of Parmigianino's virtuoso self-portrait.

"Unless, of course, under the quick establishment of difficult method the true mystery survives." Ammons does in fact limit the openness of his "suasion" by attempting to deny what the best moments of *Sphere* advertise as boldly as "Self-Portrait": that scripture differs from nature because its mystery is merely "surficial," generated from continual demands that readers observe peculiarities of the textual surface. Prominent among these, of course, is its closure from life, its being *"another life to the city"* or "something else" as Ashbery describes his text. But because Ammons more often simply defines himself, his poem, and his world as corresponding whole spheres, like Whitman's "Song of Myself" *Sphere* is quite exclusive in its claim to be inclusive. We may thus feel that it projects a "united capable/ nation, and a united nations!" (79) less capably than the "logarithm" which Ashbery derived from more sustained reading of allegories of art written and painted in other nations.

Paradoxically, the contemplation of mediatory, secondary art may induce more lively collaboration from future readers than the contemplation of mind and world, the two major components of ordinary experience which art attempts to reconcile. If the artist takes the secondariness and otherness of art as subject of his poem and as model for himself, his "suasion" can be open to innumerable potential readers.

> This otherness, this
> "not being us" is all there is to look at
> In the mirror. (81)

In contrast, if the artist takes as subject of his poem and as model for himself the primariness of self-identical nature, his suasion will be closed to potential readers to the extent that it claims to participate in reality without their help. Ammons' experiment lacks the control of reference to clearly defined visual images which enables both Revelation and "Self-Portrait" to project self-critical community.

The poet does at last translate his early pluralization of Leviathan as a vague unconscious commonwealth ("all the people . . . resting with a hugeness of whales dozing" [43]) into an emblem of *Sphere*, assigning it the apocalyptic force of the abstract but hard-edged and object-filled vision which St. John sees across a sea of glass.

> the abstract poem
> cleaves through the glassy heights like a hump
>   of a great
>
> beast, the rising reification, integration's

grandest, most roving whale: (136)

But *Sphere* never confronts us with as focused and provocative an image as does "Self-Portrait in a Convex Mirror," in which the hand of the angel-painter "looks like a dozing whale on the sea bottom." Indeed Ammons ultimately dismisses ordinary vision in favor of a pseudo-mysticism induced by technology: "in spite of the spectacularity of the universe/ even in the visual reception it appears to those who have gone above our atmosphere"—the astronauts who write poems—"that the universe is truly a great darkness" (139). And Ammons dismisses spectacularity because he has projected an apocalyptic contemplation too vast to be reflected on a glassy half-sphere—and thus not available to mortal eyes:

> I have dreamed of a stroll-through, the
> stars in a close-woven, showering bedazzlement, though
> diamond- or ruby-cool, in which I contemplated the
> universe
>
> at length (139–40)

Both Ashbery and St. John make much more effort to compensate for the limitations of mortal vision.

When Ammons "to the huge air's multiple fuzzy tongues/ . . . address[es] vague hosannas" (8), the absence of a visual spatial object which can serve as counterpart to his text helps conceal the difference between subjects and objects of contemplation and prevents the poem from generating tensions between poet and reader which can benefit both.

Certainly we may be attracted by Ammons' brash imitation of a poet whose vision also defied visualization: "I figure I'm the exact poet of the concrete par excellence as Whitman might say" (123). But just because *Sphere* so successfully resists becoming what Eliot would have called an objective correlative to self-critical interpretation, it encourages us to participate much less strongly than "Self-Portrait" or the many other modern texts we have read which elaborate the complex rhetorical strategy as well as the solar imagery of ancient choral poetry.

FOUR
Recapitulation

Reading as Reconstruction

"An Ordinary Evening in New Haven," *Four Quartets*, "Self-Portrait in a Convex Mirror": however these texts differ, they all project reevaluations of history and discourse more open and potentially generative than most proposed by contemporary theory. As we have seen, both ancient and modern poets have rigorously analyzed tensions inherent in exchange between individuals and cultures. Poetry can demonstrate the virtues of skeptical analysis as effectively as any deconstructionist essay. But because it can better explore the complex dynamics of dialogue, it can also define continual self-questioning as the matrix of extraordinarily vital community.

This diverse body of work therefore also offers challenges and opportunities that are generally not required by an approach to reading which rivals deconstruction as the conscience of the newer criticism. Semiotic analyses of literature tend not to recognize that literary texts both derive from and generate unusually intense self-awareness. In *The Role of the Reader* (Bloomington, 1979) Umberto Eco does attribute some latitude to the Model Reader, observing that he is free to choose what codes to apply to a text and to decide how to activate various textual levels (Eco refers to codes and subcodes, circumstances of utterance, discursive, narrative, actantial, ideological and "world" structures).[1] But poetry requires us to do more than reconcile discrepancies among its various combinations of structural and thematic elements. It also challenges our habitual acceptance of simpler and less self-critical codifications of experience imposed by both established and subversive ideologies and institutions.

An application of semiotics to literature more flexible than Eco's

---

[1] Eco, pp. 13–15. Eco derives his categories from Janos S. Petofi; see "A Frame for Frames," *Proceedings of the Second Annual Meeting of the Berkeley Linguistic Society* (Berkeley, 1976). It should also be noted that Eco finally demonstrates the programmatic nature of texts by claiming that even Roland Barthes' concept of the *plaisir de texte* refers to a predetermined freedom:

> Those texts that according to Barthes are able to produce the "jouissance" of the unexhausted virtuality of their expressive plane succeed in this effect just because they have been planned to incite their Model Readers to reproduce their own processes of deconstruction by a plurality of free interpretive choices. (p. 40)

helps us see how poetry can give us a rich and stimulating sense of our options as self-critical members of diverse communities precisely by insisting that it is controlled to a great extent by various cultural and literary systems. In *Semiotics of Poetry* (Indiana, 1978), Michael Rifaterre states:

> The reader's manufacture of meaning is . . . not so much a progress through the poem and a half-random accretion of verbal associations, as it is a seesaw scanning of the text, compelled by the very duality of the signs,—ungrammatical as mimesis, grammatical within the significance network. This seesawing from one sign value to the other, this alternating appearance and disappearance of significance, both in spite and because of unacceptable features on the plane of mimetic meaning, is a kind of semiotic circularity characterising the practice of signification known as poetry. In the reader's mind it means a continual recommencing, an indecisiveness resolved one moment and lost the next with each reliving of revealed significance and this it is that makes the poem endlessly rereadable and fascinating.[2]

Yet the poetry we have read demonstrates that the poetic sign is endlessly rereadable and fascinating because it is "grammatical" also in the *potential* network of interpretation by many readers who—like the poet—can provisionally free themselves from the impersonality of any semiotic system by acknowledging its constraints. Indeed when texts represent the readings which have generated them and which they in turn generate, they demand that we uncover our own secrets as well as theirs and define this mutual questioning as model for speech that is truly free.

The parody of Romans 7 in Act V of *Hamlet* which Eliot further elaborated reminds us how the most compelling texts question basic concepts of identity and authority. "If Hamlet from himself be ta'en away/ And when he's not himself does wrong Laertes. . . ." This climactic speech invites us to acknowledge that we are often unkind to others because we are always alienated from ourselves—except when such provocative deconstructions of convention challenge us to acknowledge our alienation and thus join a provisional community grounded in self-criticism. Like this sequence in *Hamlet*, the poems we have read activate three oppositions, the third a product of the other two: tension between themselves and readers; conflicts between objects and subjects of interpretation which they represent; intensifications of the resistance to reductive definition which they induce in the reader.

We can see more clearly how poetry projects more perfect union by provoking multiple division if we qualify Murray Krieger's use of a visual representation of marriage to challenge the skepticism common to deconstruction and semiotics.

---

2 Rifaterre, p. 166.

Jan van Eyck, *Arnolfini Wedding* (London, National Gallery): detail.

> The mirror plays a major self-referential role in Jan van Eyck's
> famous wedding portrait of Arnolfini and his wife. In the painting,
> hanging on the far wall behind the couple being married, a mirror
> reflects the scene already being mirrored in the picture. In that
> second-order reflection, we can make out the artist himself seated
> before the couple and painting the picture we are looking at, thereby
> visually corroborating the statement that he has written on the paint-
> ing, which testifies to his witnessing of the marriage: "Johannes de
> eyck *fuit hic*."[3]

In fact van Eyck's mirror does not portray the artist seated painting. As
Erwin Panofsky notes, if van Eyck did portray himself, it was only as one
of two faceless standing men who witness the marriage from the doorway
in which the actual viewer apparently stands.[4] The painting also in two
ways indicates that the image of union which the artist joins us in interpreting itself reinterprets the incarnate Word's sacrifice: the paradigmatic
union of Heaven and Earth, Signified and signifier. Not only do the bride
and bridegroom pose as Gabriel and Mary in an Annunciation—often read
as a *thalamus virginis*—but ten tiny images of Christ's passion and resurrection also surround the mirror in which the painter is reflected as one of
two witnesses. When van Eyck depicted himself not painting but viewing a
reenactment of the redemptive union of divinity and humanity, he in
effect provided a model for verbal as well as visual artists' attempts to
extend the redemptive project of Scripture by representing complex interaction between authorities and interpreters.

If we correct Krieger's account of the mirror-image in the van Eyck
we can develop his defense of literature. As Krieger sees the artist asserting his presence as an artist, he defines literary self-consciousness as a
means of reconstructing the illusion of identity between signifier and
signified, word and world asserted in metaphor.

> If discourse normally must find its nature by making its way from
> identity (metaphor) to difference (metonymy) literature has the role
> of earning its way back to identity from the differential nature of
> normal discourse from which it deviates. Thus literature has the
> peculiar task of becoming a kind of discourse which, as discursive,
> can yet appear to occupy the normally non-discursive metaphorical
> stage . . . Literature performs this feat, not by struggling toward an
> impossible return to naïveté in a romantic search for the origins of
> language, but by borrowing the appearance of a discourse for iden-
> tity through an ironic self-consciousness which knows the metaphori-
> cal indulgence to be an illusion.[5]

We must modify this formulation if we see that in van Eyck the artist is
explicitly "present" only as one of two potential readers of at least four

---

[3] *Poetic Presence and Illusion* (Baltimore, 1980), p. 187.
[4] *Early Netherlandish Painting* vol. I (Cambridge, Mass., 1953), p. 203.
[5] Krieger, p. 184.

systems of signification and their many possible interrelationships: the marrying couple, the signature of the artist (which indeed locates van Eyck's presence in the *past*), the death and resurrection of Christ, and their own reflections. Such allusive and self-reflexive art does more than encourage us to reconstruct the myths of authorial presence which deconstructionist criticism has rightly challenged. It also invites us to join a vast community of past, present, and future interpreters in both recognizing and acknowledging that no human-authored work either definitively interprets the world or can itself be definitively interpreted. The poetry we have read—ancient and modern, European and American— insists that there is no consistently reliable bridge between any subjective interpreter and any object of interpretation. It projects an exodus from illusion: a liberation grounded in never-ending analysis of the constraints of discourse and in respect for the power of literature to serve as an unflagging gadfly to culture.

Index